IDOL TEMPLES AND CRAFTY PRIESTS

Idol Temples and Crafty Priests

The Origins of Enlightenment Anticlericalism

S. J. Barnett

First published in Great Britain 1999 by
MACMILLAN PRESS LTD
Houndmills, Basingstoke, Hampshire RG21 6XS and London
Companies and representatives throughout the world

A catalogue record for this book is available from the British Library.

ISBN 0–333–72543–3

First published in the United States of America 1999 by
ST. MARTIN'S PRESS, INC.,
Scholarly and Reference Division,
175 Fifth Avenue, New York, N.Y. 10010

ISBN 0–312–21590–8

Library of Congress Cataloging-in-Publication Data
Barnett, S. J. 1960–
Idol temples and crafty priests / the origins of Enlightenment
anticlericalism / S.J. Barnett.
p.   cm.
Includes bibliographical references and index.
ISBN 0–312–21590–8
1. Anti-clericalism—England—History—18th century.   2. Anti
–clericalism—History.   I. Title.
BR1625.B37   1998
273'.8—dc21   98–17289
                                                    CIP

This book is printed on paper suitable for recycling and made from fully managed and
sustained forest sources.

10   9   8   7   6   5   4   3   2   1
08   07   06   05   04   03   02   01   00   99

Printed and bound in Great Britain by
Antony Rowe Ltd, Chippenham, Wiltshire

Contents

Preface: Enlightenment or Long Reformation?

One of the chief characteristics of the European Enlightenment (*c.* 1690s–1790s) was a virulent anticlericalism, the foundation for its attack upon the perceived ignorant, obscurantist and inefficient *ancien régime*. This book investigates how Christian polemic and historical thought contributed to the formation of that anticlericalism. The focus will be upon the great polemical and historical debate between Rome and English Protestants (and the internal divisions of both) from the sixteenth to the eighteenth century. This was a debate initiated by Henry VIII's withdrawal of obedience to Rome and his assumption of supremacy in the Anglican Church (1534). Much of Europe had, however, already experienced an outpouring of polemical propaganda since the initiation of the Reformation, beginning with Luther's declaration of 1517. Luther's declaration condemned what he understood as the centuries of gross spiritual and venal corruption of the Church. In so doing, Luther effected a revolution in the historical conception of Europe which soon became the dominant Protestant view. This unprecedented institutional hostility was not, however, a simple Catholic–Protestant confessional divide. The great material wealth, power and influence of the European Church was a prize eagerly sought by all monarchs. The rift was also embittered and complicated by the fact the two great confessions had their own internal lines of fracture. Catholic reformers in Italy themselves condemned the corruption of the Roman Curia. In England, many zealous Protestants condemned the Anglican Church as but little reformed. It was thought to be quasi-Catholic in ceremony and especially in structure, for it retained its episcopate, the core of the medieval Church hierarchy. This point was hardly a quibble, for elsewhere in Europe many powerful Catholic bishops and archbishops continued to dispose of almost as much wealth and power as aristocrats. In England the episcopate had been brought into submission to the monarch, but it retained much of its power in the Church, was still a force in government (in the House of Lords), and continued to be visibly very wealthy.

During and after the Reformation, the critique advanced to

condemn religious opponents was, in its fundamentals, common to all participants of the debate: to pro-Rome propagandists, to Protestants, to anti-curial (anti-Rome) Catholics and anti-Anglican Protestants. Both confessions and their subdivisions accused each other of using religion as a mask for the attainment of secular desires, namely wealth, power and prestige. Each accused the other of antichristian behaviour, of using superstition and pagan forms of worship to hoodwink the masses into quiescent obedience to a false religion.

This harsh assessment was also the essence of the Enlightenment critique of the Church: that the medieval period had been a benighted, ignorant and superstitious epoch devoid of rational thinking. Europe had fallen into a cultural abyss, one consciously brought about by the Church in order to prevent society from affording reason its just place in society. The inky-darkness of irrationality had prevented the unmasking of perhaps the greatest social ruse ever. So blinded, thought the enlightened, that in the eighteenth century European society remained backward and brutish in its outlook. Elements of this assessment could not easily be dismissed, for the Church continued to hold a virtual monopoly on education, and it often tried to limit the development of scientific and philosophical research. The Church was a great landowner, yet did little to reform the inefficient practices and often oppressively feudal structures found on its estates. Europe had thus been unable – argued enlightened thinkers, the *philosophes* – to reclaim the wisdom of the ancient classical world and put it to use as an ally of reason in order to advance European civilization. The first manifestations of the Enlightenment critique of Church history appeared predominantly in the writings of the so-called English deists of the late seventeenth and early eighteenth centuries, and this period and its writers forms the inner core of this present investigation. Paradoxically, there is abundant evidence that the historical scheme of these deists was culled from Protestant thought. Many modern historians, however, because of an overconcentration on the *philosophes* and a concomitant neglect of Christian writers, have assumed the deist historical scheme to have been one principally developed under the stimulus of anti-religious sceptical writings.

The debate on the nature and origins of the Enlightenment has simmered for decades now. This present reassessment of its anticlerical thought is not intended as an attack on the values of the Enlightenment, or to denigrate its achievements or importance in

European history. Neither is the following discussion intended as a substitute for the study of the varied influences that converged to form the Enlightenment. Yet a clear understanding of the origins of its distinctive anticlericalism is most helpful in the endeavour to understand what was at times an enigmatic and disparate phenomenon. The attribution of deist historical views is of particular importance because of the central role of the critique of Christianity in the attempt of *philosophes* to rehabilitate human reason as a tool to explain the dire shortcomings of the *ancien régime* and finally to overcome it. In a more general sense, discussion of the importance of historical perspectives held by early modern thinkers is of methodological value to all attempts to investigate history.

Today, as in the distant past, individuals and institutions decide what to do, or what not to do, on the basis of that which has already occurred, or on the basis of what they imagine will occur by analogy to a sufficiently similar past experience. The role of comparative history in the lives of ordinary individuals, the activities of society at large and of its institutions, then, is far more crucial than we ordinarily accept in the daily humdrum of our lives. We commonly take reasoning from the past to the present or future for granted, and do not conceive of ourselves as taking part in the stuff of historical research. The bigger the decision to be made, the more exacting is our need to analyse the past. What could be more daunting than, in the eighteenth century, setting out to refound European culture anew? There was a need to scrutinize, rescrutinize, debate, research and test the validity of various philosophies of history against recorded events. Why did *this* happen in history instead of *that*? Was there a general causal dynamic in history to be identified and tested against the historical development of other epochs and places?

In the eighteenth century history was the searchlight of civilization and printers were kept busy. The reading of history was fashionable in a way very difficult for us to appreciate now. It was the key to understanding the palpable ills of the past and avoiding them in the future. There were many debates, not only on the facts and philosophy of history, but upon what practical method should be adopted to study it. A characteristic of the enlightened approach to the study of religious history was the comparative method. By comparing the history of all religions – a sociology of religion – it was thought possible to identify the process of priestcraft thought intrinsic to all religions, and so more effectively to consign Christianity to the dustbin of history. How had crafty priests managed to instil their astounding fraud in society, and

how had they managed to maintain its credibility even amongst the
learned and intelligent? The deists and *philosophes* were in this one
respect, however, Johnny-come-latelies. Beleaguered Protestant and
Catholic propagandists had already developed the tool of comparative
historical enquiry in the late sixteenth century. The comparative practice of these confessional partisans has never been dignified with the
term sociology of religion, presumably because the answers to their
comparative enquiries were mostly predetermined by their religious
affiliations. But modern historians have quietly forgotten that the
comparative historical enquiries of deists also had a predetermined
outcome: the dismissal of all institutional religions as venal priestly
frauds. In any case, as in all historical enquiry (as today in some
measure), the results were heavily determined by the questions asked.

Insufficient attention has been given to the Christian origins of the
Enlightenment critique of Church history. Most importantly, one of the
significant developmental dynamics of intra-confessional conflict, that
of social class – with only one or two exceptions – has also been inade-
quately examined. In sixteenth- and seventeenth-century England, the
main opposition to the Anglican, that is to say to the state-Church and
its royal head, came from Puritans and Dissenters (Nonconformists).
These were disproportionately found amongst artisans, farmers, shop-
keepers, merchants and professionals. They sought a Presbyterian
model of Church government based upon what they considered to be
the pure simplicity of apostolic practice, where no autonomous hierarchy of priests had existed. Instead, there had been (they thought) a
series of more or less self-organizing and egalitarian collectives, where
there was no opportunity for high ecclesiastics to amass wealth and
power and distort Christian doctrine for their own ends.

In this context, religious opposition to the Anglican Church also
included political and economic – that is to say class – factors.
Powerful and wealthy bishops were often seen as natural allies of the
aristocratic class and the monarch, who was, after all, the supreme
head of the Church. In Catholic Italy the configuration of religious
opposition differed. Overt opposition to Rome and its jurisdiction in
the Church was often only practical if one of the princes of the several
sovereign states of Italy afforded critics of the Church protection and
patronage from the persecution of the Roman Inquisition. Hence
anti-curialists (intellectuals, politicians, lawyers and at times ecclesiastics) often took part in a *de facto* class alliance with sovereigns,
usually promoting the right of princes to jurisdiction within the
Churches of their own small states.

The origins of the Enlightenment have been sought in various periods and schools of thought. Some historians have held the opinion that the early origins of the Enlightenment are to be located in a Europe undergoing fundamental change as a result of new, wider intellectual boundaries opened up by the discovery of the New World and seventeenth-century scientific discovery. Others have held that the Renaissance bequeathed ideas to the eighteenth century which were fundamental to the process of forming a critique of the medieval Church and the metaphysical learning it championed. It is true that European society was undergoing important changes in the sixteenth and seventeenth centuries. But there is little or no proof these changes and intellectual bequests themselves alone initiated the Enlightenment or formed its core stimulus (although, once the Enlightenment was initiated, it is inescapable that such factors were important components in its development). There is a growing consensus that the anticlerical polemic of the so-called deists of late seventeenth-century England represented one of the first and most important steps towards the Enlightenment. English deism, however, cannot be considered as solely the belated product of Renaissance thought or of later scientific discovery. The evidence I shall present in following chapters indicates that religious division and its economic, political and historiographical reflections were determinants of prime importance to the inception and development of the deist project.

As medievalists are often quick to point out to scholars of the Enlightenment, various species of highly critical anticlerical ideas can be located in Europe in various periods and places. Thus the dominant theme underlying Enlightenment anticlericalism – that crafty priests had peddled a fraudulent religion – was hardly original. The problem still remains, however, of why the dawn of the Enlightenment began to glimmer in the late seventeenth century and (some would argue) principally in England, and not another time and another place? Research into Enlightenment origins should not only be seeking 'original' ideas then, but also the circumstances in which old ideas can be rejuvenated, so disposing of a new explanatory power far in excess of the initial idea. The crucial point is that a new context for an old idea, which is to say a new audience – one in a different political, religious and economic context – views an old idea through the spectacles of new norms, exigencies and predilections. The result can be dismissal of old ideas as anachronistic. An alternative possibility is that a stale idea with little or declining social force is transformed by a new context into something very different, holding an explanatory power and social attraction way beyond the capacity of its original. In the idealist school of historical thought, the development and transmission of ideas is seen as the main dynamic of historical change. The birth of Enlightenment anticlericalism, however, cannot be adequately explained solely by the development and transmission of ideas; the general and specific contexts in which those ideas – old or new – are located must be delineated.

The task of this book is, therefore, to trace how anticlerical polemic and historical thought developed during the Reformation and its complex aftermath, and, unintentionally, provided the core of the anticlerical historical critique advanced by the *philosophes* of the Enlightenment.

S. J. BARNETT
1998

1 Introduction: Anticlericalism and Historical Revolutions

It has been noted that a cleric, a lawyer and a herald will each recount a different historical past,[1] which is one manner of illustrating that the practical circumstances of life determine one's historical view. Yet why did eighteenth-century English deists, Protestants, anti-curial Italians as well as enlightened Europeans come to share very similar views of the medieval Church? My answer begins with the following thesis: we cannot properly understand an age if we do not understand how it regarded its own past, for every era constructs its own past anew.[2] Examples of change or re-creation of hitherto accepted historical accounts abound in modern history. Consider, since the 1960s, the change in the portrayal of colonial history, or the re-evaluation of the historical role of women in society. Consider (until the 1990s) the official history of the now defunct USSR, a notorious example of the culture-bound nature of historical writing. Equally important has been the frequent depiction – albeit often implicit – of the period from the Reformation to the Industrial Revolution as an inexorable progression to modernity.

Historians who devise and impose such historical accounts are reacting to an understandable predisposition. Because societies continually evolve and historians are of course participants in that evolution, they are often prompted to explain, justify and periodically rewrite history as a more or less lineal progress to the present. This view or philosophy of history has been termed Whig history. Changes in historical perspective are also unavoidable to some extent. This is because the efforts of historians, accompanied by the development of new, more sophisticated techniques of historical enquiry, cause the sum total of our knowledge of the past to increase. But modern societies are not always more likely to rewrite their history than older societies. In no period of European history has such a sweeping change in its past been achieved than in the sixteenth and seventeenth centuries. A new history of Christendom – a radical reinterpretation of medieval Europe c. AD 500–1500 – was devised and often imposed

1

upon large areas of Europe by Church and state. The new history of
Europe was of course that produced by Protestant protagonists and
historians of the Church such as Martin Luther, John Calvin and the
Magdeburg Centuriators.

This was an historical revolution produced partly as a justification
of the Protestant secession from Rome, and in part a reaction to the
polemical and historiographical counter-attack by Roman orthodoxy.
So what? one might say, ecclesiastics have always squabbled about
the history of the Church. To think in that dismissive vein would be
to fall prey to a culture-bound paradigm of historical change. The
relationship of state to Church, the role of Christianity in society and
in the lives of rulers, intellectuals and peasants in Europe in 1517 –
the year in which Martin Luther initiated the Reformation – differed
from modern times in fundamental respects. It was a difference of
sufficient magnitude that a sweeping revolution in the historical foundation of Christianity could be expected to presage great change in
the outlook of European thinkers in both religious and secular terms.

By the sixteenth century a gradual erosion of Church power in relation to princely power was already evident, and there was often bitter
dissatisfaction with the nature of the Church. Nevertheless, there still
existed no socially approved moral code or broad societal conceptions
outside those of Christianity and the teachings of the Church. Canon
(Church) law and the Christian concepts it embodied still regulated
or heavily influenced most fundamental collective and personal social
mores. This was a fact most apparent to Rome and defenders of the
Catholic faith. It was, as we shall see, precisely the basis upon which
Catholic propagandists launched the initial counter-attack against the
Reformation. Luther and Calvin were lambasted for abandoning the
moral precepts of Christianity. They and other Protestant protagonists were accused of submitting themselves to the iniquitous
temptations of the flesh and the earthly corruptions of religion. These
were dangers against which Christendom had hitherto been guarded
only by Rome and the Catholic Church.

In this century, the dispensation of princely or imperial power was
still legitimized in Christian terms as a reflection of the heavenly hierarchy of power. Vast Church lands were still directly administered by
monks, and universities were led by clerics of one kind or another.
There was little effective separation between Church and state.
Cardinals and bishops held high political office and political conceptions were very often at least ostensibly justified upon religious
grounds. Yet many Europeans then began to learn, via the polemical

and historiographical onslaught of Luther, Calvin and others, that Rome could no longer be considered as the legitimate and hallowed primary point of contact between European Christendom and God. After 1517 the old Catholic certainties which had hitherto informed almost all aspects of European culture had gone or were at least increasingly thrown into question in Protestant lands.

It was to be fateful for Christendom that this revolution in historical thinking was proclaimed at the very time Europe was assimilating the potential of the printed word. From various Protestant protagonists came numerous printed accounts of the gross spiritual betrayal and fleshly corruption of the beating heart of European Christianity. Christians were informed that the sanctity of Rome and the popes had been only a tale concocted to lull the suspicions of Christians, whilst the popes had pursued worldly and antichristian goals. Believing the actions of the papacy to represent divine will, Christians had unwittingly allowed popes and prelates to rule the Church despotically. High ecclesiastics had amassed great wealth and power and, as aspiring tyrants are wont, had undermined and challenged the legitimate secular powers of kings and emperors. All had been justified by a body of Church law designed to deceive the faithful and draw Europe steadily away from its rightful Christian heritage. In a word, Rome was guilty of priestcraft.

For most Protestants, religious outlook and historical understanding became inextricably meshed together. To defend overtly, for example, the pre-Reformation historical status quo on the medieval Church, was to risk appearing to most Protestants to be Catholic in sympathy, if not in religious allegiance. This was a tricky problem, one experienced by some English seventeenth-century High Churchmen, that is to say staunch episcopalian Anglicans who claimed legitimate descent from the medieval Church. In general, however, because of the intimate link between the new and dominant Protestant view of Church history and Protestant identity, the impulse to continue and deepen the historical attacks upon the medieval Church was more often unflinchingly merciless. The historical development of medieval Christianity was frequently reduced to little more than a tyrannous and licentious process of religious fraud, which had exploited the ignorance of the masses – an accusation also turned upon the popery of the bishop-ridden Anglican Church by Dissenters. From the pens of hundreds of Protestant polemicists, the attack on the medieval Church was so profound that English late seventeenth- and eighteenth-century enemies of the Church and the continental *philosophes* who followed them had little need to develop their own critique of the Church. Dissenting Protestants such as John Toland (1670–1722), when abandoning the Church for deism or natural religion in the late 1690s, having already condemned the Anglican Church, simply extended their historical critique backwards in time from the medieval period to include most or all of the post-apostolic Church. For such thinkers all hierarchical established Churches had been and still were merely religious frauds instituted by the clergy for gain; they thus advocated a non-institutional belief in God. That comprehensive dismissal of Christian institutional history from the apostles to the present is something historians have come to term the Enlightenment critique of Church history.

Enlightened thinkers such as Hume, Voltaire, Diderot and Condorcet, to name but a few, wished to dispel the trance in which superstition and religious despotism had long held Europe. In its stead they wished to usher in a period characterized by the rational evaluation of existing social, political, economic and religious forms. Peter Gay demonstrated in his *The Rise of Modern Paganism* (1966) that, as critical thinkers, the *philosophes* focused their attention on the philosophical lessons found in the works of pagan classical writers. From the wisdom of those writers *philosophes* believed they would be able to develop further their own critical powers and emancipate society from a nightmarish dungeon of ignorance to the light of rational progress. Christianity was perceived to be but one example of the crafty and nefarious priesthoods of time immemorial which continued to dominate all religion in order to further their own worldly ambition.

In practice – that is to say whether individual *philosophes* wished to acknowledge it or not – they focused on classical learning through Protestant spectacles. As one philosopher has expressed it, all ages have some ideas fundamental to their self-identity, which lie so far back in the mind, 'that they are never really conscious of them at all. They do not see them, but other things through them. It is ... the things which they take for granted, that characterize a period'.[3] After all, the *philosophes* were able to write philosophical history – that is to say accounts that sought general explanations for events – precisely because Protestant historical analysis had provided them with an adequate empirical base with which to demonstrate the priestcraft of institutional Christianity.

Peter Gay's work focused upon the narrow band of *philosophes* and, although in subsequent years the field of Enlightenment studies has widened to include more than just the famed few, there has been relatively little systematic analysis of the plethora of Christian accounts of Church history and associated polemic. Compared to the few elite *philosophes*, a very large number of little known Protestants and Catholics felt moved to write polemical history in the seventeenth and eighteenth centuries. But epithets such as minor or unknown ought not to connote lack of influence. Despite the fame of *philosophes* such as Voltaire, Montesquieu or Diderot, it would require a bold or indeed reckless historian to claim that the small intellectual elite of *philosophes* represented the characteristic thought of millions of eighteenth-century Europeans. Most ordinary eighteenth-century individuals retained some level of allegiance to institutional Christianity. In addition, Wesleyan Methodism attracted a growing flock to Christianity in the decades after 1740. In Italy there was a widespread call for reform of the Church rather than its abolition, a call which comprised the thought and actions of large numbers of individuals.

Posterity thus continues to endow prominent *philosophes* such as Voltaire with just fame, but rather obviously with questionable validity as typical representatives of society-wide eighteenth-century thought. There is no reason to presume that a wide selection of minor or 'non-enlightened' writers had any less collective influence (outside elite intellectual circles) upon the general populace than Voltaire and other *philosophes*, and every reason to consider the possibility of the reverse. Already in the sixteenth century, the partisan use of the pulpit, the advent of print culture and the upheaval of the Reformation had produced an attentive audience for historico-religious polemic the extent of which the *philosophes* could only dream. Albeit unevenly, the corrosive Reformation conflict over the history and contemporary nature of the Christian Church and its prolonged and divisive aftermath had entered into the minds of all sections of European society. Indeed, the popularity or perceived importance of religious literature hardly diminished in the eighteenth century.

For each and every *philosophe* in every European country, there were hundreds of Christian writers, and for each and every enlightened tract, there were hundreds of diverse religious tracts that found a widespread audience: those who continued to believe, on one level or another, in the Bible, the efficacy of prayer and collective worship. This did not mean the *philosophes* were uninfluential. They were most influential in shaping and promoting a secular and scientific view of economics, politics, history, philosophy and social development. Their influence was, however, primarily upon the intellectual elite, the growing intelligentsia and, to a lesser extent, upon some rulers and legislators. Their goal, the secularization of society, was to become a more tangible reality only in the nineteenth century. In the seventeenth and early eighteenth centuries, the little island of deists and *philosophes* was still surrounded by an immense and very turbulent river of Christian thought, containing contradictory currents which threatened to burst the theological confines of its banks. It was only natural and logical that some early deists and later *philosophes* took the opportunity to appropriate and borrow from some of those contradictory currents, but with a view to dissipating the whole Christian river.

Having established the proposition of a Protestant historical revolution, it is now necessary to reject the notion of a purely Protestant priestcraft theory aimed exclusively at Rome. The first point is that there was not one single target of Protestant polemic but several. Various competing Protestant tendencies also used the priestcraft accusation against each other. In turn, Rome accused Protestant protagonists of priestcraft: of being in league with the Antichrist and of breaking away from Rome to indulge their sexual and political ambitions. This was an indictment most prolific during the Counter-Reformation period (*c.* 1550–1650), but one extending into the late eighteenth century. The final element in the matrix of Christian polemic which forms its European character was the construction of a Catholic anti-curial (anti-Rome) historiography remarkably similar to that of the Protestants. For anti-curial Catholics and Protestants, the reality of the priest-king enthroned at the Vatican – simultaneously the sovereign of the Papal States and head of Christendom – was living proof of the degeneration of the medieval priesthood. Rome was seen to constitute concrete proof of the use of religion as a Trojan Horse pushed into civil society in order to usurp its power and wealth by stealth. In short, there existed a pan-European polemic consisting of thousands of publications, in which the essential and explicit subject matter was the historical and contemporary chicane and deceit of priests.

It ought to become a truism then, that in exploring religious attitudes, to focus upon only one of the two great religious confessions or upon one region without reference to the wider European perspective is to court error. One recent example is the claim that Catholics were unable to reciprocate the Protestant Antichrist and idolatry charge.[4]

The first step in avoiding such error, naturally, is the identification of the principal fulcrums of the debate and the subjection of their output to comparative analysis. The Catholic centre of the debate was, not surprisingly, the Catholic heartland of the Italian peninsula, Rome and the Papal States. England soon came to be, in historiographical terms, one of the major production centres of Protestant historical polemic. As F. Levy has commented: 'of all the "Reformations" of Europe, the English one was, in terms of its justification, the most historical.'[5] The ideas of the religious radicals of late seventeenth- and eighteenth-century England had great influence upon the development of European enlightened thinkers. This was especially so in France, which came to be gripped by what has been termed Anglomania, although the ideas of John Toland made the early work of Voltaire seem quite tame by comparison.

One reason for the underestimation of the importance of religious thought and Christian historiography in studies of the eighteenth century has certainly been the result of an undue concentration on the small band of *philosophes*. As Dale Van Kley noted in 1987, '[t]he notion that a movement so secular as the French Enlightenment might have had other than purely secular origins would have until recently raised scholarly eyebrows'.[6] But in one important respect that neglect was a legacy of the Enlightenment's own view of medieval history. In eighteenth-century Britain, as in Europe, enlightened thinkers dismissed the medieval period as one of barbarous darkness engendered by the self-interest of priestly despots and fanatics. Such summary dismissal meant enlightened British writers rarely wrote systematic studies of medieval Church history. Edward Gibbon's *Decline and Fall of the Roman Empire* (1776–88) is exceptional in the quantity of its analysis devoted to the medieval Church, and has therefore been the subject of considerable (although sometimes misconceived) study.

Gibbon aside, this ostensible lacuna in the historiography of the *philosophes* has usually been interpreted by modern historians to indicate that enlightened thinkers considered the history of the medieval Church to have been relatively unimportant to their contemporary concerns. As a consequence, the medieval Church has been understood as a subject that did not have significant positive influence upon Enlightenment conceptions of religion and Church history. It is true that religious thought has, to a degree, relatively recently been reinstated as a legitimate part of Enlightenment studies. But the polemical use of the history of the medieval Church has rarely been considered a useful part of the discussion, and has consequently never been systematically analysed. Instead, searching for 'positive' influence, some historians have unduly stressed the influence of openly sceptical and atheistic works – often printed and circulated clandestinely – upon the anticlerical culture of the Enlightenment. However, these efforts have so far failed to demonstrate adequately either the circulation of such texts or evidence of their influence upon religious thought over and above the destructive inter-Christian anticlerical climate of the sixteenth and seventeenth centuries.

For early English deists such as John Toland, and the many European deists and radicals subsequent to him, it was paramount that the history of institutional Christianity should be thoroughly desacralized, that is to say exposed as the all too mortal history of priestcraft. We must remember that the search of the *philosophes* for the wisdom of ancient pagan writers proceeded from the assumption of the priestly craft of the Church. Cunning clerics had held Europe static in their dark thrall since the decline of the Roman Empire. To ensure the spell could not be broken, the clergy had never allowed reason to claim its rightful role in society. The philosophical truths and insights of the ancients which the *philosophes* wished to embrace had been ignominiously and criminally buried from view. The task of undermining the sacrality of the medieval Church and contemporary Catholicism, however, had already been successfully accomplished by scores of English Protestant writers since the mid-sixteenth-century works of Bishop John Bale (1495–1563) and John Foxe (1516–87). For French *philosophes*, subject to a Catholic Church and state, this was most convenient indeed; especially so because many of the plethora of Protestant tracts were written with a sectarian venom the *philosophes* would have been hard-pressed to better. In the seventeenth century even moderate English authors thought that 'Roman priests deliberately kept the people in ignorance in order to preserve their own authority'.[7] Nevertheless, the startling similarity between deist and Protestant (and, as will be seen, Italian anti-curial) analyses of Church history has hardly been commented upon. One can only assume that this coincidence of historical outlook has not been noticed, or has been regarded as so obvious it has been taken for granted and not systematically studied and placed within its proper European context.

The religious map of early modern England, like that of Counter-Reformation Italy, was riven with divisions. In England the major division was that between varieties of Presbyterianism and Anglicanism. The Anglican Church was episcopalian and its position as the Church of the state gave it dominant status. It was, therefore, save for the occasional protestations of a few nonjuring High Churchmen, mostly Erastian in its outlook (i.e. favouring the authority of the state over the Church). Presbyterians – from the Elizabethan Puritans (Calvinists) through to the varied Dissenters of the late seventeenth century – advocated Church independence from the state, where ministers were subject to local parish control. The Presbyterian view, in practice, also embodied aspects of social class, for Presbyterians were frequently disproportionately drawn from the middling sort, the middle classes and lower gentry. As we shall see, this was important, for the nexus of religious, economic and political grievances provided a powerful spur to polemical innovation, and was to be a decisive factor in the formation of what is known as deist historiography.

Equally important as the Anglican-Presbyterian divide was anti-Catholicism, which Patrick Collinson has described as the 'sheet-anchor of England's nationhood' in the sixteenth and seventeenth centuries. In 1600, the Puritan Andrew Willet had urged anti-popery as the main vocation of the Church of England. Such shared anticlerical prejudice was thought to promote unity between Puritans and bishops, and limit conversion to Catholicism. In the years 1605–25 the pamphlet controversy with Rome saw over 500 anti-Catholic publications. Anti-popery was thus a stock-in-trade of early modern English Protestantism, an outlook only a little attenuated in High Church thought – most notably during the decade of Laudian ascendancy (1630s) when a more openly conciliatory attitude was taken towards the medieval Church by some Anglican writers.[8]

It has already been seen that Italian Catholic polemicists responded vigorously to the challenge of Protestantism and the European crisis of religious authority which that challenge provoked. Propagandists such as Jacopo Moronessa, Vicar General of the Celestine Order, characterized Protestant reformers as religious impostors intent only on self-gain and self-aggrandizement. But, behind the unity in the face of adversity displayed by Catholics, religious division in the Italian peninsula was historiographically decisive to a degree unparalleled in England. Religious dissent in Italy was often the product of or was exacerbated by the multiple political divisions of a polycentric peninsula. Rulers of relatively small sovereign states fought for control of their Churches against the jurisdictional claims of nearby Rome. This jurisdictional struggle, despite the repression and centralizing tendencies of the Counter-Reformation, was a central component in the development of an embittered anti-curial Catholic historiography.

Anti-curialists, like Protestants, concentrated upon re-forging the history of medieval Christendom, repeatedly hammering at its superstition, corruption and above all at its priest-king, the pope. In the last decades of the eighteenth century, the culmination of Catholic dissent was to be found in the development of what has been termed the Catholic Enlightenment, a partly Jansenist-inspired reform movement that reached its peak in the Synod of Pistoia (1786). So it was that the Archbishop of Taranto in the southern Kingdom of Naples, Giuseppe Capecelatro (1744–1836), reminded his readers in his 1788 critique of Church history that, if one wished to reform the Catholic Church, it was necessary to forge a new Church history.[9] His proclamation was a rallying cry, although his historical critique – while astounding in its venom – was hardly original in its substance. Capecelatro was, in fact, augmenting an anti-curial historiography, the fundamentals of which had been mostly constructed decades before and had anyway been common in Protestant thought since the Reformation. This was an historiography freely drawn upon by radicals in the Italian Enlightenment, just as the fundamentals of Protestant historical thought were utilized by English deists such as John Toland.

Because of the *de facto* continuity between the medieval and contemporary papacy and Papal States, the history of the medieval Church became a central battleground in the polemic between Roman orthodoxy and reform-minded, pro-regal propagandists (often termed jurisdictionalists). Sovereigns of the various states of the peninsula therefore – to one degree or another – supported and protected anti-curial reformers who polemicized against Rome on the terrain of medieval Church history. Nevertheless, despite the contemporary centrality of Church history to pro-curial propagandists and anti-curial reformers, the importance of Church history in Italian Enlightenment studies has to some extent been neglected. The neglect can partly be attributed to the fact that Italian Enlightenment studies have at times also been conducted within a retrospective framework with Whiggish overtones. This tendency was candidly summarized by Furio Diaz, in his review of European Enlightenment studies *Per una storia illuministica* (1973). Diaz noted, uncritically, that the years *c.* 1955–70 had been ones in which hope for economic, political and cultural reform and improvement had been dominant. It was 'natural', therefore, that historians searched in history for 'times and processes' which reflected their own objectives of progress – and they found them in the *philosophes*.[10]

Not surprisingly, then, the result has been an undue concentration on a small elite of enlightened thinkers, and on those historians and jurisdictionalist figures who have been considered as precursors of High Enlightenment thinkers: men who had reached the first rung of the ladder of progress leading to modernity. Hence the anti-curial writings of the outstanding Modena-based scholar Lodovico Muratori (1672–1750) and the brilliant Neapolitan lawyer Pietro Giannone (1676–1748) have been viewed as forerunners of enlightened thinkers such as Cosimo Amidei (d.1784) and his *La Chiesa e la repubblica dentro i loro limiti* (1768). It is undeniable that Muratorian and Giannonian historiography was later used by enlightened Italians as evidence of the spiritual and material degeneracy of the Catholic priesthood in general, and that Muratori did great service to the study of medieval history. However, one result of placing Muratori on the ladder of progress has been a reluctance, by some historians, to accept that his historiography was not wholly secular in its orientation. As a consequence, the providential elements of Muratori's historical critique have often been quietly passed over, because they were elements of his thought not in keeping with the supposed process of Enlightenment secularization. For similar reasons, the Christian piety of Giannone has been denied by omission.

A consequence of this attitude has been to erect an artificially stark division between the thinking of Muratori and Giannone, and that of anti-curialists of the previous century. This fanciful division has also partly been the result of a pronounced and strangely negative view of seventeenth-century Italian culture as a stagnant period of no histor-ical worth. The history of seventeenth-century Italy, something obviously important for an understanding of eighteenth-century Italian thought, has only relatively recently been rehabilitated as an object worthy of study. Its recent rescue has meant there has yet been relatively little systematic effort to determine the nature of the some-times clandestine anti-curial – often termed libertine (a commonly used but uselessly vague term) – historiographical traditions of the seventeenth century bequeathed to eighteenth-century writers. This is to say the context in which eighteenth-century anti-curial histori-ography underwent gestation has rarely been warranted sufficiently important for discussion.[11] Similarly, there has been no methodical research dedicated to charting and defining the radical and

Protestant-like critique of the medieval Church developed by less renowned and virtually unknown Catholic dissidents in the later eighteenth century. Nor has there been any systematic comparison of dissident Catholic historiography with that of Protestants. Comparative studies are important because they allow historians to generalize on the European context in which the Christian priestcraft critique was developed, and gauge the nature and influence of that critique.[12]

If relatively moderate critics of the Church such as Muratori are to be considered precursors of the Italian Enlightenment, what can be said of Protestant critics of the Church, such as Luther and Calvin? After all, these men produced a more devastating critique of Church history than Muratori not far short of two hundred years earlier. If the difference between Muratori and enlightened Italians is only a matter of degree, then perhaps the English Enlightenment and its distinctive attitude to Church history should be traced back to the most influential Protestant propagandist John Foxe? Other than the fact that Foxe and Toland were both English Protestant propagandists, it is, of course, impossible to trace any linear intellectual or theological influence between them. It is possible, however, to explore the diversity of the Protestant historiographical and polemical tradition from sixteenth- to eighteenth-century England. It was a development rooted in and responding to the complex realities of post-Reformation England, one which was devoted to purifying the Christian Church. But we know that in the late seventeenth and eighteenth century one part of the English Protestant tradition – radical Dissenters – turned upon itself and condemned all the contemporary and historical hierarchical Christian Churches as antichristian frauds. This should be a salutary warning to those who wish to simplify the history of intellectual development, for Protestants had created deist anti-Church historiography.

Luther and Calvin had produced an historical revolution. In his *Christianity not Mysterious* (1696), Toland – not yet a deist –was one of the Presbyterian-minded Dissenters who set about initiating a second historical revolution or, depending on one's view, decisively completing that of Luther and Calvin. In this work he dedicated himself to demonstrating that only a non-hierarchical Presbyterian Church could ensure Christianity was not infected with priestly mysteries.

As we shall see below, Foxe would certainly have recognized Toland's splenetic accusations of priestcraft as decidedly Protestant. He would certainly not have understood why the early Church was

condemned equally by Toland as by the medieval Church. It is, therefore, most likely Foxe would have approved of the fact that Toland's
book was condemned by the Irish Parliament, burnt by the hangman,
and Toland forced to flee.

In their historical writings, Toland and other like-minded
Protestants were drawing – most effectively – upon a Protestant religious commonplace. They exploited and extended anti-Catholic
historiography in order to advance their claim that the career of
traditional hierarchical Churches was manifestly at an end and a new
Presbyterian age was the only solution for the ills of Christianity. The
crisis of the European mind in the decades 1680s–1720s (delineated
in P. Hazard's *The Crisis of European Consciousness*, 1935) ought,
therefore, rather to be considered a final facet of the crisis of the
Church initiated by the Reformation. For all historians now accept
that in the Europe of the Enlightenment there was only a very limited
change in or crisis of faith. The faith of the English masses changed
little, even if in some respects they demonstrated more ambivalence
to the institutional Church by turning to an alternative pole of religious attraction such as provided by Methodism. The only convulsion
in the faith of the masses, or at least in sections of their ranks,
occurred in revolutionary France and, although dramatic, it was but
a brief interlude in eighteenth-century European history.

The distinction between a crisis of the Church and that of faith is
important. This dichotomy helps to explain why, in the seventeenth
and early eighteenth century, new scientific ideas, such as those of
Isaac Newton, which had the potential to undermine the biblical view
of the cosmos were at first mostly assimilated into Christianity.
Inevitably, a crisis in the Church, if sufficiently profound and
protracted, nevertheless contained the possibility of a crisis of faith,
because the teachings of the Church allied to the Bible have always
constituted the major influence upon the Christian conception of
God. Such an incipient crisis in faith was eventually naturally
bolstered rather than retarded by alternative, scientific explanations
of the cosmos. Not surprisingly then, later – mostly after the mid-
eighteenth century – a narrow and elite section of an increasingly
numerous and confident intelligentsia began to overtly question
Christian fundamentals. These thinkers were impatient to free
scientific and philosphical inquiry from traditional Christian
epistemological boundaries. Consequently, some went beyond questioning the historical and contemporary legitimacy of the Church, to
query the very fundamentals of Christianity.

With regard to the Whig historical tradition, Herbert Butterfield has noted, it is precisely 'in reference to the great transitions in European society that the Whig view holds hardest and longest', whereas the real historical process is much more complex[13] – which is an observation of great significance in this discussion. In late seventeenth-century and for some decades of eighteenth-century England, scientific discovery, rather than acting as a secularizing force, more often sustained the idea of a world governed by providence. Newton's discoveries explained much about the fundamentals of the operations of the universe. But he himself, and many of the Christian recipients of his work for decades – no less in England than in Italy – viewed his work as evidence of the ineffable creative power of God, the watch-maker-God who set all in motion and continually maintained the laws of nature.

The prominent Italian philosopher and political economist Antonio Genovesi counterposed Newtonian science against the doubts of sceptics and libertines. Indeed, Voltaire said that when he thought of Newton, he automatically thought of God. In England, the congruity of empirical scientific research and Christianity was defended by such thinkers as Robert Boyle, as he did in his *Christian Virtuoso: Shewing that by being Addicted to Experimental Philosophy a Man is rather Assisted than Indisposed to Be a Good Christian* (1690). This was a view echoed by Samuel Clarke in his *A Demonstration of the Being and Attributes of God* (1705). Newton's work, therefore, came in a period when the autonomy of science from religion was still in its embryonic stages. Science can thus hardly be seen as the sole parent giving birth to the Enlightenment. We also know a successful alliance between religion and science could still be forged at the end of the eighteenth century by scientists such as Joseph Priestley (1733–1804). This was not an unusual phenomenon of the High Enlightenment, in which it cannot be said there was any straightforward or necessary conflict between religion and scientific materialism. In Christian terms (and for some deists), no one 'doubted that the forms of living things were related in some harmonius way to fulfilling God's purposes in his creation'.[14]

We do know that scientific and philosophical discovery were nevertheless vital components of the High Enlightenment (after about 1750), and were eventually important vehicles for the very gradual and uneven (in geographical and chronological terms) secularization of intellectual thought. Nevertheless, as we have seen, scientific ideas do not in themselves necessarily possess a *de facto* power of intellectual change. This is graphically illustrated by the fortunes of the Copernican revolution in astronomical thought, which eventually displaced the biblical notion of the Earth as the centre of the universe. The ideas of Copernicus were not officially proscribed by the papacy until 1616, more than seventy years after their appearance in 1543. The lengthy delay is accounted for by the fact that his ideas were not then perceived as a significant threat to Church doctrine. His ideas were not then widely held or defended, and anyway the papacy had other pressing concerns during the Counter-Reformation.[15] That is to say, in 1543, Copernican ideas did not find an audience sufficiently prepared to break with Church orthodoxy. The crisis of the Church in 1543 was not yet profound enough to prise loose the bonds of ecclesiastical intellectual tutelage, or encourage or permit widespread and open defiance of biblical conceptions. Some degree of maturation had yet to take place. Yet, as we shall see, there is no evidence that even in 1616 the Curia was overly concerned with the actual scientific threat of Copernican or Galilean ideas. Clearly one must ask what happened in those seventy years: what was the change in religious context which prompted Rome to defensive action?

By far the most dominant factor in religious experience in those years was the protracted post-Reformation aftermath of internecine religious polemic and warfare, in which the credibility of the Christian Church as a spiritual guide was slowly eroded. Hence Rome felt the need to make a practical statement of its status as traditional defender of the faith. As the seventeenth century progressed, the foundation of institutional Christianity was increasingly called into question by the continued development and propagation of a ferocious priestcraft accusation wielded by Catholics, Protestants and their various subdivisions. In a pious age it was only natural that some of the intellectual elite, increasing in number and degree of intellectual independence from the Church, searched for a solution to the palpable and seemingly ineradicable ills of institutional Christianity. As will be seen, the writings of Charles Blount and John Toland, which many historians consider to have marked the beginning of the English Enlightenment, were not about the building of a new European future in harmony with scientific advance. Rather they were at pains to resolve the long-term crisis of institutional Christianity by extending the reach of the traditional anticlericalism of the Protestant priestcraft critique to include almost *all* of the history of all established hierarchies of Christianity. This development meant it was possible to sidestep the intractable problem of corrupt priesthoods, and substitute their own

Presbyterian vision. In Christian terms this was a radical and risky project.

The writings of Blount, Toland and others have often been referred to as anticlerical. In general terms, Enlightenment anticlericalism was predicated on an unremitting view of the history of religion as a long-term religious, political and economic fraud. However, if the term anticlerical is used as a precise term of definition for deist or otherwise sceptical enlightened thought, as has been the case, there is a danger of a lack of conceptual clarity. The term anticlerical denotes an attitude of hostility to the power and influence of the clergy, in social, economic and political terms. This is as true of the unremitting anti-clericalism of early modern Catholics directed towards the Protestant Church, as that of Protestants against the Catholic Church, and of Protestant and Catholic dissidents against their respective established Churches. A recognizably anticlerical and very public broadside could equally well be delivered by a *philosophe,* a Catholic, or a Protestant. A good deal of Protestant and dissident Catholic polemic was often more laden with vitriol than the most rabid declamations of Enlightenment propagandists against the Church. Hence statements that English deists harboured 'a barely disguised anticlericalism' are unintelligible and only serve to cloud the conceptual clarity necessary in an already complex field.[16]

Anticlericalism then, is a matter of degree and specificity, and is not a term sufficient in itself to indicate any general hostility to Christianity or its Churches. If anticlericalism is implicitly assumed to be the trait of antichristian or deistic thought, the historian, when encountering a vicious anticlerical diatribe, may well risk mistaking Christian factional critique for Enlightenment hostility to Christianity. The result of such misapprehension has been that some radical Protestants have been transformed into deists, while others have been given the hopelessly vague appellation of 'anticlerical writer'. This type of confusion is not only a problem for modern historians, for in Paris the anti-Catholic polemic of the Huguenot Pierre Bayle (1647–1706) was understood by some as an attack upon Christianity in general. Such were the dangers of the Reformation's institutionalization of Christian conflict, a destructive phenomenon of a magnitude not before experienced in Europe.

The writings of the *philosophes* were read across Europe by a narrow and often elite section of the reading public. The Christian diatribes against the perceived priestcraft of their religious opponents, however, were printed with a view to a very much wider audience. This was an audience that had grown as literacy rates rapidly climbed in most of post-reformation Europe, and access to pamphlets and tracts became more frequent as printed material tended to cheapen in the context of a burgeoning vernacular print culture. Jacopo Moronessa was typical of the period when he wrote his vicious accusation of Protestant priestcraft, *Il Modello di Martino Lutero* (1555), in Italian rather than Latin in order – so he explained – that even peasants would be able to comprehend the awful and antichristian truth about Luther. The perceived exigencies of successful religious polemic changed little in the coming centuries. More than two hundred years later, John Wesley decided to keep his bitterly destructive *Concise Ecclesiastical History* (1781) at a deliberately low price in order to ensure maximum readership. In this crude, but nevertheless important sense, the splenetic and pervasive anticlericalism spawned by the Reformation was the *de facto* general context surrounding the audience for unorthodox theological and philosophical polemics, whether of the wider dissenting type or the narrow elite writings of *philosophes*. Orthodox polemic itself had thus partly prepared the conceptual terrain for unorthodox polemico-historical thought. In the history of mentalities, this is a point too often dismissed and denigrated as little but a commonplace.

Amongst some historians, once the shibboleth of intellectual progress had been invoked as an explanation for the origin and nature of the Enlightenment, it was only natural that there should have been a hunt for identifiable stages in its development. This has been a search that has provided historians with some elegantly simple historical schemes. One such example is the notion that the roots of the Enlightenment are to be found in the Renaissance as, amongst others, Peter Gay has argued in his *Modern Paganism*. This might be considered an idea less than helpful to the student of the Enlightenment who finds his or her subject dissolved into a vague long-term trend. It is a notion which can provoke legitimate outrage in students of the Renaissance, who find their not inconsiderable object of study relegated to the prologue of the Enlightenment. Such problems have not gone entirely unnoticed by historians. Patrick Collinson has noted that political history has suffered from a retrospective approach, with the construction of developmental stages which may only be the invention of historians.[17]

Gay contended the Enlightenment ought to be viewed as a break with the Christian past, rather than as an organic development from within. But such a formulation of the problem of Enlightenment origins is somewhat of a red herring. It would be very difficult indeed to find an historian who would argue that in the Renaissance (or earlier periods) there were not sceptics and atheists. Some of these certainly regarded the Christian priesthood with fundamental misgivings; even, as the Albigenses of thirteenth-century France argued, that the papacy was a religious fraud. Some materialist ideas – such as atomism – were similarly old news and had been known by early modern scholars to have existed in ancient Greek thought. The point, then, is not always to find an original idea or tradition, but also to assess how the power of ideas can change in different prevailing circumstances and be infused with new vigour or a radically different significance. Thus the proper subject of Enlightenment studies is the political, social, economic and religious context of seventeenth- and eighteenth-century Europe. Historians should not concentrate unduly upon the importation of a 'pivotal' idea from the Renaissance or ancient Rome at the expense of assessing the wider social consciousness into which such an idea is placed. It was the perceived reality of priestcraft, personified by the priest-king at Rome and epitomized in the bloody wars of religion, which for many gave Protestant anti-Catholic and Catholic anti-curial propaganda its manifest truth.

As Roy Porter has argued in reference to Gibbon's *Decline and Fall*, it is misleading to examine historical writing without establishing the context of its audience. This is to say the context in which an idea is raised can, at times, be as important as the idea itself.[18] In the context of the Reformation it can be said – and as the event and its aftermath proved – old anticlerical ideas were reinvigorated by the experience of chronic confessional division. In this period the pedlars of anticlerical diatribes were no longer enraged but isolated individuals, or protagonists of small or impermanent religious sects. Christian anticlericalism had become official, had become the hallmark of respectable Catholic or Protestant piety. Some of the finest minds of the period were engaged in manufacturing and researching polemics and historical accounts which purported to contain factual proof of their accusations of priestcraft.

Until the eighteenth century most states were confessional, and significant and sustained religious conciliation rare. Permanent national and international religious institutions were still sufficiently endowed with wealth and prestige to attract the services of first-rate propagandists, whose task it was to find new polemical or historical avenues by which to undermine the religious credibility of their opponents. To stress, therefore, the similarity of pre-Reformation – that is

to say necessarily mostly clandestine – anticlerical ideas or unorthodox philosophical theories with those of post-Reformation Europe is
not to compare like with like. If we are interested in the magnitude of
an idea's impact (and clearly we are when considering the origins of
Enlightenment anticlericalism), it is no less than to compare the
proverbial chalk with the cheese. It would be to remain within an
abstract frame of reference with little bearing on the long-term reality
of religious change and experience. In the hands of early English
Protestant reformers, the charge that the Catholic Church had taken
its model from the priestcraft of the pagans was a severe indictment.
As we shall see in later chapters, one and a half centuries later, in the
writings of various English Dissenters, the same charge was considered by most readers to apply to the Anglican Church, even though
the Anglican Church was often not itself named. The difference of
perception did not lie in the idea, but in the context into which the
idea was received. It is to that context we must now turn.

In late seventeenth-century England the most virulent anti-
Catholicism was periodically legitimized in the minds of Protestants
by widespread fears of invasion by Catholic powers and numerous
real or alleged popish plots (such as that leading to the Exclusion
Controversy of 1679–81). The accession of the Catholic King James II
(1685–8), who publicly attended Mass, appointed Catholic officers to
the Army and had, as Lord High Commissioner of Scotland, overseen
the bloody persecution of the Scottish Covenanters, naturally reinforced fears of Catholic tyranny. The sober fact of renewed
Protestant–Catholic war in Ireland (1689–91) only served to further
heighten Protestant fears of an eventual victory of papal despotism.
In this atmosphere, where Dissenting Protestants also suffered persecution and discrimination (and we know Toland was a Dissenter until
1697) twenty-four Catholics were hung, drawn and quartered
between 1678–81.[19] In Scotland in 1696 a young student, Thomas
Aikenhead, was tried and executed for blasphemy for allegedly
denying the divinity of Christ. This was still a very pious period, then,
and religious passion could still run very hot. Indeed the religious
situation at the end of the century has been described as near religious anarchy, in which various dissenting tendencies simultaneously
contended against the domination of the Anglican Church and each
other for the allegiance of the faithful.

Dissenters were bitterly disappointed at the failure of the
Protestant succession of William and Mary in 1689 to herald comprehensive toleration and end religious discrimination in public life. In

this superheated religious climate, an inherent possibility was religious exhaustion, manifested by some in a defection to a non-institutional and therefore non-partisan and non-dogmatic natural religious system such as deism. In the life of John Toland, we know the process of moving from dissenting Christianity to deism was preceded by an earnest yet unsuccessful struggle for a less divisive and bloodstained Christianity.[20] Modern historians, however, have not so far noted that the disaffection of Toland evident in his *Christianity not Mysterious* was justified with historiographical and polemical views that bore a startling similarity to the usual dissenting Protestant historical view. Toland's work should not be singled out for criticism as unoriginal, because eminent Englishmen also produced analyses of the medieval Church which were less than original, including that contained in Gibbon's *Decline and Fall of the Roman Empire*. In any case, we are not here too concerned with originality, but with the intellectual impact of ideas.

SOME PARAMETERS AND ASSUMPTIONS

This book does not seek the origins of the Enlightenment itself, nor does it aim to provide a detailed account of post-Reformation theological development. Rather it seeks to explore the nature, efficacy and broad context of the Christian priestcraft theory, the most common vehicle by which religious opposition was then expressed. To establish the existence and nature of the Christian priestcraft discourse – something hitherto not accomplished – Chapters 2 to 5 will necessarily discuss in some detail its nature and historical chronology via a wide variety of writers. The analysis contained in these chapters will provide the basis for an understanding of the extent to which it was practical for enlightened thinkers to appropriate the comparative polemic and historical critique of Christians. The possible avenues for the investigation of the priestcraft accusation are diverse. The discussion will focus upon various subjects of importance to early modern Christian thinkers: state and Church; papal supremacy; the main aspects of Church doctrine; clerical wealth; heresy; superstition; forgery and idolatry. In order to demonstrate the continuity of the Christian priestcraft polemic and, most importantly, its independence from Enlightenment thought, British and Italian Christian historical writing from the mid-sixteenth century until 1800 will be examined, although the main focus will be the period *c.* 1690–1800.

The question of which writers to select for study poses a problem. Clearly, the historical view of an age cannot be adequately assessed if only a select few distinguished historians are chosen for study. To assume that intellectual elites necessarily reflect the thought of society as a whole would clearly be an untenable assumption. Nevertheless, as Laird Okie has stated, the 'tendency of scholars to focus on a few big names has produced an incomplete and somewhat distorted picture of eighteenth-century historiography'.[21] The relatively large number of unknown and 'minor' writers reviewed in this book is a product of the need to broaden the scope of enquiry into early modern conceptions of Church history in order to redress past concentration on the thought of the *philosophes*. Thus most writers included for discussion, aside from perhaps Muratori, Giannone, Priestley, Toland, Gibbon and John Wesley, will be unfamiliar to readers.

Despite the importance of the term deism to many studies of the Enlightenment, it continues to represent serious terminological difficulty. The term deism connotes such a divergent set of seventeenth- and eighteenth-century attitudes to religion that, as we shall see, the use of the word is apt to be to be very misleading. Unfortunately, its uncritical use has led to a blurring of delineation between Christians and deists. For the purposes of this study, Christians are defined as those whose religious views included an acceptance of the revelation of Jesus Christ and his tenets as expressed in the New Testament, as well as a belief in the role of Christian collective worship whether expressed in formal institutions (Churches) or gathered congregations. Some so-called deists too believed in the revelation of Jesus Christ, and others that the Creation and nature itself proved the existence of a God otherwise unknowable – a God who in both cases no longer intervened in human history. But most rejected the need for collective Christian worship and its institutions.

So, risking another attempt to define something not amenable to definition, that rejection will express the content of the term deism as used in this book. However simplistic this definition may seem to some, it does at least provide us with the possibility of using the term deist – if only in this present discussion – with less confusion than might otherwise be the case. It is also a working definition with considerable practical application to the task of exploring the enlightened view of Church history and its origins. Some more remarks on the problem of defining deism will be made in Chapter 7.

2 The Priestcraft Theory: Text and Context

The imposition by Church and state of a revolutionary history of Christian culture on much of early modern Europe was itself a factor in the matrix of tension that led to long-term political destabilization and military conflict in Europe. In the French Wars of Religion, as in other conflicts of the period, supposed religious precedent often served to reinforce and justify the economic and political goals of kings and princes. After all – and it is worth stressing this often undervalued point – the stakes were high. Protestant secession meant control of the Church, which usually meant at least a short-term injection of funds for hard-pressed sovereigns and better prospects for taxing the wealth of the Church. More importantly, control of the Church and its power over the hearts and minds of the masses was still a principal factor in a sovereign's ability to maintain adequate control of his/her realm in a politically and militarily unstable continent. That Rome supported most of the bellicosity of Catholic powers was understandable: faith coincided with the protection of the secular wealth of the Church from Protestant hands. In this sense, a Catholic battle for the defence of empire lay behind and at times coincided with the material goals of Catholic powers. The carnage and turmoil of the various so-called Wars of Religion in the sixteenth century gave way to that of the Thirty Years War (1618–48), in which huge areas of Europe were devastated and peoples displaced amid the slaughter. The monarchies of Europe did not emerge from this maelstrom and regain political and religious balance until the wave of Europe-wide wars and revolutions of the mid-seventeenth century had subsided.

That the highborn protagonists of such conflicts very often engaged in battle under the more or less covert goad of politics and economics, but overtly under the colours of religion, is clear if usually understated by historians. Much less appreciated is how the flag of religion in this period was also an ensign for implicit yet fundamental social and political outlooks shared by peasants and townsmen alike. Protestants fought the historical enemy: the betrayer of Christendom, the usurper of princely prerogatives and the engineers and advocates of despotic rule. Catholics fought the modern traitors of Christianity, which they considered to be the latest version of the Manichaeist heresy. The leaders of this heresy were wholly corrupt, their claimed reforming aim was but a guise for venal goals, and Europe was being led into iniquitous rule and bloody conflict. For Catholics this assessment was all too plainly verified by the reality of religious persecution, which in England accounted for the execution of almost two hundred Catholics in the reign of Elizabeth I.

For the first time two established European Churches contended against each other, and the scale of the conflicts fought under religious banners dwarfed medieval enormities such as the slaughter of the Albigensians in the thirteenth century. Europe was gripped by a religious conflict that went to the very roots of society. This was still a period in which political and economic disagreements between and within social classes were usually expressed in religious terms. Luther learnt this lesson to his cost in the Peasant War of 1525, when German peasants extended his accusation of long-standing Catholic oppression to include their own temporal lords, and revolted against both Church and nobility (that is Church and state) in the name of true Christianity. In seventeenth-century England, the Civil War, despite its economic and political roots, was also fought in religious clothes and often within an impassioned religious frame of reference. The ill-fated Charles I (1625–49) himself recognized that without control of the Church effective rule was unlikely. In Europe Catholics and Protestants fought and died with different concepts of the past, different historical systems and paradigms they had themselves created in order to better understand, explain and justify the present. The overtly didactic use of historical writing as validation for given religious and political positions was common, considered legitimate, and persisted into the late eighteenth century. Joseph Priestley could thus write that 'Being a unitarian', he differs with the historical interpretations of Trinitarians,[1] even 'when there is no dispute about the facts'.[2]

Confessional historians narrated an historical story in which, as in all written history, there were more or less discernible chains of events constituting the dynamic or unfolding of historical development. Some causal factors, however, were never explicitly stated by the writers. Facts may have been presented, but the identification or attribution of causality for a particular part or facet of the historical account was often left to the acumen of the reader. Behind what might therefore seem to have been pure empiricism, of course, lay the highly subjective realm of the historian's choice, stress and mode of depiction of historical events. Historians were also able to rely on the conceptual evidence of the reader – that is to say shared religious, political and social conceptions – to supply some of the contextual and even causal elements of the historical account.

Reading historical accounts is, therefore, rarely purely a passive undertaking. For example, to read a history of the popes without knowing something about Jesus Christ and the Apostles would almost certainly limit one's understanding of the text, or bias comprehension, as the reader flounders for the fundamentals of Christianity. But, whether more or less ignorant or conversant with the fundamentals of an historical narrative, the readership still possesses a value-laden context or conceptual framework into which the account is integrated and assessed. Naturally, historians strive to anticipate the manner in which a particular account may be received by readers and adjust the content in order to maximize the intended comprehension. However, if the context or conceptual evidence brought to bear by the audience is very different to that imagined by the author, there is potential for a misreading of the meaning or significance of the account. As we have seen, such was the fate of some of the writings of Pierre Bayle, whose work has been considered by some as marking the first stirrings of the French Enlightenment. In Paris, Bayle's attacks upon the perceived idolatry and superstition of the Catholic Church were assumed to be attacks upon Christianity itself. In a dialectical turn of history, therefore, 'anti-Catholic controversy was read as anti-Christian polemics'.[3]

The possibility of such confusion – or the conscious exploitation of ambiguity – in seventeenth- and eighteenth-century England was greatly augmented by the complexity of its religious life. In religious controversy, the term deist was widely applied by thinkers of various outlooks as a term of opprobrium for a diverse spectrum of individuals deemed deficient in their Christianity. By uncritically accepting and repeating this appellation, some writers have mistakenly been considered by modern historians as non-Christian because they were hypercritical of the history of the Church and the claimed frauds of priests. Neither was this a problem restricted to historical texts, as the varied reception of the scientific works of Isaac Newton demonstrated. Figures such as the French deist Voltaire interpreted Newton's work as indicating that God had created the universe, but had then left humanity to its own devices, free of divine interference. This was an interpretation certainly not intended by the very pious Newton, who held a profoundly providential and prophetic view of historical development, yet who has been termed a deist by some twentieth-century historians.

It has been said, therefore, and with good justification that, in France, 'English writers appeared more radical than they were at home'.[4] Similarly, Domenico Ferrone has noted there was 'a profound difference' in the meaning of the same Enlightenment ideas in France and Italy, because they were received into 'backdrops of very different historical realities'. At times, even the attempts of Rome to counter Enlightenment ideas had, in part, quite the reverse effect. In order to train clerics to fight new heretical ideas, it was sometimes considered necessary to provide frank and detailed lectures upon the ideas of perceived Church enemies such as Baruch Spinoza, Herbert of Cherbury and Thomas Hobbes. Some of these lectures were published – such as those of Abbot Bencini in 1720 – and in Turin served to heighten interest in Spinozan thought.[5]

Nevertheless, however heretical the pantheistic ideas (that God and the universe are identical) of Spinoza might have been, in terms of their religious and intellectual impact, his ideas had comparatively little impression upon the psyche of Europe as compared to those of Luther and Calvin. How could it have been otherwise? Their ideas and historical critique quickly became the ammunition for extensive and tenacious propaganda machines. We should also recognize that the message of the Reformers was just as subversive and radical as Spinoza's. Although ideas such as Spinoza's might be considered inimical to the Church in general, Luther's ideas could be considered by some to represent an implicit and immediate incitement to revolt against Church and (as in 1525) sometimes secular authority. For Luther, Calvin and subsequent generations of Protestants, the history of medieval Christendom was the history of priestcraft: a systematic and criminal deception that Christians had to expunge by toppling the edifice that had protected and nourished it.

It is true that not all Luther's ideas were new,[6] but his analysis, as a whole, can nevertheless be considered a new historical insight. It was Luther who first produced a grand scheme of papal priestcraft, one sufficiently erudite and in harmony with contemporary political and theological dissatisfactions with Rome to constitute a pole of attraction for hitherto mostly submerged dissent. For Luther, Calvin and others there was no doubt about the assertion of the deep-seated priestcraft of Rome, for they perceived that before them they had the hard and baleful facts of contemporary Catholicism as conclusive proof of its historical nature. This new insight into Church history was amplified and consolidated in the work of the Magdeburg Centuriators, led by Matthias Flacius Illyricus (1520–75). The publication of the *Magdeburg Centuries* (1559–74),[7] a systematic attack on orthodox Church history, provoked the Catholic Cesare Baronius (1538–1607) to write his *Annales ecclesiastici* (1588–1607) in order to counter the Europe-wide Protestant offensive.

Luther repeated his historical schema in his preface to the *Vitae romanorum pontificum* (1536) written by the English martyr Robert Barnes (1495–1540). Subsequently, in the writings of various influential writers, the English Protestant tradition of the priestcraft theory was developed, remaining prevalent in much Protestant thought beyond the year 1800. The medieval consensus on the intervention of God in the medieval Church and in the lives of Christians was shattered as sixteenth- and seventeenth-century Protestants denied the divinity of medieval miracles. From the pulpit or in print, medieval miracles were derided as naught but tricks perpetrated upon the laity in order to increase the ungodly power of popes and prelates.[8] In the late eighteenth century, John Wesley (1703–91) still typified Protestant thought when he wrote that false medieval miracles had been promoted for gain and from a desire to be 'reverenced by the multitude'.[9] Additionally vexed by attacks of sceptics on the credibility of miracles, some eighteenth-century Protestants, anxious to ensure that genuine apostolic miracles were not lost with the dross of the medieval fakes, strove ever harder to demonstrate the fraudulent authorship of medieval miracles. It was for this reason that Bishop John Douglas of Salisbury wrote *The Criterion: or, Miracles examined with a View to Expose the Pretensions of Pagans and Papists* (1754).[10]

Sixteenth- and seventeenth-century Protestants had so thoroughly vilified Church history as the history of clerical fraud that very little remained of sacred Church history – that is to say of the actions of the faithful guided by divine grace.[11] As already noted, for Protestants the fraud and cruel religious oppression of the medieval Church continued in the form of the contemporary Catholic Church. In this situation, Protestant historians and polemicists naturally and increasingly translated tangible Protestant fears and religious differences into a Church history that gave causal precedence to the venal actions of popes and prelates at the expense of primary (divine) causes. Primary causes or providence – the interventions of God in the world – were increasingly denied, whether in the form of miracles, natural wonders or events considered to have been directly brought about by God's hand. Protestants concentrated on the task of identifying medieval priestcraft, tracing the various social, economic and political motives of its clerical perpetrators. At most, only the first three centuries of

Christianity escaped the full blast of Protestant damnation: the early Church, in which for some the hand of God was considered evident and priestly fraud relatively undeveloped.

In practice, then, exemplified in such works as William Crashaw's *Falsificationum romanarum* (1606), secondary or human causes frequently came to dominate historical accounts, even if the tone of those accounts was still overtly pious. Increasingly, the traditional direction and intervention of God in the historical development of the Church became reduced to a vague, long-term and negative form: the amorphous machinations of the biblical Antichrist. In the second half of the seventeenth century, in such works as Henry Care's anti-Anglican periodical *A Pacquet of Advice from Rome* (1678–83), despite mention of the Antichrist and the care taken to identify it with the pope, the *de facto* dominance of secondary causality is marked. After all, the Westminster Confession (1643) had asserted decades before that God 'ordereth [events] to fall out according to the nature of second causes'. Subjected to the exigencies of Christian factional conflict, Protestants had made unintended yet tangible progress towards the English deist project of the late seventeenth century: the desacralization of Church history.[12]

Yet, in the literal sense, *A Pacquet of Advice from Rome* might be still held to demonstrate that (as Roy Porter has commented) 'for Christian history the proper study of mankind was Providence', while the history of the *philosophes* took as its proper subject the actions of humanity. Similarly, Peter Gay has stated that the developmental dynamic of history as understood by Christians lay 'in the shadow of the supernatural'.[13] Such formulations, most common, and to an extent useful in order to demonstrate the difference between trad-itional Christian and Enlightenment historiographical conceptions, are yet potentially most misleading. The uncritical acceptance of such stark divisions has led historians to underestimate the importance and extent of the impact of Christian historical understanding upon the formation of social, political and economic attitudes.

We know both sceptical and Christian historians and polemicists of the sixteenth to the eighteenth centuries pursued their own goals. It has also been said '[n]ever in the palmiest days of classical or human-ist writing was more feverish activity exhibited in scanning records of the past'[14] than that brought about by the Reformation. Yet are we to say the only goal the myriad of authors of that great and prolonged polemical outpouring succeeded in was to confirm the existence of a God who had given some vague direction to long-term historical

development? Was there no comment presented upon the nature of
the priesthood, the Church, the political outlook of Catholic states
and the relationship between Church and state? The Protestant
historical polemic portrayed the all too human history of the medieval
Church as one of priestcraft. Orthodox Catholics and many dissenting
Protestants did likewise for the short history of the new Anglican
Church. We cannot forget that the actors in the polemico-historical
dramas presented were human. Their misdeeds and the bloody and
baleful consequences of them were fully comprehensible and recognizable to readers as the human drama of everyday life.

Modern historians must grit their teeth and admit that these historical conceptions were often reinforced by the palpable intolerance of
Church and state, and the perceived existence of the priest-king at
Rome. The less than laudable aims and behaviour of European political and military alliances which were presented in confessional terms
also undoubtedly contributed to tarnishing the reputation of the
Church. The fundamental point is this: when Catholics and Protestants
delved into historical thinking they could not damn medieval spiritual
failings without damning human and institutional behaviour and their
contemporary parallels. In Protestant thought this was of course the
origin of anti-Catholicism, a term so hackneyed by over-use it is all too
easy to forget the momentous context of its birth.

So dominant a part of the Protestant psyche was the priestcraft
theory, that its logic was in good part inescapable even for those
tending towards High Church conceptions. High Churchmen wished
to rescue something from the wreckage of the medieval Church in
order to provide historical continuity for the Anglican Church. Yet
Richard Field, High Church chaplain to Queen Elizabeth and James
I, pointed out in his *Of the Church* (1606) that after Pope Gregory I
(590–604) the superstition, barbarity, corruption, ignorance, forgeries
and false miracles of the Church were no longer opposed. The pope,
'taking all into his owne hands by innumerable sleights, and treading
down under his feete the crownes of Kings, and iurisdictions of
Bishops', corrupted the Church.[15]

Some modern scholars of the Enlightenment have argued (sometimes
inadvertently by failing to consider the practical significance of Christian
historiography) that the new profane historiography of the *philosophes*
marked a revolution in the potential of historical writing to influence
historical and contemporary conceptions of religion and, by implication,
of European civilization. This claim is, at least in part, without foundation. Perhaps the clearest expression of this misconception has been

made by Peter Gay. Gay explained that anticlerical criticism of the Church had existed for centuries, 'but it was far from dangerous to religion or even to the clerical establishment'. Similarly, the doubting of miracles was 'relatively innocuous', because such criticism emanated from a narrow circle of men[16] – although it is difficult to see how the opinions of millions of Protestant men and women can be considered a narrow circle of men. But, of course, Gay's 'family' of *philosophes* was exactly that, a narrow circle of elite men.

Perhaps we should now acknowledge that the paradigm of progress has had a far more insidious impact on historical thought than has hitherto been admitted. How can Gay's assessment be reconciled with the understanding of historians that, in post-Reformation Europe, the new fracture lines of religious conflict considerably exacerbated the instability of an already politically and economically unstable Europe, whose kings continued to fight for survival and material advantage? Besides the banner of religion in secular warfare, large-scale religious persecution for secular ends also meant blood-letting and massive social upheaval of various kinds. Is it possible the religious justification of these horrible events did not contribute to a deepening of cynicism concerning the role of Church hierarchies? Sometimes, as in the case of Huguenot refugees in England in the late 1680s, refugees fleeing Catholic persecution came to a land in which state and Church continued to take part in gory religious repression, as for example the long-standing persecution of Scottish Presbyterians. English and Scottish Dissenters could be forgiven for wondering about the difference between the Anglican and Catholic Churches.

It is now time to examine the classic example – in Peter Gay's terms – where Christian historiography lay 'in the shadow of the supernatural': the use of the Antichrist concept to explain the development of tyranny and antichristian doctrine in the Church. Both Martin Luther and John Calvin had identified the papacy with the Antichrist, that of the *Book of Revelation* in which the defeat of the Antichrist was to presage the Millennium. English Protestants soon adopted and continued that identification. Somewhere behind the venal actions of popes and prelates in history was the Antichrist, the inspiration for priestcraft. For some his presence had apparently been confirmed by the onset of papal supremacy in the Church, often understood to have commenced in 607 when Pope Boniface III accepted the title of universal bishop from the eastern Emperor Focas. Contemporary events also confirmed the existence of an apocalyptical struggle presaging the Millennium. John Foxe and other Marian exiles struggled to understand why God had allowed the accession of the Catholic Queen Mary (1553–8) and the subsequent persecution of Protestants, of whom nearly three hundred were sent to the stake. Their conclusion was that English Protestants were being subjected to a divine test, an apocalyptical and final struggle between good and evil.

In the seventeenth century, the Thirty Years War (1618–48) was interpreted by many English Protestants as an apocalyptical struggle between Christians and the Antichrist – the fraudulent priest-cum-king at Rome and his allies.[17] Other events of this century, the Gunpowder Plot (1605), the widespread fear of other Catholic conspiracies, the Civil War of the 1640s, regicide and religious massacres on the continent, were similarly identified. Puritans, not slow to realize the polemical force of an implicit parallel with the papacy, also used the Antichrist charge against Anglican episcopalians. Even in the thought of some exponents of the use of reason in religion, such as the Cambridge Platonist Henry More, there was a continued belief in biblical prophecy, as there was in that of the scientist Isaac Newton.

In historical analysis, the mere mention of the word Antichrist invoked a vague scheme of historical development, ratifying the human apparition of Catholic priestcraft as a truth verified by prophecy. One word could go a very long way indeed, which is to say the Antichrist concept quickly arrived at the status of conceptual knowledge. The Revocation of the Edict of Nantes (the 1598 concord ending the wars of religion in France) in 1685 and the cruel oppression of Huguenots which followed, was similarly understood as the product of Catholic priestcraft. This event only needed to be but fleetingly linked to the Antichrist in order to summon from the reader's mind an unseen causality behind the earthly actions of popes and Catholic princes. It was, therefore, often necessary only to prune away a few phrases, sentences or pages of identifiably Christian thought in a text to be left with an account of priestcraft sufficiently secondary in its causality to be appropriate for easy adoption by deists, sceptics and atheists.

For those still tempted to agree with the unqualified statement that Christian historiography lay 'in the shadow of the supernatural', and so summarily deprive it of the power to influence secular conceptions of the world and its history, a comment on Catholic anti-curial historiography is necessary. Anti-curial Catholic analysis of the Church, very similar indeed in its essentials to that of Protestants, did not sport any such concept as the Antichrist. Neither is there one whit of evidence that the efficacy of the anti-curial attack on Rome was thus diminished or that anti-curial historiography was more easily utilized by the enlightened Italians than that of Protestants by English deists. The Antichrist concept was simply not needed by reforming anti-curial Catholics. To have accused the papacy and prelates of historical collusion with the devil would have been to denigrate beyond salvage that which they wished to rescue by reform.

Both dissident Catholic writers and Protestants in general – despite disagreements on how to reform the Church – could agree that the first centuries of the Church were to be exculpated from the unchristian hand of priestcraft. Both parties viewed the simplicity and perceived purity of the early Church as the original model Jesus himself had prescribed: a period often understood as before the state adoption (or at least toleration and Imperial favour) of Christianity by Emperor Constantine (d. 337) and not extending after Pope Gregory I (590–604). For some Anglicans, a vestige of Church purity remained until the antichristianism of Pope Gregory VII (1073–85). But by pioneering a radically new history of Christendom, Protestants had allowed a distinctly wayward genie out of the proverbial bottle. From early in the post-Reformation period, competing Protestant tendencies had incorporated some of the elements of the priestcraft tirade in their own polemics against each other. The form of that critique was comparative: English polemicists compared Catholicism to the heathen iniquities of paganism and Islam, and a similar comparative technique was also used by competing Protestant tendencies against each other and against the Anglican Church. It is surprising that, although there is copious evidence of this practice, the important consequences of its increasing use have been given little attention.[18]

Despite the five-year reign of Bloody Mary (1553–8), and enduring until the arrival in 1625 of Charles I, post-Reformation England experienced a degree of religious freedom comparatively greater than elsewhere in Europe. Combined with bitter factional division, such relative freedom was conducive to the early development and circulation of a range of printed historical analyses and polemical weapons. From as early as the Vestiarian Dispute (*c.* 1550–69), the deepening divisions of the English Protestant Church were evident. In this dispute some Anglican clergy were accused of inculcating pagan ceremonial forms by wearing vestments smacking of Catholicism, and therefore of Catholic idolatry. It was the Vestiarian dispute that provided one of the foundations for Puritanism. Use of this type of comparative polemic gathered pace, as is evident in the work of the Anglican Oliver Ormerod (1580?–1626). Against the two main religious opponents of Anglicanism – Catholicism and Puritanism – he wrote two comparative works: the *Pagano-Papismus: wherein is proved ... that Papisme is flat Paganisme* (1606); and *The Picture of a Puritane ... or a Discoverie of Puritan-papisme* (1605). Puritans too repeatedly invoked the spectre of paganism and, in the decades leading up to the Civil War, Anglicans complained they were accused of having the mark of the biblical Beast, the mark of pagan idolatry.

Protestant polemicists had recognized the power of the comparative technique to undermine religious opponents. It thus became the dominant polemical tool in the various bitter religious divisions and crises permeating the history of seventeenth-century England and Europe. Those who were to become deists and sceptics, surrounded as they were by such polemics, could not but notice the efficacy of the technique. This comparative religious discourse has, however, been viewed as a secular development of the Enlightenment, partly because its polemical power was put to great effect in dismissing the priesthoods of all religions – so much so that it became the signature of Enlightenment anticlericalism.

It is true that the cause of the Civil War of the 1640s (which has wider economic and political roots) cannot be attributed to any Puritan–Anglican split. Nevertheless, the schism in English Protestantism certainly found its major expression in that struggle against the absolutist tendencies of King Charles's regime. Charles, married to a Catholic, had been seen to promote what was perceived by many as the growing quasi-Catholicism of the Anglican Church under Archbishop Laud, and had oppressed Puritans in the name of Anglicanism. For Puritans and other Dissenters who aligned themselves against him in the Civil War, this was further proof of the tyrannical nature of Catholicism. At the end of the seventeenth century the Civil War was still within living memory, and Restoration religious persecution and discrimination had done little to unite British Protestants. The Toleration Act (1689) did reduce the exclusive power of the established Church, but the restrictive and punitive acts of the Clarendon Code of 1661–5 remained.[19] It is sometimes noted that religious persecution in England after 1688 was, in fact, minimal compared to elsewhere in Europe, and the Anglican Church was not as influential in the state as it had been. Whether this is more or less true is not the most important point. For this discussion, the overriding issue is how Christian participants perceived the contemporary religious status quo, for we know, without doubt, there was great and widespread bitterness felt in the last decades of the seventeenth and the first decades of the eighteenth century. In addition, the destructive competition between Dissenters and the Anglican Church was, for the first time since the Civil War and Protectorate period, ushered into the public domain via the expiry of the Printing Act in 1695.[20]

The spectacle of such destructive competition for the souls of the laity represented for some Protestants an intolerable situation. By some, the institutional credibility of the priesthood was seen to be under threat, as indeed it potentially was by the advent of deist thought in the 1690s. Commenting on the cause of the rise of deism in England, William Stephens, a Whig cleric, wrote in 1796: having seen 'that Popery in all its Branches was only a device of the Priesthood, to carry on a particular Interest of their own', gentlemen 'could not forebear to see that both these Protestant parties [Anglicans and Dissenters], under the pretence of Religion, were only grasping at Power'. As a result, such gentlemen refused to countenance both parties.[21] Nevertheless, despite the disastrously self-destructive splits and feuds in Protestantism, or how vacillating royal religious leadership might have seemed, the one shibboleth that still periodically united Protestants was anti-Catholicism. The fears of a state reconversion to Rome were kept vivid by the memory of the conversion of James II to Catholicism (*c.* 1670), the fears of a Catholic succession to Queen Anne (1702–14), and the armed Jacobite rebellions of 1715 and 1745. Anti-Catholicism had also been heightened by the *Dragonnades* (brutal visitations by dragoons) of 1683–6 against the Huguenots in France, as well as reports of the renewed devastation and death visited upon the Vaudois (Waldenses) in their Piedmontese valleys in 1686. The latter was an especially bitter pill for Protestants to swallow. The Waldenses had been revered since the Reformation for having supposedly preserved an untrammelled Christianity uncorrupted by the medieval papacy and were, therefore, considered to be the spiritual forebears of Protestants.

Not surprisingly, then, priestcraft was considered to be a contemporary reality, one crucial aspect of which was the existence of the Papal States in Italy. For Protestants and for anti-curial Catholics, the despot-priest ruling the Papal States was self-evident proof of historical and contemporary usurpation of princely prerogatives. One result was that Jacobite Catholic plots or alleged plots (which came thick and fast: 1696, 1700, 1706, 1715, 1722),[22] and the perceived apostasy of the Stuarts were understood by many as events transcending purely religious concerns, and were implicitly linked to notions of human and national liberty. So powerful was the fear of Catholic tyranny and the concern for a Protestant Europe, that not only Anglicans but even oppressed Presbyterians and deists could favourably contrast the Protestant liberty of England with the supposed deeply despotic Catholicism of the French King Louis XIV (1654–1715). In this manner, what is in part the myth of French absolute monarchy was created, a myth that persists even to this day;[23] while the then equally fearsome concept of the hierocratic centre of European tyranny at Rome has become more elusive.

The religious and political context in which the post-Reformation historiographical traditions of Italy developed was more complex than that of Britain, in good part because of the polycentric nature of the Italian peninsula. It was an unstable region and its instability originated from political struggles between competing sovereignties, as well as from the territorial predations of extra-peninsular powers.[24] That instability was in direct contrast to Counter-Reformation attempts by the Curia to secure religious homogenization, and militated against the exercise of an effective Roman jurisdiction over the Churches of the various sovereign states. The strict controls on printed matter and other forms of intellectual censorship of the Counter-Reformation, and the continuance of such controls into the eighteenth century could not, therefore, eliminate all efforts at an anti-curial critique of Church history. It is, however, true that Rome did manage to significantly inhibit the publication of anti-curial accounts of Church history.

Anti-curial writers who, on behalf of their sovereigns, opposed Roman jurisdiction over their national Churches and consequently risked the ire of the Roman Inquisition, could exploit the polycentrism of the Italian peninsula. Thus the influential Venetian jurisdictionalist and theologian Paolo Sarpi (1552–1623) could write and publish with less fear than dissident Catholics resident in the Papal States or Italian states more closely tied to Rome. Yet Sarpi was excommunicated, seriously wounded by assassins, and was constrained to publish his *Historia del Concilio Tridentino* (1619), his most well-known critical work, in London under a pseudonym.[25] Furthermore, his *Historia ... sopra li beneficii ecclesiastici*, a work trenchantly critical of the papacy and the medieval Church, was only published in 1675, long after his death.

The papacy was not, however, always purely defensive in its approach to heterodoxy. Between 1669 and 1670 proponents of materialism at the University of Pisa had been harshly repressed. In 1688 the Neapolitan clergy, alarmed at the continued spread of heterodoxy, had set in motion what can be seen as a preventative nine-year trial of individuals accused, amongst other charges, of advocating materialistic and atomistic ideas. It should be no surprise, however, that in the Italian states, the desperately poor occupants of which had the most intimate view of the conspicuous parasitic consumption, ostentation and spiritual failings of Rome, there existed (according to contemporary reports) significant numbers of radical Christians and sceptics. For anti-curialists and religious radicals, the scandal of Reformation and Counter-Reformation polemic and its bloody aftermath, combined with a papacy declining in influence yet still persecuting dissidents, could not but verify the continued existence of Christian priestcraft. Amongst some, such circumstances also served to put the existence of providential guidance into doubt, and to reinvigorate old ideas of a purely rational and naturalistic assessment of human existence.

In the eighteenth century, the tone of the demands of Italian sovereigns and jurisdictionalists for control and reform of their Churches grew more strident. The Neapolitan Allesandro Riccardi indicated this intensification when he told his readers in 1708 that, if necessary, Naples would seek by the sword the aid not forthcoming from the canons of the Church.[26] We know there was some clandestine traffic of books critical of the Church into Italy. The papacy was unable to exert sufficient and consistent pressure to stem the flow completely. Nevertheless, for anti-curial writers the watchful eye of the Roman Inquisition continued to be a periodic worry. For most reformers the secular sovereign state represented the possibility of rational reform against the superstitious and despotic rule of the priest-king at Rome. Papal temporal dominion was considered by even the most timid anti-curialists as wholly inconsistent with the teachings of Jesus Christ. But sovereigns of the patchwork of small Italian states were often very reliant upon alliances to ward off internal and external aggression, and could unexpectedly withdraw their protection and patronage of anti-curialists if improved relations with Rome were deemed necessary. It was such a shift in attitude towards Rome which forced the author of the influential anti-curial *Istoria civile del Regno di Napoli* (1723), Pietro Giannone, to flee Naples after its publication. Giannone later found his protection withdrawn in Savoyard Piedmont, after which he was finally to die in prison. Similar shifts in circumstances also forced the exile of the radical Alberto Radicati (Count of Passerano, 1698–1737) from his native Piedmont.

So treacherous were these political sands, that a text not formally considered particularly radical by the papacy might, in new political circumstances, be considered dangerous. A typical case in point was the anti-curial historiography of the German Justinus Febronius (Johann Von Hontheim). Contemporary historians recognized that the critique of the Church in Febronius's *De statu ecclesiae et legitima potestate romani pontificis* (1763) contained nothing new, but it represented a more threatening aspect than other similar accounts because it came at a time of strained relations between Pope Clement XIII (1758–69) and the states of Europe. In 1764 the book was placed on the papal Index of prohibited books. In 1766 Rome issued an edict decreeing a ten-year prison sentence for those who replied to an advertisement of the Venetian printer Giuseppe Bettinelli for subscriptions to a proposed Italian translation of Febronius's work.

To both orthodox propagandists and anti-curialists alike, the question of Church history was central, not least because the papacy and those who opposed Roman jurisdiction both used the history of the Church as one of their major propaganda weapons. It could not have been otherwise, because of the historical connections presented by the continuity of relationship between medieval history, Roman supremacy within the Church, and the continued existence of the medieval Papal States. Eighteenth-century orthodox historiography was, in form and content, mostly still reliant on the Counter-Reformation work of Cesare Baronius, his *Annales ecclesiastici*. Baronius had set out to prove Roman legitimacy by demonstrating that the Catholic Church was continuous with the apostolic Church. The voluminous historical works of eighteenth-century writers such as Cardinal Orsi (1692–1761) and Bishop Becchetti (1742–1814), were restatements of Baronian orthodoxy. In historical and theological terms it was an orthodoxy based on the divine legitimacy of the supposed episcopal successors of St Peter at Rome (the Petrine theme), to whom Peter had transferred the keys to heaven and purgatory. In practical terms, orthodox writers also based their arguments upon the historical role of Rome as the defender of the Church against all the earthly enemies of Christ.[27] For anti-curialists too, the separation of the contemporary Church from the medieval papacy in their analyses was not desirable or practical. Given the catalogue of medieval enormities, the evident continuation of the medieval and contemporary Church provided a seemingly endless quantity of critical ammunition supremely suited for incorporation into an accusation of priestcraft.

In the Papal States, the status of the Curia as the religious centre of the state and also of Catholic Europe, was not easily divorced from the Curia as the supreme secular authority in its domain. To deny Rome as the executive centre of Catholicism was also tantamount to denying the doctrinal and providential foundation (the Petrine theme) of its temporal rule. Such a critical intermeshing of secular and religious imperatives naturally served to create doctrinal and historiographical inertia in orthodox thought. In the hostile and unstable environs of the Italian peninsula, only with substantial risk to the Roman status quo was it possible to contemplate any significant change in the fundamentals of orthodox historiography. Rome's many able propagandists, therefore, such as Francesco Antonio Zaccaria and Giovanni Marchetti, had limited room for innovative manoeuvre against incisive anti-curial attacks upon Roman jurisdiction and secular dominion.

The growing weakness of the papacy was manifest in its inability to assert its authority over the Church of even a small Italian state such as the Duchy of Parma. It was a weakness also exemplified by the success of French and Spanish pressure for the dissolution of the Jesuits, finally achieved in 1773. Personally responsible to the pope, and performing a major role in the education of much of the European elite, the Jesuits were seen as the epitome of a foreign body exercising undue influence in a nation state. There is also evidence to show that at times the papacy, conscious of its decreasing influence, preferred not to take official measures against anti-curial historical works, lest the measures inflamed an already difficult situation. One consequence of this vacillation was that the Gallican and fiercely anti-curial historiography of Claude Fleury (1640–1723) was able to circulate through much of Italy relatively freely.[28]

The growing call for the reform of Catholicism, bolstered by the spiritual challenge of Jansenism (on which see below), naturally extended to the condemnation of the past and present activities of the Roman Inquisition against heterodoxy. But despite influential calls for a reform of the European system of justice, especially that of Cesare Beccaria (1738–94) who wrote the classic Enlightenment text *Dei Delitti e delle pene* (1764) on the subject, the curial defence of the Inquisition was intransigent, exemplified in the work of Tommaso Pani. Pani had the misfortune to publish his reactionary defence of the Inquisition in the very year of the French revolution, which has left to posterity the worst possible assessment of curial backwardness.[29] To have abolished the Inquisition would have been for the Curia to weaken its hand in relation to the policing of its own state, and to a degree the policing of its religious jurisdiction over the Churches of its sovereign neighbours. The current Tridentine doctrine (that derived from the Council of Trent, 1545–63), it can be said, remained locked in a stultifying embrace with the imperatives of papal secular dominion and curial jurisdiction. The inability of Rome to concede reform without self-jeopardy is vital in understanding the practical weakness of Rome and the growing confidence of anti-curialists in the second half of the eighteenth century.

The desire for spiritual renewal had not, however, been the exclusive property of anti-curial reformers. Jansenism, derived from the thought of Cornelius Jansen (1585–1638), bishop of Ypres, was essentially an ascetic and theologically pessimistic search for the renewal of Christian piety. Jansenists were in conflict with what they perceived as the lax casuistry of the Jesuits, they consequently came to be opponents of the papacy and were duly condemned by Pope Innocent X in 1653. Nevertheless, a call for a renewal of faith, at least in the first half of the eighteenth century, could appeal to both pro-curial and anti-curial Italians. Even in the Roman Curia there were those such as Cardinal Polignac who were prepared to encourage Jansenist-inspired reforming tendencies. Polignac was representative of orthodox Catholics who recognized the need for reform of the Church in order to neutralize the most threatening aspects of Enlightenment culture.

In the second half of the century, the conciliatory attitude of Pope Benedict XIV (1740–58) was replaced by that of the more hard-line Clement III (1758–69). The prospect of reforming the Church from within now became very remote. Rome, it is clear, found itself in a no-win situation. To concede some measure of reform and limited autonomy to Churches in the peninsula would only signal the weakness of Rome and lead to further demands. Yet to remain unyielding was to court unilateral action by princes and their supporters and risk a public display of papal weakness – which was to be the case. In response to the now unremitting refusal of Rome to even consider reform, anti-curial Jansenists became more insistent in their calls for change. They increasingly turned to Italian princes as instruments to advance both Church reform and the jurisdictionalist struggle for control over their own Churches. In this environment any remaining support for Jansenist ideas amongst pro-curialists naturally evaporated. In 1761 Pope Clement, humiliated by the prospect of princes enforcing reform in their Churches with no reference to Rome, forced the pro-Jansenist

Cardinal Passionei to sign a condemnation of Jansenism. But the coming storm could not be halted, and the height of Jansenist influence was reached in Tuscany under Grand Duke Leopold in the 1780s. In alliance with Jansenist clergymen such as the Gallican-regalist Bishop Scipione de'Ricci, Leopold wanted to impose a Jansenist reform on the Tuscan Church independently of Rome, a movement epitomized by the Synod of Pistoia (1786).[30]

Crucial though the complex context of the eighteenth-century Italian peninsula might be, to explore properly Catholic anticlerical theories it is necessary – as with Protestant thought – to return to the Reformation. In orthodox opinion the Reformation was apostasy. It represented the advent of the Antichrist in the guise of Manichaeist heretics, personified by the fraudsters Luther and Calvin who were pursuing a self-interested and premeditated corruption of religion. These reformers, as early as the 1520s in Italy, were popularly depicted as impostors, even idolaters.[31] In the Counter-Reformation period, various pro-curial writers[32] more fully developed the theory that the Reformation was to be understood as the product of priestcraft. Catholic propagandists denounced as iniquitous fraud the claimed Protestant miracles. Tommaso Campanella in his *Atheismus triumphatus* (1631) revealed, for example, that Protestants had manufactured false miracles in order to further their own ambition. Like the Protestant priestcraft charge, once established, the Catholic anti-Protestant onslaught endured, becoming the dominant Catholic paradigm for explaining the religious nature of Protestantism and the motives of its protagonists. It was an indictment that continued until at least the mid-eighteenth century and the work of Vincenzo Gotti.[33]

As with Protestant polemics, however, it is not only the content of the debate that is of interest, but also its comparative form. Propagandists such as Thomas Bozio in his *De signis ecclesiae* (1591) compared Protestantism to Islam and Judaism, just as Protestants had done for Catholicism. We know the same polemical developments were occurring in France, as in the *Calvino-Turcismus* (1597) of the priest William Rainolds and the Archbishop of Rheims, William Gifford. Many English Catholics too held that Protestantism was a venal fraud, including Catholic Queen Mary Tudor (1553–8).[34] When, in addition, we remember the *Pagano Papismus* (1606) of Ormerod, we can note that one hundred years before the appearance of deism in England, therefore, a milestone had already been put in place on the road to the creation of a pan-European historical and polemical culture of comparative religion. As Giorgio Spini has commented, this no-holds-barred vilification, in which the most unscrupulous sexual and political slurs were hurled – via print, pulpit and university – could not help but provide contemporary social confirmation of the existence of priestly fraud.[35] For how could both confessions be legitimate representatives of God's will, when each claimed to have sole divine blessing for their creeds and opposed each other mercilessly, even militarily? Clearly, at least the claims of one side were fraudulent. For anti-curial Catholics implacably hostile to the worldly corruptions of Rome and convinced the papacy was a religious fraud, the response of Rome to the Protestant reformers was a struggle to defend an ecclesiastical empire more than a theologically principled dispute.

In seventeenth-century Italy, as elsewhere in Europe, there were various shades of religious disagreement with Rome, ranging from the pious such as that of Sarpi, to that of less pious and sometimes sceptical propagandists, often referred to as libertines. The term libertine is notoriously imprecise and unhelpful, because the ranks of so-called libertines included a wide variety of writers. A good proportion of libertines were not atheists, but more or less radical anti-curial Catholics (I shall henceforth refer to such writers simply as anti-curialists). The city of Venice offered to such men a relatively free press and a more open intellectual atmosphere and was, until the eighteenth century, one of the important publishing centres of Europe. Nevertheless, as already noted, anti-curial writers often led a precarious existence, at times forced to publish their works clandestinely and sometimes writing in exile; although, as we have also seen, at least some of their works circulated in Italy.

The religious opposition of the more radical anti-curialists was expressed in a wide variety of literary forms. In polemical, historical and allegorical works such as *Il Nipotismo di Roma* (1667) of Gregorio Leti or the *L'Inquisizione processata* (1681) of Lamberti Arconati, the Catholic hierarchy were proclaimed as impostors. These writers and others focused sharply on secondary causes, unfavourably comparing contemporary prelates with the clergy of the early Church, the Holy Age of Rome, the 'centuries of sanctity'. This was a period before gold and ambition had corrupted the Christian priesthood, an age which, for Leti, began to decline under Pope Urban I (222–30),[36] and for most since the fourth-century Constantinian adoption of Christianity. Since that Golden time, prelates had been but crafty priests who preached that which they did not themselves believe and used religion for self-gain. Arconati's *L'Inquisizione processata* was, however, plagiarized from Sarpi's *Historia della Sacra Inquisitione*

(1638, but written at least fifteen years earlier). Given the exigencies of polemical battle, Sarpi too – like eighteenth-century anti-curialists – had paid very close attention to secondary causes at the expense of primary ones. In his *Trattato delle Materie Beneficiarie,* Sarpi explained that, in contrast to the fervour and charity of the early Church, the present Church was only diligent, even ruthless, in acquiring and retaining riches.[37]

As one might expect, for Italian anti-curial Catholics of the seventeenth and eighteenth centuries, polemic with Protestants was of little importance compared to the pressing battle against Rome. In any case, anti-curialists rarely aligned themselves fully with the Protestant assessment of the Curia, which was not so much aimed at reform of Catholicism as at its abolition. It is possible that some anti-curialists wished to go further than challenging the perceived corruption of Rome and its jurisdiction, and proceed towards a Protestant-style reform of the Church. The problem for such thinkers – whether they overtly acknowledged it or not – was that they formed part of an alliance with princes, aristocrats and prelates against Rome. Princes and their supporters were acutely aware of the dangers of more radical religious reform, both in terms of the role of the Church in the maintenance of social stability, and the potential perils of even a moderate shift in the complex series of alliances that rulers of small Italian states relied on for their continued existence.

If anti-curialists had advocated a Protestant-like secession from Rome – especially if they advocated the independence or abolition of the episcopate – it is most unlikely that sovereigns of the peninsula would have supported such a radical step. Even to have posed publicly such a question would have been to put at risk the royal support that anti-curialists badly needed. Thus, even though most anti-curialist thinkers held Erastian views in favour of their particular temporal rulers, most were not Erastian in the Anglican sense of owing religious allegiance solely to the prince as head of the Church. Such writers were dissident Catholics, but Catholics nonetheless, and therefore most (at least formally) still recognized Rome, via its Petrine claims, as the spiritual head of the Church. This was, of course, a recognition of a spiritual leadership only, one devoid of jurisdictional qualities and the exercise of any temporal dominion. Executive leadership of sovereign Churches was reserved to their respective princes and prelates. For these writers the medieval popes had not only usurped supremacy over their episcopal coadjutors and seized temporal rule, but had also meddled in the affairs of states and denied the rightful share of the sovereign in the jurisdiction of the Church. Hence, appended to the title of the *Della Monarchia univer-sale de'papi* (1789) written by the Neapolitan Marcello Eusebio Scotti, is the line *Respondit Jesus: regnum meum non est de hoc mundo* (Jesus replied: my kingdom is not of this world). Giannone too spoke for many when he argued 'the Church is in the republic ... and not indeed the republic in the Church'.[38] On Earth, the kingdom of the Church was only a spiritual one; but as the earthly Church existed in civil society, it had to be subject to civil laws.

Protestants had always contrasted their reasonable creed against the superstition and irrationality of Catholicism. In the late seventeenth and eighteenth century, under pressure from the Enlightenment appeal to rationality, however, the reference to reason became the litmus test in much historical writing. In the historiography of Muratori and to some extent in that of Giannone the growing formal appeal to reason in historical evaluation was common. Recourse to reason added ostensible weight to both anti-curial and Protestant arguments dismissing miracles as more likely to have been of human invention than divine, as well as appearing to increase the gravity of general condemnations of superstition. Hence 'Several Gentlemen', the anonymous editors of the periodical *The History of Popery* (1735), a re-edition of Henry Care's periodical *A Pacquet of Advice from Rome* felt they should state: 'This paper ... goes thro' the principal branches of the Popish controversy, in a way so rational and historical, plain and scriptural', and thereby gives 'clear answers to the artful sophistry of priests and Jesuits, and others of the popish clan.'[39] Despite possible appearances to the contrary, such appeals to reason did not, it must be stressed, have any innovatory or significant impact upon the traditional critique of the medieval Church propounded by Catholics or Protestants.

Muratori's recourse to reason was often little more than a genuflection. In his *De ingeniorum moderatione in religionis negotio* (1714) he confronted the relationship between reason and religion, and argued religious truth must be sought primarily in faith and revelation, ensuring that the use of reason in his historical thought was limited. Not surprisingly, then, the outcome of Muratori's attempt to balance his orthodox piety against his antipathy to the jurisdiction of Rome was that he accepted as genuine the considerable orthodox tally of miracles. In his *Antiquitates italicae medii aevi* (1738–42) he noted it 'is certain that in those times the true prodigies, miracles and favours operated by God through the intercession of the saints were never less'.[40] Yet, beyond officially sanctioned miracles, Muratori condemned some other medieval miracles as fraudulent. As we shall see, the application of the test of reason only made significant appearance in the thought of some of those radical Christian thinkers about to cross the Rubicon towards deism: in the work of those who were concerned to extend their historical condemnation to include virtually all Church history, such as that of Alberto Radicati and John Toland. But even for many such men, reason was not initially exploited to doubt revelation, rather priestly fraud was asserted.

Regardless of the intensity of any formal appeal to reason, however, in the writings of most anti-curialists, the attitude adopted towards medieval miracles is very often as sceptical as that of Protestants. In most, mention of medieval miracles is scant and, as in Giannone's *Storia civile*, miracles are often dismissed as fakes manufactured in order to inflame the devotions of the faithful and procure riches. In some accounts miracles are altogether absent, as in the *Storia del papato* (1796–1802) of the republican Paolo Rivarola. Rivarola explained that the popes claimed to have operated miracles so that 'their blind adulators would believe as an article of faith everything the popes said and did was good, just and holy'.[41]

We know the enlightened Cosimo Amidei explicitly acknowledged the historiography of Giannone and Muratori in his work, yet, if he had wished to draw upon a very much wider anti-curial historiography emanating from the first half of the eighteenth century, he would not have found it. How, therefore, can one account for the relative paucity of anti-Rome historical accounts in the first half of the eighteenth century? To do so necessitates a re-focus on the concept Paul Hazard outlined in the 1930s, that of a crisis of European thought in the late seventeenth and the first two decades of the eighteenth century. In this period there is no doubt there was a perceptible increase in the number of individuals across Europe prepared, from a wide variety of standpoints, to more openly question and reinterpret many of the fundamentals of Christianity. For Hazard and others, this emerging climate of free religious enquiry signalled the first signs of the European Enlightenment. To assume there was just one Enlightenment, however, would be to overlook important, even crucial, factors in the development of Enlightened thought in various regions and states. Nowhere is this more apparent than in the Italian peninsula.

In the first half of the eighteenth century, Italy, in common with other parts of Europe, experienced an intellectual ferment that

questioned central elements of traditional theological thought. This
was accompanied by a call for Christian renewal amongst wide
sections of the clergy, both anti-curial and pro-curial in orientation.
Reforming prelates such as Celestino Galiani (1681–1753) and other
thinkers attempted to harness new scientific and philosophical ideas
to the service of Catholicism. The very limited confines of that project
are evident in the fact that Galiani felt unable to present his views in
print.[42] It must be noted, then, that before mid-century there was no
consistent and overt enlightened challenge made in Italy to the heart
of Catholicism: the historical legitimacy of Catholic doctrine and
Roman supremacy. One notable exception was the *Storia civile* of
Giannone, on account of which Giannone was hounded, imprisoned
and ultimately paid with his life because his historical analysis had
been too far-reaching. His work was an open challenge to Rome,
rather than a forthright plea for reform, and could not be tolerated.
This was an unpleasant reminder of the harsh curial repression
directed at anti-curial and unorthodox thinkers in Naples in the last
years of the seventeenth century and in Tuscany in 1669–70.

The panorama was clear: overt, highly public challenges to Rome
would end in tears, and even the orthodox Muratori only narrowly
escaped persecution. So, despite the ferment of philosophical, scientific and theological thought in the so-called years of crisis of the
European mind, the Achilles heel of the papacy, its historical legitimacy, was not significantly challenged in Italy. After the mid-century,
the broad movement for Church reform ran into the sands of curial
intransigence and repression. The papacy, given the burgeoning
provocative influence of the European Enlightenment, feared even
mild calls for reform might turn into potentially dangerous flashpoints.

As already noted, the result was that anti-curialists not only turned
to Italian princes as agents of reform independent of Rome, they also
realized it was absolutely necessary to openly declaim against the
historical legitimacy of Roman supremacy. Opponents of the Curia
could not but be given added confidence to do so by the forced renun-
ciation of its elite spiritual troops, the Jesuits. In the last two decades
of the eighteenth century, in alliance with princes, Catholic opponents of Rome returned more resolutely to the anti-curial
historiographical traditions of Giannone and seventeenth-century
opponents of the Curia. This was a tactic by no one more succinctly
affirmed than Capecelatro who (we may remember) told his readers
a new history of the Church was necessary in order to reform it.
Similarly, from about 1600 or before, dissenting English Protestants

(Puritans), goaded by the repression of the nascent Calvinist Church by Queen Elizabeth, had also arrived at the need for open polemic against the established Church. The climax of Dissenter opposition to the Anglican Church did not, however, occur until the late seventeenth and early eighteenth century, more or less seventy years before the open confrontation between anti-curial Catholics and Rome.

This differential of seventy years delineates the beginning of the English Enlightenment and that of the Italian High Enlightenment. The Italian High Enlightenment was more or less coeval with that of France (although no strict comparison is valid), which meant its participants could draw upon the thought of the leading *philosophes* of Europe. Having stated this, the fact that reforming Catholics were then in the forefront of the challenge to the historical legitimacy of Rome was most significant and must be accounted for. Because of the relatively weak nature of the Italian Enlightenment, in which intellectuals were at times more dependent on princely support than elsewhere, reforming clerics could still be vital components of enlightened reform (as they were – although under very different conditions – in Scotland). A more important factor, was that, for anti-curial Catholic reformers as for enlightened Italians, the primary stumbling block to the secularizing programme of the Enlightenment was Roman jurisdiction and its temporal rule. To sweep away the worst elements of superstition – enshrined in orthodox Roman Catholic doctrine – and advance scientific thinking and research, it was above all necessary to reform the obscurantist Church. But Rome, as any other Italian state, could still exploit diplomatic means to frustrate the desires of neighbouring princes and their enlightened advisers. To curb properly the power of Rome to stultify the minds of Italians, it was necessary to dismantle its power base: to remove the Church from its position of temporal rule.

The attack against the Church, then, if not the cutting edge of the Italian Enlightenment (for some writers avoided the problematic and still dangerous question of religion), was nevertheless unambiguously central to its programme. In this situation, the broad coalition that was anti-curialism – even if its programme of Catholic reform was very old news – was integral to the programme of the Enlightenment as it could not be elsewhere in Europe. When enlightened Italians joined the chorus against Rome, they reiterated the historical critique of dissenting Catholics. To talk of the development of the Italian or indeed the English Enlightenment without talking of religious division is, therefore, not possible.

3 From Free Christendom to Papal Despotism

Early modern enemies of Rome were well aware that medieval princes – royal piety aside – had often been hostile to the practical reality of papal supremacy in the Church. It was only to be expected that a wealthy and very influential international institution such as the medieval Church, which was often mostly tax-exempt, would at times have found itself in conflict with the economic and political desires of kings. The political support of Rome had often been a decisive factor in international relations and the domestic fortunes of kings and emperors. Those kings not in favour with Rome naturally resented Roman control over their prelates more rather than less.

The power of the medieval pontifical throne and its promise of wealth was a prize to be fought for, both by competing factions of cardinals (from the eleventh century the electoral college of the pope), and kings and emperors. Disputes over the outcome of papal elections or the continuing legitimacy of an incumbent led to schisms, in which two popes contended for legitimate rule, each usually supported by different kings. Schisms were of course potentially disastrous for the spiritual credibility of the papacy. The Great Schism (1378–1417), during which for a brief time three popes had existed, each doggedly fighting for sole recognition, was calamitous for the concept of papal supremacy. The direct result was the rise of Conciliarism, an attempt to subject popes to councils of the whole Church. Ostensibly, the Great Schism and even the Reformation were, in terms of duration and geographical extent, however, small affairs compared to the permanent schism between the Eastern (Orthodox Church) and Western Churches which had occurred in 1054. But the eleventh-century East–West schism did not occur on territory over which the papacy had ever had any jurisdiction or – perhaps more importantly – from which it had ever drawn financial support. The permanent East–West schism might have been a tragedy in terms of the unity of Christendom, but it posed no actual loss to Rome in terms of wealth, influence or the care of souls. The result was that the East–West divide never produced the long-term, pervasive and destructive rancour in Europe that typified the Reformation and its aftermath, in which the ripe plum of Church wealth and influence over the laity often became the focus of princely ambition.

In the sixteenth century, for the first time, the European authority of Rome found itself pitted against permanent rival centres of ecclesiastical authority in the form of national or otherwise independent Churches. These Churches, as Rome itself, were allied or tied to various and sometimes shifting political and economic formations and exigencies. The potential for a crisis of religious authority in Europe was therefore unprecedented, especially in a period of burgeoning print culture. For the first time the internecine squabbles of prelates and theologians were made widely available in a propaganda war of an unheard-of size, and to an unprecedentedly large reading audience.

In practice, the Reformation did not only attack papal supremacy and the medieval Catholic hierarchy. In the revolutionary new account of Church history the pope was the epitome, the embodiment of all that was perceived as rotten in medieval society: its superstition, ignorance, barbarity and the venal corruption of the Church – its doctrine and morality. To attack the authority of the pope then, was to attack the very bone marrow of European culture from about the sixth to the sixteenth century. The stakes in the struggle for a new history of Europe were high, and not just in religious or historical terms. For a sovereign to acknowledge the supremacy of the pope in the Church was, more or less, to limit royal authority in the Church in a period when the Church was still a primary means of royal legitimation and propaganda. To deny papal supremacy also opened a possible avenue to the lands and wealth of the Church, which monarchs such as Henry VIII used to sustain royal authority by largesse to the nobility.

Martin Luther and John Calvin[1] had identified the tyranny of the popes in the Church as one of the main causal factors in the corruption of Christian doctrine, an assessment that had immense influence on subsequent Protestant historians. Although very critical of Pope Gregory I, Luther exempted him from total condemnation because he had protested against the title of universal bishop. But in 607 Pope Boniface III accepted that very title. For Protestants this date was a landmark in the corruption of the Church. Nevertheless, for Luther and others, papal jurisdiction in the Church had still been constrained by imperial (Holy Roman Empire) and royal intervention. Beginning with Gregory VII (1073–85), it was thought, the popes broke free of secular control by objecting to the imperial disposition of episcopal elections. Papal tyranny over the Church, according to Luther, was then codified and stabilized by the development of canon law contained in collections of decretals produced from the twelfth to the fourteenth century.[2] Much of the Lutheran scheme was adopted by writers such as John Foxe and was reproduced in his immensely influential *Actes and Monuments* (1555). Other writers, such as Bishop John Bale in his *Acta romanorum pontificum* (1558), also served to imbue Luther's view of Church history into the English Protestant tradition. Luther's outline became – with only a few partial exceptions[3] – the general scheme of papal history to be found in sixteenth- and seventeenth-century English works. As already noted, even staunch seventeenth-century High Church Anglicans such as Richard Field felt constrained to reproduce most of Luther's scheme of papal descent into superstition, barbarity, ignorance, corruption, forgeries and false miracles.

In the eighteenth century, the English and Scottish Church and the various dissenting Protestant tendencies still continued to identify and legitimize themselves in good part in contrast to the perceived evils of the medieval and contemporary popes. High Churchmen too continued to expose the fraudulent and antichristian deeds of the popes and in so doing, for example, the Nonjuror[4] Laurence Howell (*c.* 1664–1720) was continuing an old Protestant preoccupation. Howell was following the tradition exemplified in such works as Thomas James's *Treatise of the Corruptions of Scripture, Counsels, and Fathers, by the Prelats, Pastors, and Pillars of the Church of Rome* (1611). Howell's own work, *A View of the Pontificate* (1712), was dedicated to exposing the forgeries of the *Liber pontificalis*, the official Roman biographical register of popes dating from the sixth century. For Howell the *Liber pontificalis* was 'for the most part a heap of fictions', a book forged and adulterated with no other end 'than to make the world believe not only that the bishops of Rome in all ages made the greatest figure in the Church, but that their very presbyters [assistants of the Roman bishop who constituted the college of cardinals in the eleventh century] bore pre-eminence over all others'.[5]

Howell's account might be considered more radical than Luther's as to the imputed inception of papal attempts to usurp supremacy, which for Howell commenced in the pontificate of Pope Leo I (440–61). As we shall see, the tendency to push the origins of papal priestcraft further back into history in order to illustrate the intrinsic nature of papal corruption was an early feature of Protestant historiography. It was certainly an avenue of deepening the attack on Rome, yet also one of the methods deployed to demonstrate one's own impeccable Protestant credentials against other Protestant detractors.

But this progressive backdating was eventually to prove a calamitous phenomenon for Christianity. As more of Christian history became understood by Protestants as only that of priestcraft, the historical evidence for non-corrupt priesthoods grew thinner and thinner.

For Howell, the history of the papacy was one of desperate scenes, for many popes 'have been known to wade through blood and bribery' to obtain the pontifical honour, and they had 'sacrificed all that lay in their way to serve the ends of their aspiring ambition'. But the popes did not fight all their battles alone, and were supported by the Church hierarchy, led by the cardinals, 'the princes of the Church', who were similarly only motivated by personal gain. In addition, from the thirteenth century, the mendicant friars, continually favoured by the popes, pretended piety and poverty, but 'chous'd the silly people of their money'. They evaded episcopal control by being responsible only to the popes, and thus provided the papacy with loyal allies. Scholasticism, the medieval method of philosophical and theological speculation, was also understood to have been developed in order to defend the 'encroachments and usurpations of the court and bishop of Rome'. The development of indulgences (the remission of temporal punishment for sin, the papal sale of which had occasioned Luther's protest in 1517) had similarly aimed only at papal profit. The foundation of the Inquisition too was 'a project of the court of Rome to establish their usurped supremacy', and bishops and councils were 'forced to submit to the arbitrary determination of a few regulars [Dominicans]'.[6]

Another Anglican Nonjuror, Bishop Jeremy Collier (1650–1726), author of *An Ecclesiastical History of Great Britain* (1708), proffers substantially the same priestcraft analysis, but one tailored to his pronounced episcopalian outlook. In his analysis Collier manufactures a precedent of a Saxon Episcopal Church relatively free from papal corruptions, until subsequently corrupted by Norman invasion and papal influence. In the seventh century, therefore, English Christians still had 'Spiritual Sovereignty within themselves, were under no Foreign Superintendency, nor us'd to apply to the See of Rome to pay their homage to the Popes' Primacy'.[7]

In the seventeenth- and eighteenth-century Church of England there was a fear of fanaticism either of the papal or the Protestant Dissenter variety. Consequently, Anglican prelates were inclined to stress the eirenic *via media* of a path between Rome and Dissenters inclined to Presbyterianism. As we have just seen, this moderation did certainly not extend to papal history. The writings of George

Gregory (1754–1808), vicar and prebendary at St Paul's, were also typical of Anglican anti-Catholic thought. Gregory intended his *History of the Christian Church* (1790) to be a manual of Church history for use by the junior clergy, and he supplied his students with substantially the same account of priestcraft as Howell seventy-eight years earlier. However, outside the hard-line Episcopalianism of some High Churchmen, Anglicans such as Gregory vilified the medieval episcopate as licentious, of having colluded in papal usurpation of supremacy and of emulating the venal ambition of the popes. The antichristian bent of the popes, he thought, knew no bounds, and they did not scruple to prostitute the heresy charge in order to combat any challenge to the institutional or spiritual power of the pope. Gregory also indicted the collusion of medieval kings and emperors in priestcraft, damning the Carolingians (the dynasty of Charlemagne) for legitimizing and materially supporting the despotic ambitions of the Roman priest-kings via their eighth-century donations of territory to Rome. The 'entire agreement' between Charlemagne and the pope, 'was the political connection of mutual interest, not of religion'.[8]

Another Anglican vicar and writer who intended his work to be a textbook for the young was Thomas Gisborne (the elder, 1758–1846). In Gisborne's *Familiar Survey of the Christian Religion* (1799) the historical schema is again that of priestcraft, differentiating itself only by the relatively early date of papal supremacy, which he alleges was awarded in about 379 to pope Damasus by the emperors Valentinian and Gratian. Thus the popes usurped the 'supreme authority in religious affairs, [which was] originally possessed by the temporal ruler'. As many other Protestants had angrily noted, the supremacy of Rome and the pope was also supported by the imposition of the 'unknown tongue' of Latin in the Church.[9]

Outside the pale of the Anglican Church, thinking on the history of the Church was little different. Dissenters, hostile to the Anglican Church, nevertheless fully shared the Anglican accusation of papal despotism. After 1689 Dissenting ministers and chapels enjoyed some protection by the law, and in many parishes the Anglican clergy were in open competition with Dissenting ministers. One sure sign of Protestant credibility and zeal was of course exemplary anti-Catholicism. For those many Dissenters of a Presbyterian inclination, their anti-papal views were reinforced by the anti-hierarchical element common to the Presbyterian religious outlook, itself reinforced by the frequently pronounced 'middling' social composition of

Dissent. In a sermon of the dissenting minister James Bicheno (d. 1831), *A Glance at the History of Christianity and of English Nonconformity* (1798), the pope and his hierarchy are damned. As 'idolaters ... had their superior and inferior priests ... in imitation of these the debauched Christian Church began ... to have her bishops and arch-bishops'.[10] As a consequence, the democracy and liberty of the Church began to vanish, and from the sixth century the 'inferior people' were excluded from any role in the Church. The business of Christians then was not to search the scriptures, but 'to learn the mind of the pope'. Thus 'Black darkness succeeded and for some centuries, we scarcely discern a ray of light. The priests were everything and the people nothing'.[11]

One of the most bitter accounts of clerical tyranny and fraud is found in the periodical *History of Popery* (1735). This was a re-edited edition of Henry Care's periodical *A Pacquet of Advice from Rome* (1678–83) by the anonymous dissenting editors 'Several Gentlemen'. For these men, the pope was the Antichrist, the monks were the popes' standing army, and St Augustine's mission to England in 597 only had the aim of rendering 'the *latria* and the *dulia* to Rome'.[12] In common with most other Protestant writers, the editors describe the corrupting influence of wealth upon the papacy, which spurred on the ambitious drive towards a papal monarchy. This notwithstanding, the history of papal despotism began with the City of Rome itself: '[f]or the advantage that [the popes] ... had by inhabiting the imperial city, was a main temptation that at first induced them to affect a supremacy'. Usurpation of power was also aided by the ignorance pervading the medieval mind. The 'silly souls' of the ignorant and illiterate barbarians who overran Europe, were 'taken up in devout amazement' at the status of the Bishop of that 'renown city'. Similarly, ignorance was exploited by the use of forgery. The texts of ancient authors were corrupted, laws invented, acts of councils falsified and canons forged in order to justify papal superiority – a subject to which many pages are devoted. The editors also make use of the paganism critique, the accusation 'that the popish hierarchy ... is no other than the old pagan hierarchy revived',[13] a common verdict and one expressed similarly by Joseph Priestley.

Priestley, in his *General History of the Christian Church* (1802–3) and his *History of the Corruptions of Christianity* (1782), professed some sympathy for the history of the Church. But his passing sympathetic comments are drowned by the deep gloom of his priestcraft analysis. For Priestley

the popes derived much advantage from the ideas of the northern
nations in their state of paganism. For they considered the bishop
of Rome in the same light in which they had before done their arch-
druid, and transferred to him that boundless reverence with which
they had been used to regard the other. Hence the force of papal
excommunications, which, as under the druids, deprived a person
of all the common rights of humanity.[14]

The popes, according to Priestley, also employed forgery and fraud to
grasp power. Amongst the examples he cites is the forgery of the
Pseudo-Isidorean Decretals (supposedly compiled by Isidore of
Seville [d. 636], but written possibly as late as *c.* 850) which were
utilized to provide historical legitimacy for papal despotism in the
Church. Such abuses meant many suspected 'the whole system of
Christianity had its origin in imposture, and had no other object than
the emolument of the clergy'.[15]

Another Dissenter, John Angell, considered that in the fourth
century the Church was already corrupt and had become 'modelled by
assuming priests'. It was then that the popes rose to pre-eminence and
'laid the foundations for that monarchical power and grandeur to
which they afterwards rose'.[16] Angell's *The History of Religion* (1764),
published in forty weekly parts under the pseudonym 'An Impartial
Hand', was no more nor less bleak in its historical outlook than the
estimation of the founder of Methodism, John Wesley. Wesley wrote
an Abridgement of Johann von Mosheim's *Institutiones historiae eccle-
siasticae* (1726) entitled *A Concise Ecclesiastical History* (1781).[17] It
has been said that Mosheim's account of the papacy was particularly
bleak and was described by Gibbon as rational and correct. But use of
Mosheim did not transform or significantly deepen the sectarian ire of
the usual English Protestant priestcraft theory, which had already
reached its critical apogee before the publication of Mosheim's work.
In Wesley's abridgement the usurping popes were part of the 'rapacious priesthood' who, as in the thought of Priestley, took advantage
of the fact that the newly converted barbarous nations looked upon
the pope as their Archdruid. This fact 'swelled the arrogance of the
roman druid to an enormous size', and gave him a 'despotic authority,
in civil and political matters that was unknown to former ages'. This
calamity came about because the pagan nations 'had been absolutely
enslaved to their priests, without whose counsel they transact[ed]
nothing, either in civil or military affairs'.[18]

The profound influence of the priestcraft paradigm is also attested to by another attempt to write a more sympathetic account of the medieval Church, that of the evangelical curate and headmaster Joseph Milner (1744–97). Milner's *History of the Church of Christ* (1794–1809) became an important text in Evangelical circles, and in it he declares his disapproval of writers who exaggerate the vices of Christians. But his objections to Mosheim's account – as for example when Milner rejects Mosheim's view of missionary monks as 'covering ambition with the cloak of mortification' – are annulled by the pervasive gloom of Milner's own analysis. Milner himself explains that the 'princes of the earth, as well as the meanest persons, were ... enslaved to popedom'. The friars were the tax gatherers of the pope, and the profession of Franciscan poverty was part of their 'deep laid plans of hypocrisy', avowed merely in order to dupe the people into enriching the papacy and increasing its authority.[19]

The conception of papal history held by Scottish Protestants differed little from their more southerly co-religionists. The Scottish Enlightenment, renowned for the erudite and 'philosophical' historiography of such figures as David Hume and William Robertson, was not surpassed in Enlightenment Europe in the degree to which the principles of the Enlightenment were espoused by the leaders of the established Church. In terms of Church history, of course, this mattered little, because we know the enlightened had appropriated the fundamentals of their view of Church history from the Protestant critique. The brother-in-law of William Robertson, the Kirk cleric Patrick Nisbet (1722–1803), wrote *An Abridgement of Ecclesiastical History* (1776), in which the factors leading to papal supremacy include: the exploitation of the confusion engendered by barbarian invasions, the 'riches and honours' received from Gothic princes, and the deliberate emasculation of the power of the episcopate. Two other factors are stressed. As in the accounts of other Protestants, the pope was considered by newly converted European peoples to be the 'great arch-druid', which gave the pope boundless power over them. The appearance of 'Mahomet' and his wars and conquests also 'roused the zeal and emulation of the Roman pontiff', and 'furnished occasions for the more ample exercise of despotic power, and rendered many more humble supplicants to his [the pope's] authority'.[20]

A similar, if more heated, analysis is found in the work of John Brown (1722–87), minister of the staunchly Calvinist Scottish Secession Church. Brown was accused of having gained his precocious learning from the devil, and was persecuted for five years on that account, although he certainly did not himself advocate tolerance. In

his *General History of the Christian Church* (1771), Brown relates how
the popes – those 'clerical impostors' – had 'greedily embraced' the
common belief that they possessed the power of the chief druids and
had 'rioted in luxury and wickedness'. Equally antichristian, 'the
working of pretended miracles were considered as unanswerable
arguments against every doubt' laid upon the corrupt nature of
worship and papal power.[21]

The work specifically written in order to refute this kind of accusation, and which had championed papal supremacy during the
Counter-Reformation was the *Annales ecclesiastici* of Baronius. The
intended eighteenth-century replacement for Baronius was the *Della
Istoria ecclesiastica* (1746–96) of Orsi and Becchetti; but in its fundamentals it differed little from the historical scheme of Baronius.[22]
Various other pro-curial historians, such as Giuseppe Piatti and
Antonio Sandini[23] also reiterated the analysis of Baronius on questions regarding papal supremacy, which rested upon an assertion of
the Petrine theme, the apostolic succession of bishops.

For Italian anti-curial yet conservative writers such as Lodovico
Muratori, the Petrine basis of papal claims to spiritual supremacy in
the Church was not contentious. But it also marked the line at which
Muratori's theological conservatism gave way to the imperatives of
jurisdictional struggle in his own state, the Duchy of Modena.
Muratori was adviser to the Dukes of Modena in territorial and
ecclesiological disputes between Rome and Modena. His opposition
to the jurisdiction of the Curia over the Church of Modena was based
upon his loyalty to the ruling Este dynasty and his conception of the
near absolute role of the prince. Muratori wished to challenge the
historical legitimacy of Roman jurisdiction, yet leave the formal
petrinal supremacy of Rome intact and so retain a degree of Catholic
orthodoxy. In his *Antichità Estensi* (1717), following the lead of his
predecessor and mentor Benedetto Bacchini,[24] Muratori first under-
took a revision of the role of secular power in the jurisdiction of the
Church. He commenced with the seventh-century Lombard Kings,
whom he also imputed to be forebears of the Este family. Against
the prevailing image of the Lombard and Gothic kings as heathen
barbarians, in his *Annali d'Italia* (1744–9), Muratori again depicted
them as religiously tolerant and law-giving lovers of justice.

In his *Antiquitates italicae medii* (1738–42) Muratori declared there
'is no doubt' that in the early Church 'the Roman Pontifex, the
[Church] councils and metropolitan bishops', had supremacy over the
episcopate. In this tactful formulation, which of course actually

denied papal supremacy, the popes shared power with other prelates. Muratori's major objective, however, was to illustrate how the pope was then still subject to the will of the Lombard and Gothic kings and Frankish emperors. Up to the early ninth century, he illustrated, these rulers had the power to intervene in matters of ecclesiastical justice. Then he felt able to write: 'Deny now, if you are able, that the kings, although pious, judged it their own duty to intervene in the correction of the ecclesiastics and in their government,' against which the popes did not protest.[25]

Unlike the relatively moderate Muratori, most anti-curialists were stridently overt in their denunciations of the despotic usurpation of Church authority by the popes. For these writers, as for Protestants, papal supremacy was proof of medieval priestcraft, confirmed by the continued reality of the legislator-priest at Rome. The same reality had also been perceived to confront seventeenth-century critics of the Church, and was censured to one degree or another in the works of various anti-curialist writers. Lamberti Arconati, for example, in his *L'inquisizione processata*, angrily denounced the tyranny, bloody cruelty and frauds of the inquisition, 'erected on the throne of impiety by papal cunning'.[26]

As already noted, the inspiration for Arconati's *L'inquisizione processata* had come from Sarpi. In his *History of the Council of Trent* (1619) Sarpi had demonstrated how the papacy had consistently and cynically manoeuvred in the council in order to preserve and assert its dominance over the entire Church. In another work, his *Historia ... sopra li beneficii ecclesiastici*, Sarpi condemned the monarchic usurpation of Church government by the pope. He opined that in 'its origin the government of the Church was completely democratic involving all the faithful in its deliberations'. When the Church had grown in number the government was 'aristocratic', in the hands of the ministers only. Everything was then resolved by local synods at least twice a year and bishops and clerics met 'almost daily', although elections were 'popular'.[27] Like other anti-curialists, he also demonstrated how Papal supremacy had anyway been limited by royal intervention in the Church.

Of Pope Paul V (1605–21), Sarpi wrote that in his youth he had dedicated himself to studies 'which did not have any other aim than to acquire the spiritual and temporal monarchy of the whole world for the Roman pontefice'.[28] Despite the incisive nature of their critique of papal craft, Sarpi and some other early seventeenth-century Venetian jurisdictionalists, such as Giovanni Battista Leone and

Tommaso Zefiriele Bovio, were at some remove from some of the consciously inflammatory anti-curial works of the period. Nevertheless, Battista could note in his *Due Discorsi sopra la liberta ecclesiastica* (1606) that the popes used fraud and deceit in temporal claims, abused spiritual power by claiming the pope was God on the land, and so terrorized the rude masses into obedience.[29]

The tone of the seventeenth-century anti-curial critique of the papacy thus stretched from impugning the papacy as a cabal of greedy and unscrupulous men who used religion to deceive the laity for self-gain, to an institution headed by a priest-king intent on world power. These and similar evaluations formed an important component of the cultural legacy that seventeenth-century writers bequeathed to ardent eighteenth-century jurisdictionalists such as the Neapolitan Pietro Giannone, whose historiography was to have significant influence upon subsequent anti-curial writers.[30] The Kingdom of Naples, still semi-feudal in character and in desperate need of economic reform, suffered from the inertia of a richly endowed and conservative Church, which used nearby Rome as a counterweight to the Neapolitan alliance of nobles and intellectuals. Not surprisingly, Giannone's conception of state–Church relations was, like Muratori's, a regalist formulation. Giannone too rehabilitated the Gothic and Lombard Kings and elevated their role in the government of the Church in order to counter claims for the antiquity of papal supremacy. But, unlike Muratori, Giannone underpinned his historical analysis with the providential evidence of Mosaic Law, using elements of it to establish the legitimate pre-eminence of civil law over the Church.[31]

For Giannone, in the fifth century the popes had obtained supremacy over all the patriarchs of Christendom on account of the status of Rome, and then began to usurp the rights of European metropolitan bishops. The Church, however, was still 'entirely' subject to the will of the Lombard and Gothic kings and 'as members of civil society ... [the popes] obeyed the civil laws, by which they were also judged and punished'. The donation of Pepin III in 756 (of territory in north-eastern Italy), which laid the foundation for the States of the Church, and its confirmation by his son Charlemagne, represented an act of momentous importance in Giannone's writings – as it did in the thought of most anti-curialists. The territorial donations meant that the popes and bishops became powerful temporal lords; consequently they became concerned with worldly rather than spiritual matters. In order to regulate the ensuing abuse and spiritual corruption, princes intervened in the life of the Church, and so still substantially limited papal supremacy in the eighth century.

Not to be so easily restricted, argued Giannone, the popes so organized the discipline of the Church (over permitted degrees of consanguinity in marriage for example), that the dispensation of Rome was increasingly necessary, thus rendering papal supremacy an ever greater practical fact. Canon law was created only 'in order to better establish [the dispensation of] ecclesiastical justice', enabling it to more effectively compete with secular courts, and thus promote 'pontifical greatness'. The same canonists conspired with scholastics in order to produce a corpus of Church writings designed to more securely establish the monarchy of Rome; while the Inquisition was founded to police and protect that monarchical supremacy. The popes also had staunch allies. By granting 'so many privileges and prerogatives' to monasteries, which were responsible to the pope rather than bishops, the pope had 'acquired many defenders of his authority and power, since the monks ... in order to conserve them were obliged to sustain the authority of the concessor'.[32]

More than half a century later, the jurisdictionalist struggle in the Kingdom of Naples, as elsewhere in the Italian peninsula, had not abated but increased in intensity, and had found an advocate in Archbishop Capecelatro,[33] who received economic support from the sovereign of Naples. As in Giannone's writings, those of Capecelatro uphold the rule of the state against the jurisdiction of the popes. Unlike Giannone, the archbishop did not rest his case on Mosaic law, but rather on the biblical evidence of the obedience of Jesus to the emperor. In his *Discorso istorico-politico* Capecelatro also lamented that the popes had usurped, by forgery and fraud, the ancient rights of sovereigns, bishops and metropolitans. Nevertheless, the popes still cynically used the episcopate as a support for the extension of papal supremacy.

Another Neapolitan clergyman and contemporary of Capecelatro, accused by the Curia of spreading Jansenist ideas, was Marcello Eusebio Scotti (1740–1800).[34] In his *Della Monarchia universale de'papi,* the origin of papal supremacy is located partly in the Petrine legacy, but also in the deeply corrupting effects of the enrichment of the Church. For Scotti, at Rome, the richest of Churches, corruption by wealth went furthest. The result was greater ambition, leading to the antichristian usurpation of supremacy, which was steadily promoted and defended by the monastic orders. In order to defend the supremacy and prestige of the Court of Rome, the Curia became a workshop of falsity and imposture. The popes cultivated a corrupt 'external' religion for the ignorant masses, one reliant upon hypocritical formalism, while they consistently concealed the true Christian doctrine. Indeed, rather than venerating elements of Judaism as Giannone had done, Scotti exploited the New Testament Pharisees, biblically depicted as the chief opponents of Christ, as a direct analogy with the papacy. In case readers had missed the significance of his comparison, he also declared that the eleventh-century cardinalate, composed of the princes of the Church, was the 'Sanhedrin of the new Judaic temporal monarchy', and had been raised on the ruins of the episcopate (the Sanhedrin was the supreme Jewish council at Jerusalem and pronounced the death penalty upon Christ).[35]

Extreme as the rhetoric and accusations of Scotti might seem, the Catholic reform movement in northern Italy in the 1780s produced some equally bitter denunciations of papal priestcraft. The development of the jurisdictionalist struggle there, as in the south, was cut short in the last years of the century by French occupation, with the formation in the north of French-style revolutionary republics, and in the south of the Parthenopean Republic. But before the outbreak of the French Revolution in 1789, the tone of some of the northern anti-curial rhetoric was already ominous. According to the anonymous author of the *Istoria del pontificate romane* (1785), in the early Church 'the bishops and abbots formed the senate' but later the 'republic of the Church become an absolute monarchy'. The popes had suppressed the independent power of the episcopate, the senate of the 'republic of the Church'. They then claimed infallibility to increase their despotic power, and created the Inquisition to maintain their supremacy.[36]

While under French protection after the entrance of the Republican Army into Lombardy in 1796, Paolo Rivarola – possibly an ex-priest – translated the *Mystére d'iniquité, c'est-à-dire l'histoire de la papauté* (1611) of the French Huguenot leader Philippe Du Plessis-Mornay.[37] The *Mystére d'iniquité*, a monument to the nature of the priestcraft theory current amongst early seventeenth-century Huguenots, was promoted as official propaganda against the Church by French and Italian Jacobins. Rivarola's translation of (and additions to) Mornay, the *Storia del papato*, is couched in a ferocious and sometimes prolix republican invective which, unsurprisingly, does not always spare the royal order. Rivarola too notes the use made by the popes of pagan priestly prerogatives, and for him '[t]he Holy Spirit of the papacy consisted of cunning, fraud, deception

[and] imposture'. These diabolical but relatively restrained methods were used for as long as was possible. But then, in order to maintain despotic rule over the Church, peoples, kingdoms and empires, there entered 'threats, declamations, claimed infallibility and finally open violence, excommunications and the fire of the Inquisition'.[38]

The *Storia cronologica de' papi* (1798), penned by the Jansenist Pier Delle Piane,[39] has a comparatively conciliatory and regalist tone. His analysis exhibits a combination of vestigial spiritual respect for the Curia combined with damning indictment, a recipe of the type found in some other northern Italian works.[40] Some popes are lauded for their piety, charity and erudition. Yet, in general, most are castigated for using fraud and forgery to become monarchs of the Church, some of whom ruled tyrannically and employed fraud and forgery to level the road to the 'solemn imposture' of the papal monarchy. Piane does not deny that the pope is the 'ministerial head' of the Church, yet he vigorously defends the attempts by the late fourteenth- and fifteenth-century Conciliar movement to subject the popes to general councils of the Church.[41] Similar in many respects, although not so concili-atory, is the analysis of the pro-Gallican Carlo Denina (1731–1813). Denina, an ex-priest, theologian and historian at Turin University, under pressure from Rome first left Italy for the protection of Frederick II in Berlin. In his *Discorso istorico sopra l'origine della gerarchia* (composed *c.* 1779–80), he describes how the popes usurped the power of the episcopate to become an 'absolute monarchy', aided by the popes' cardinals and the Inquisition.[42]

THE PITFALLS OF THE PRIESTCRAFT POLEMIC

As early as the beginning of the seventeenth century, some Anglicans had felt uneasy about the strident claims of priestcraft aimed at the medieval and contemporary papacy by Puritans. Such devastating polemic could also be turned against the Anglican prelacy. In the opinion of late sixteenth-century Puritans, the Anglican Church had failed to reform itself fully and retained dangerous elements of Catholicism. Not least was the survival of the episcopate and Catholic ceremonial forms and practices which smacked of idolatry, superstition and tyranny. In the 1580s and 1590s many Puritans despaired the Anglican Church could ever be properly reformed on the Calvinist theological model and non-hierarchical presbyterian polity. Consequently, many had retreated from it and formed a clandestine

Presbyterian organization. But Church and state under Elizabeth firmly persecuted the growing rival Church.

At the beginning of the seventeenth century, therefore, the political and theological ground for a comparison of the despotism and perceived ceremonial corruption of the Anglican Church with that of the papacy was prepared. A work of Henry Ainsworth (1571– c.1622), directed at the perceived paganism of the Anglican Church and containing echoes of the Vestiarian dispute, is a typical example of the tenor of Puritan anti-Anglicanism: *Certayne Questions concerning* (i) *Silk or Wool in the High Priest's Ephod*; (ii) *Idol Temples commonly called Churches* (1605. An ephod is a Jewish ecclesiastical vestment). Not surprisingly, by 1606, some Anglicans were beginning to realize that an unfettered anti-popery polemic could be dangerous. It was warned that some complex theological debate 'could lead unsophisticated ministers astray, and should be left to experienced divines.... It was no longer an area into which radical Protestants' zeal could safely be channelled'.[43] Consequently, some Anglicans now pursued an offensive against Puritans.

By the last decades of the seventeenth century, despite the momentous events and vicissitudes of previous decades, there was no change in the virulence of Protestant anti-Catholicism and the dissatisfaction of Dissenters with the perceived popery of the Anglican Church. On the contrary, the complex polemical climate was hotter and, in the late 1690s, more public than ever. The frequent and strident public proclamations that there had been more than a millennium of Catholic priestcraft, an accusation extended by Dissenters to the Anglican Church, prompted some to question whether priestcraft was not innate to all hierarchical priesthoods. Dissatisfied Presbyterian-minded Dissenters such as John Toland, whose zeal had not yet been dissipated by the oppression of Church and state, certainly posed such questions. We know that some answered such questions in the affirmative, because they promulgated historical evidence (as they saw it) demonstrating that traditional, hierarchical Christian priesthoods had all been corrupt and antichristian for all or almost all of their existence. From the Presbyterian womb, the pugnacious Protestant infant who would in turn give birth to so-called deism had emerged, already upon its lips an historical challenge.

In 1710–11, the Convocation of Canterbury attributed the growing scepticism, deism and Dissenter dissatisfaction partly to the evils of the Civil War and the Toleration Act of 1689. Convocation too recognized the danger posed by Protestants who extended the ubiquitous anti-Rome historico-polemic to the contemporary Anglican Church:

> The Frauds of *Pagan* and *Popish Priests* have been display'd, in order to represent all Priests as Imposers upon the Credulity of Mankind; and draw Infamy upon the *Priesthood* in general, and to render the Order itself, in what Religion soever it was found, equally the Object of publick Aversion and Contempt.[44]

The assembly opined that the forged treatises of the earliest ages of the Church have been enumerated,

> which they [Dissenters] represent as Times of great Fraud and Imposture, on the one hand; of great Ignorance and Credulity, on the other.[45]

Even some decades later, after the decline of the deists in England, the Anglican priest Conyers Middleton in his *Free Inquiry* (1749) continued to indicate the dangers inherent in using the history of the medieval Church against Rome.

In the opinion of Abbot Bencini, who played a role in combatting heresy in the college De Propaganda Fide at Rome, the real enemy of the faith in 1720 was not to be found in the ideas of sceptics such as Spinoza. Rather, it was the 'libertine theory of the fraudulence of religions, from which every heresy had derived' – of which of course anti-curialists such as Leti, Pallavicino and Arconati were exponents. For Bencini, Spinoza, Hobbes and Cherbury all 'accepted the Libertine thesis of the imposture of religions'.[46] However, it would be most misleading to uncritically accept Bencini's assessment that all manifestations of scepticism and heresy had a common root. For Hobbes and Cherbury can hardly be termed dangerous sceptics – even though Cherbury has been considered the father of deism – but were rather Dissenting Protestants who were prepared to use the priestcraft accusation in the cause of reform. Similarly, in Italy, those wielding the club of priestcraft against Rome were hardly all atheists or even radical sceptics, as even a cursory examination of anti-curial thought reveals. It was, of course, only to be expected that pro-curialists such as Bencini would lump together all those accusing Rome of contemporary and historical priestcraft. By depicting them all as antichristian atheists, it was hoped would-be moderate dissidents might think again before joining their ranks and branding themselves as enemies of Jesus Christ.

To accept the categorization of Bencini, that all critics of the Church (who were indeed numerous) were sceptics or worse, would also be to accept that seventeenth- and early eighteenth-century Europe was suffering from a widespread crisis of faith, for which there is no evidence. What can be asserted, is that the crisis in the Church provoked by the Reformation had progressively deepened somewhat in proportion to the manifest duration and bitterness of religious division and antagonism. Only as the eighteenth century progressed, nourished by the increased availability of alternative, rational explanations of the universe, did a narrow section of the intelligentsia – and then mostly in France – experience a crisis of faith.

That enemies of Rome shared a similar polemical and historical critique was hardly a perceptive insight by Bencini. The shared perspective was an early and rather obvious response to religious conflict, using comparisons drawn from common religious prejudice (against Islam, Judaism, and ancient idolaters for example) to slander religious opponents. Seventeenth- and eighteenth-century anti-curial Catholic and Protestant propagandists could draw upon a ready made European corpus of such comparisons, either more or less erudite or stylistically efficacious. If we wish to discuss the influence of Christianity's critique of itself, we should examine the scheme of medieval Church history in Edward Gibbon's *Decline and Fall*. His scheme, in its fundamentals and disregarding his famous style, was only a repetition of the common-or-garden Protestant priestcraft analysis (a point which will be returned to in subsequent chapters).

Protestants and dissident Catholics shared a perspective in which theology and historiography were intertwined with questions of nationhood, of freedom against despotism and of social and economic justice. Democrats inspired democracy, powerful despots inculcated despotism; it was regarded as a simple lesson, one confirmed by the copious evidence of history. Once the popes had stripped the episcopate of its power, they had proceeded (as we shall see in the next chapter) to usurp the rights of kings and emperors. Even when Protestant kings had finally assimilated the hard truth about papal tyranny, in the Protestant mind the popes continued to be the instigators of and goads to royal despotism and a threat to the freedom of Protestants. This much was clear, manifest in the continued menace of the alliance of European Catholic powers and in the sailing of the Spanish Armada against England in 1588. The terrible persecutions of Protestants across Europe and the barbarous wars fought under the false banner of Catholicism were thought to be the result of sinister papal influence upon Catholic kings. They were telling symptoms of a deep antichristian fervour, excited by the thirst for power and the bloodlust of ambition. As one writer put it in 1709, if the Gospel had been followed rather than Priestcraft, there would not have been so many wars and a 'Christian Peace' would have been possible.[47] Catholics, therefore, were tainted by a long-inculcated urge to tyranny and a bellicose ambition. It was thus unthinkable that Catholicism could be tolerated in any free, rational and humane society.

For most English Dissenters, Roman supremacy naturally represented the mother, the archetype of the priestly tyranny they had long experienced at the hands of the repressive English state and its Church. In early modern Europe, political and religious views were so braided together that religious dissent was closely woven with the sharp barbs of political, economic and social exigency. It is for this reason that the gulf between most pro-curialist and anti-curialist Italians was unbridgeable even, in the final analysis, by the moderate Muratori. Anti-curial Catholic historiography had more in common with its Anglican cousins than with its ostensible close relative in the Curia.

Giorgio Spini has noted that, despite the intentions of Counter-Reformation pro-curial propagandists, the widespread use of the priestcraft paradigm against the protagonists of the Reformation paradoxically served to contribute to the social reality of papal priestcraft. He has suggested seventeenth-century Italian anti-curial thought was the 'illegitimate son' of the Counter-Reformation, and that such thought had a significant influence on men such as Pietro Giannone and the self-confessed freethinker Alberto Radicati.[48] According to Spini, such anti-curialists needed, like the Protestants, to return to the original teachings of Jesus to justify their opposition to papal supremacy to themselves and to their readership.[49] In practice, a New Testament foundation for unorthodox Catholic thinkers was hardly as requisite as Spini indicates. The works of seventeenth-century anti-curialists contained minimal references to the Bible and the teachings of Jesus. The ascription of a simple democracy and pure doctrine to the primitive Church was strongly evident, however, and remained so in eighteenth-century anti-curialist thought. Neither does one find a return to the original teaching of Jesus in the thought of Giannone; rather he returned to the Mosaic teachings of the Old Testament and the evidence of the early Church. There was, then, no great theological step to be taken from the thought of many seventeenth-century libertines to eighteenth-century anti-curialists.

It would have been unthinkable that anti-curial Catholics would not sometimes have made generalized references to the New Testament, and sometimes have exploited biblical phrases such as *regnum meum non est de hoc mundo*. The exploitation of that phrase reflected growing tension between Roman domination of the Church, the increasing trend in the peninsula towards religious self-determination, and a Church reform movement also spiritually opposed to the secular dominion of the popes. Even at the height of the Catholic Enlightenment, exemplified in an important collection of tracts compiled by Bishop de'Ricci, the *Raccolta di opuscoli interessanti la Religione* (1783), there was no reliance on biblical exegesis. Of course, it was precisely an aversion to the anachronism of the Papal States and the force of intellectual darkness it represented, which was also the engine of the enlightened Italian critique of Christian history. It is not surprising then, if at crucial moments it was difficult to determine where the radical Catholic priestcraft indictment ended and the enlightened one began.

4 Church, State and Priest-Kings

In his *Dictatus papae* (1075) Pope Gregory VII (1073–85) proclaimed that his personal sanctity was inherited from St Peter, and vehemently asserted papal legislative and judicial supremacy over all Christians, not exempting the princely order. He denied the right of kings to intervene in Church matters, and proclaimed his superiority over, and right to depose all princes. Whether the *Dictatus papae* were ever read by kings and emperors is not known, but the momentous events of Gregory's pontificate served in good measure to confirm his exalted view of the papacy. This stance was maintained by many subsequent popes – most notably Innocent III (1198–1216) and Boniface VII (1294–1303) – and the clash of Church and state continued at various times and intensities until the Reformation. Not surprisingly, during the Reformation the volatile history of state and Church provided rich pickings for propaganda-minded enemies of Rome – whether of the anti-curial Catholic or Protestant type – who wanted to champion the rights of kings against Roman interference. Despite various theological differences amongst Protestants, of necessity, most looked to the historic and present sovereign state as a bulwark against Rome and its allies. In vitriolic assaults, all shades of reformers repeatedly accused the medieval and Catholic Church hierarchy of using religion as camouflage to conceal their intent to usurp divinely ordained princely power.

The most consistent Protestant defenders of the prerogatives of state were usually Erastian in outlook, in England Anglicans. For Anglicans, kings were the historic victims of Rome's antichristian designs and present defenders against Catholic aggression. But, most importantly, from King Henry VIII, the state was also defender of the Anglican Church's privileged relationship with the state against its English Protestant detractors. From Queen Elizabeth these critics were mainly Presbyterians, usually termed Puritans until the Restoration, and afterwards, because of their diversity, Dissenters or Nonconformists. Puritans, we may remind ourselves, were staunch Calvinists who stood for the independence of the Church from the state, the abolition of the episcopate and Church rule by Presbyters (local elders). Nevertheless, Puritans too felt the need to defend the historic rights of kings and emperors in the Church against despotic rule from Rome. In history, kings were seen to be performing their Christian duty, protecting and promoting the Church against antichristian rule. Puritans were certainly not defending the concept of royal supremacy in the Church.

The same accusation of priestly transgression upon divine princely prerogatives was also sustained in the seventeenth and eighteenth centuries amongst anti-curial Catholics and by many enlightened thinkers of Europe. Protestant critics also focused on the contemporary Catholic persecution of various Protestant Churches in alliance with Catholic monarchs. All was understood by Protestants as self-evident proof of the tyrannical nature of Catholicism and, by analogy, the liberty of Protestant states. The final proof of this assessment – if more was needed – was the formidable reality of the antichristian temporal dominion of the pope still ensconced in the Vatican. For dissident Catholics, it was no coincidence that the Papal States were amongst the peninsula's most autocratic, backward and inefficient states. Terrible poverty shouted outrage against Rome's parasitical splendour. In Ravenna, for example, according to a local magistrate, nearly 6000 of the 13 000 inhabitants lived wholly upon charity.[1] Beyond theological questions, for anti-curialists from humble backgrounds and for others from higher up the economic scale yet with some social conscience, an attack on Rome was also an attack upon the blatant luxury of prelates in general and the unjustifiably great landed possessions of the Church. Popes and prelates did, after all, claim to revere religious austerity. It was thus an attack upon the most obvious hypocrisy of society and one likely to find a sympathetic hearing even amongst some of the conspicuously rich and powerful laity.

The absence of comprehensive religious toleration in Protestant states often did not completely destroy the favourable comparison of Protestantism with Catholicism. The discrimination and persecution of Dissenters in England could always (although, as we shall see, frequently not with entire success) be portrayed as a relatively lesser evil when compared to the military and religious menace of a European Catholic alliance. The reality of such threats had been attested to by many events, not least the assault of the Spanish Armada and the Thirty Years War. The practical evidence of the tyrannical and antichristian nature of Catholicism thus continued to mount in the minds of Protestants. The reply of the Curia to its various and numerous critics, however, remained static. Its official response to such accusations was still based on the work of Baronius, in which papal temporal dominion and the influence of Rome over princes, emperors and secular matters proceeded from the Curia's role as the defender of the Petrine legacy and consequently of the overall Church. Cardinal Orsi's defence of papal temporal dominion in his *Dell'Origine del dominio e della sovranità de'Romani Pontifici* (1742) is typical of pro-curial arguments mounted by other writers, such as Count Alfonso Muzzarelli in his *Dominio temporale del papa* (1789).

To anti-curialists such as Pietro Tamburini, the situation could not have been more plain. Tamburini, a partisan of the Reformism of Emperor Joseph II (1765–90) in Lombardy, proclaimed in his *Vera idea della Santa Sede* (1784) that there was a glaring contradiction between the pope as a temporal monarch and as the head of the universal Church. Nevertheless, all Catholics were constrained to follow the pope, even in such antichristian errors. Sovereigns of Italian states, as part of the drive to reform the Church, often had some interest in sponsoring attacks upon the temporal dominion of the popes (as long as political exigency permitted it). Attacks on the temporal rule of Rome could justify more intervention in their own Churches in search of extra revenue and the influence of the Church over hearts and minds. At the same time monarchs could appear progressive in the eyes of enlightened intellectuals, so helping to cement them to the service of the state.

Pro-curial anti-Protestant polemic had not changed since the Counter-Reformation, and was as unsparing as that of Protestants against Catholics. Propagandists such as the Jesuit Paolo Segneri, in his *L'Incredulo senza scusa* (1690), continued to declare Protestant Church–state relations unholy conspiracies. State and Church had colluded to choose the path of 'reform' from economic and political motives. This thrust may have formed a component of anti-Protestant propaganda, but it was not empty rhetoric. Pro-curial propagandists – as ordinary pious Catholics – knew only too well that the Reformation had, from the outset, posed the question of the ownership of very extensive Church lands, treasures and incomes. It was difficult to deny that some Church wealth had found its way into the hands of Protestant kings and their supporters. The accusation that the reformers and their state sponsors were motivated by the prospect of material gain was, therefore, convincing to many sincere Catholics. As was often the case, a kernel of truth served to underpin much of the greater volume of allied hyperbole.

For some Catholics, such as Odorico Rinaldi, the continuator of Baronius's *Annales ecclesiastici*, Luther had not only wanted to destroy the status of the Church hierarchy by arguing that all Christians were priests, but also to abolish all political hierarchies and the kings who led them.[2] Nevertheless, the same propagandists also held religion was to be regarded as a justifiable and useful tool of state with which to regulate civil life, providing divinely legitimized social and spiritual mores. Neither were anti-curialists always hostile to the idea of the state's use of religion as a brake on the passions of the masses – part of the oligarchic rule of the wise; although they were more often cynical about the state use of religion. In his *L'Alcibiade fanciullo a scuola* (*c.* 1650) for example, Don Antonio Rocco argued that most laws were made in the interest of the state, and religion was used to give them a veneer of divinity and respectability in the eyes of the plebeian masses. Wise legislators thus propagated their own capricious motives as the will of the gods.[3] The fear of a social and political order not founded upon Christian precepts and policed by the Church was, nevertheless, a consideration which occasionally exercised anti-curial and pro-curial thought in the eighteenth century. It was, for example, a fear sufficient to prompt Sicilian thinkers to draw back from proposing enlightened reforms that might have disturbed the delicate but essential symbiosis of Church and state.[4] Such considerations, however, rarely impinged on the anti-curial attack on Rome.

In the first years of the seventeenth century, Paolo Sarpi stated that Pope Paul V had dedicated himself to studying how to advance the clerical order by 'withdrawing it from the power and jurisdiction of all the princes and raising it even above kings'.[5] In his *Historia ... sopra li beneficii ecclesiastici*, Sarpi also declared that the enrichment of the Church by grants, tax exemptions and donations upon its state adoption under Emperor Constantine had been a turning point in the decline of Roman spirituality. That influx of wealth and prestige had excited the thirst of the clergy for even greater riches. They began to adopt any means to procure lucre, even to inducing widows to donate to the Church and thus depriving their own sons and relations of their rightful inheritance.[6] Under Constantine (it was understood), Christianity for the first time formed the established Church, and this became – as we have already seen in Chapter 2 – the dominant point of departure in anti-curial chronologies of papal descent into sustained spiritual fraud. This periodization, as we shall see, also loomed large in the Protestant psyche.

In the eighteenth century the nature of the anti-curial critique of the papacy, although more vehement, did not undergo significant change. As the century progressed, the papacy reached its nadir in international prestige and influence, and its ability to stamp out the frequent brush-fires of anti-curial dissent in the peninsula diminished correspondingly. Nonetheless, as we have seen, the papacy could still at times persecute individual writers when it acted resolutely and when regal protection wavered or was withdrawn. Changing political, economic and religious conditions were thus more responsible than historiographical innovation for the growing efficacy of the anti-curial critique, imbuing old ideas with a new significance and explanatory power. After all, important elements of the anti-curial position on Church–state relations had been outlined many years before by writers such as Marc-Antonio Sabellico (1436–1508) and Francesco Guicciardini (1483–1540).[7]

Conscious of the backward nature of the Italian states as compared to the rest of Europe, eighteenth-century Italian sovereigns and their progressive advisers began to be more overtly in favour of economic and religious reform. To reform their Churches meant a twin-pronged attack upon the legitimacy of papal supremacy and temporal dominion. Consequently, the biblical theme – if not the actual words – of *Regnum meum non est de hoc mundo* became an increasingly common refrain in anti-curialist attacks. It was an argument with which most sovereigns of the Italian peninsula could agree, and with which it was possible to counter the various territorial claims of Rome without sanctioning potentially more destabilizing religious dissent.[8] As such, it was deemed suitable for use against Rome by imperial propagandists such as Count Giovanni Battista Comazzi, historian to Emperor Leopold I at Vienna.[9]

In the writings of Muratori there is of course a similar condemnation of Church trespass on state prerogatives. He nevertheless studiously avoided an explicit denial of the legitimacy of papal temporal dominion *per se*, and never went beyond the formulation explicit in the title of his posthumous *Della Fallibilità dei pontefici nel dominio temporale*. In the territorial disputes between Rome and Modena, Muratori produced several pro-Este publications that reflected his own regalist conception of Church–state relations.[10] In these and related works the imperial donations to the Church were re-examined. The Donation of Constantine, in which Emperor Constantine was held to have given the entire Western Empire to the Church was derided as a forgery. But Muratori was careful to exculpate the popes and attributed the fraud to princes or nobles. The denial of the

Donation of Constantine had been, however, a feature of anti-curial and Protestant polemic for a long time. The Donation had already been proven a fraud by Lorenzo Valla in 1440;[11] and had been dismissed by Protestants since the Reformation. The Donation of Pepin Muratori also considered illegitimate, because at that time (754) the Exarchate of Ravenna did not belong to Pepin but to the Greek emperor. In any case, for Muratori 'high dominion' was always retained by the emperor, a theme common to all Modenesi and Imperial polemicists, and the pope ruled only as an exarch or vicar imperial. Moreover, Muratori carefully noted, until the pontificate of Pope Alexander II (1061–73), the pope elect was still required to obtain imperial confirmation of election.

Despite such constraints, Muratori told his readers that, boosted by the Donation of Pepin, the popes became masters of cities, castles and countries. Worse still, 'just as true temporal princes' their ambition to increase their temporal dominion 'did not neglect any of the solutions of peace or war'.[12] That Muratori's arguments did not extend to denying the legitimacy of papal temporal rule did not matter greatly. In practical polemical terms, his message – bolstered by his profound erudition – was at one with that of other anti-curialists: the papacy had deserted its spiritual role and had attempted and partly succeeded in usurping the rights of princes and instituting hierocratic rule. His work was naturally warmly greeted by virtually all anti-curial writers.

Giannone's conception of Church–state relations was one of a separation of powers: one purely spiritual, and the other purely material, but with Church, in practice, subordinated to state. Founded upon his appreciation of the Pentateuch (the five books) of Moses, Giannone's is a more secular, constitutional vision of statehood, in which early medieval popes were obedient to civil laws. On the status of the various donations of territory made to the Church, Giannone's analysis coincides substantially with that of Muratori, where high dominion was retained by the emperor.[13] Yet the donations still marked the beginning of papal usurpation of princely rights to temporal rule. By the eleventh century, he opined, 'mostly through the lack of the royal line of Charlemagne', and by uniting the 'Crosier and the sword' (unity of spiritual and secular power), the papacy had shrewdly achieved that which the eastern and western emperors were not able to obtain with long wars: the feudal investiture of princes. Kings became vassals of the pope, whose kingdoms were *feudi* of the Church. Popes were secular rulers superior to kings and possessed the power to depose them. In the twelfth and thirteenth centuries, their potency boosted by various devices, the popes extended their grasp over all kings and into every kingdom and province.[14]

Fifty years subsequent to Giannone, the Neapolitan Marcello Scotti shared many aspects of his critique, including his regalism. After the fall of the Roman Empire, Scotti related, the popes were intent on fishing in the troubled waters of those momentous times, searching for all means – even the most illicit – in order to acquire temporal dominion. From the eighth century, the popes meddled in the affairs of sovereigns and, 'the temporal promises of the ancient laws', those given to Moses on Mount Sinai, '[were] confused with those of the Gospel'. The princes were ignorant and illiterate, thus all the affairs of state were in the hands of clerics and monks. These ecclesiastics 'were intent only on the acquisition of temporal goods', using underhand and illegal techniques learned from the 'Pharisaic Gospel of Rome become carnal'. From the mid-eleventh century princes were vassals of the pope. Pope Gregory VII thus constituted the great apostle of the carnal Messiah and prostitute of Rome, usurper of the God-given power of kings. The boundless ambition of the popes had been aided by canonists such as Gratian (d. *c.* 1159), whose great compilation of canon law, the *Concordantia discordantium canonum* (*c.* 1139), confirmed 'the authority of the popes to depose sovereigns'.[15]

For Archbishop Capecelatro, the teachings 'of Jesus were founded upon perfect obedience to the laws of government', which 'tends to strengthen the social bonds and political rights of society'. But the popes proceeded to trample upon the royal prerogative. As a consequence – and slyly veiling his accusation with a feigned disapproval – Capecelatro reports 'the Church has been unjustly compared to the cunning system of the druids', who disposed of 'an unlimited and tyrannical religious power', and even with 'the scourge of the Saracens'. For this most ardent prelate, the 'great colossus of priestly power' came about via territorial donations and the 'infinite superstition' of the people, with the result that powerful bishops 'distanced themselves from the immediate subjection of the princes, and became sovereigns of the [people]'. The many exemptions from civil jurisdiction granted to the Church proceeded from princely piety and their belief in 'the maxims of the ancient priesthood of the Jews' of the Old Testament. It was in the chaos of territorial wars that popes became temporal competitors, and their designs were augmented by the strange fantasies of princes. The princes, 'wished to be anointed and crowned' by the vicar of God and head of the Church, 'following the example of the ancient kings of Israel'. But

> [t]he popes took advantage of this strange fantasy ... in order to believe themselves not only ministers of that pure ceremony, but despots of kingdoms and even of the Empire ... This is the true primordial origin of all the famous dominions of Europe which were reputed to be feoffs of the Roman Church.

He explains that this strange fantasy was in reality the princely need for Christian legitimation in order to render their rule more secure. This need, combined with the ignorance, superstition and weakness of secular government, all exploited by the unrestrained ambition of the popes, ensured the liberty of peoples and principates was given a 'fatal blow'. There thus arose that 'great machine of clerical power' which extracted copious treasures from all kingdoms of Europe.[16]

In the north of the peninsula, the anonymous author of the *Istoria del pontificate* – a little similar in his gloomy tone to that found in Voltaire's *Essay on the Manners and Spirits of Nations* (1754) – provides an overview of the Carolingian period as the veritable Dark Ages. This was, he tells us, an epoch of constant chaos, of wars and risings, and even Charlemagne's 'taste and ideas were more inclined to destroy the human race than refound it'. Nevertheless, the author goes on to stridently accuse the Church hierarchy of defrauding princes of their temporal rights and that, after Charlemagne's death, the situation worsened. It was then that the popes suddenly made their claim

> to the kings of Europe: 'I prohibit you to have an unlimited power in your states and I advise you to divest yourselves, in my favour, of a part of your estates. You, peoples, listen to my commands. You will not eat unless I permit it ... You will blindly obey me in everything'.

Subsequently, kings made it their duty to submit to the pope, were stripped of their crowns, and temporal power was 'entirely subjected to the spiritual'. Because too much energy was expended contemplating life after death rather than in productive activity, medieval Europe fell into a 'universal inaction' and became under-cultivated. Popes and emperors jointly ruled Europe, and deliberated upon disputes between kings. While kings were ruining each other in war, the popes' ambition proceeded more cautiously, deploying excommunication, the Inquisition and papal representatives in the courts of kings.[17]

In his *Storia del papato*, Rivarola's accusations against the papacy are liberally coated with a bitter republican rhetoric. The popes, those 'conquerors of the world and ministers of war' with an 'unrestrained lust', claimed the power to create or depose kings. From the year 1000, they claimed direct or indirect dominion over all states of the world, fomenting intestine wars, sackings and massacres. He proclaims 'despots have always used the mantle of religion and the veil of imposture to cover their treacherous designs', a tactic 'which the popes made use of to arrive ... at their desires'. The principal occasion for this state of affairs was not just papal iniquity, but the 'treachery, the imbecility and worthlessness' of kings who, 'prostrate at the feet of the popes', granted the popes temporal dominion. Almost immediately, as the papal despots 'deified' their plunder, there arose, 'favoured by ignorance and superstition', the 'monstrous colossus of the papacy'.[18]

Despite his occasionally conciliatory tone, Delle Piane too declaims against the legitimacy of Rome's combination of earthly and spiritual rule. He reminds his readers that Jesus Christ denied any earthly kingdom, yet popes such as Gregory VII aimed at 'a universal monarchy, as much in the temporal as in the spiritual'. Delle Piane thus harks back to the pre-Constantinian purity and simplicity of the Church, when Christianity was not yet the state religion of the Romans: before the acquisition of wealth and temporal dominion which brought antichristian ambition in its wake. Constantine's adoption of Christianity, declares Delle Piane, resulted in a strange and monstrous mix of the temporal and the spiritual, in which even the cardinals of the pope were the equals of kings.[19] Antonio Montegnacco, one of the major publicists of the Venetian reform of the 1760s, is equally robust in his argument. His *Ragionamento intorno a' beni temporali posseduti dalle chiese* (1766) is dedicated to disproving the temporal rights of the popes, arguing that the Apostles' possessions were only an embarrassment and a hindrance to their spiritual mission and hence shunned.

We have seen how ardent were anti-curialists in their polemics against the papal combination of temporal and spiritual rule, designating it the result of antichristian ambition. Paradoxically, most anti-curialists were, in practice, prepared to grant executive power in the Church to their own princes. They did not fear, it seems – and probably with good reason – any retort by Rome on their own Church–state proclivities. By usurping temporal dominion, Rome had gone beyond an acceptable Church–state relationship to embrace antichristian values, leading – in Delle Piane's terms – to a strange and monstrous mix of the temporal and the spiritual. Denina's Gallican estimation, it could be said, is more Realpolitik, yet contains the same accusation. The fulcrum of his analysis is that 'God divided the government of the Church amongst priests and kings'. But the nature of the balance between papal and royal government of the Church had been dependent upon the potency of secular power in relationship to clerical power. In this balance, wrote Denina, the issue of temporal dominion was decisive. It first began to shift in favour of the papacy as a result of the role played by north Italian and Gallic bishops in the fifth- and sixth-century defence against barbarian attack. From the tenth century, secular power intervened less in the spiritual because it had less repute in the temporal. The popes disputed temporal power with the emperor, and bishops had wished 'to treat rulers ... as novices or public penitents'. The pope had claimed to be the 'prince of princes and universal monarch in temporals and spirituals', claiming the right to depose and raise kings, which was the cause of civil wars. Only with Philip II (1180–1223) was the mantle of Charlemagne resumed and the Gallican Church reborn.[20]

In many important respects the Protestant view of medieval Church–state relations echoed that of Catholic dissidents, both equating Rome and its agents with treason and despotism. In his *De servo arbitrio* (1525), Luther dealt directly with Church–state relations when he formulated the concept of the two regiments: the purely spiritual regiment of the Church and the purely worldly regiment of princes and peoples. For Luther, and similarly for Calvin, the popes had 'established the most terrible tyranny over both the spiritual and the worldly orders'. In Luther's scheme, papal escape from imperial control and the drive to hierocratic rule, trampling on the high dominion of the emperor in Italy, dated from the eleventh century and Gregory VII.[21] We have already seen how Luther's general historical scheme quickly became dominant in sixteenth- and seventeenth-century Protestant conceptions of the medieval Church, and the subject of Church–state relations was no exception. In his *Actes and Monuments* – which came to be known as *The Book of Martyrs* – Foxe followed Luther's assessment of Church–state relations, as did seventeenth- and eighteenth-century Protestants, some of whom still used Foxe as their model.

Typical of contemporary attitudes to Rome, Richard Field told his readers in 1606 that popes even now

with harlottes fore-heades and execrable boldnesse, doe endeavour
to subverte imperiall and regall power, and to overthrowe all Lawes
both of GOD and man.... they are the elders of the people, high
Priests, Scribes, Pharisies, and doctors of the Lawe, as they were
that crucified Christ.[22]

Denunciations of the usurpation of princely prerogatives by popes
were attractive to High Church Anglicans such as Field, especially in
the Laudian period (1630s). Such men could be seen publicly excori-
ating the papacy – so earning valuable anti-Catholic kudos – on an
issue upon which both Puritans and Anglicans could without difficulty
agree. In his *Antidiatribae* (1625), the Laudian Bishop Richard
Montagu naturally rejected the powers of the popes to depose kings
or interfere in princely matters. Nevertheless, Montagu followed his
staunch Episcopalianism to a logical conclusion, arguing that, as a
bishop, the pope was to be allowed his own bishopric: the Papal
States. But outside the Laudian episcopalian circle, the very idea of
the pope as a priest-king exercising temporal power was anathema to
the vast majority of Protestants. After the downfall of Laud in 1641
such brazen High Church arguments were only very rarely voiced.

For a Protestant to accuse the Church of hierocratic usurpation of
the state was to accuse it of treason in the most profound sense of the
word. The proofs of the charge were both historical and contemporary: historical in the outrageous annals of Roman Catholic history,
contemporary in the fear of the perceived Catholic-engineered absolutism of the French Catholic state. This was treason by French
prelates against the prerogative of the French monarchy as well as
against the rights of its subjects. This was the same state which had
persecuted Protestants in the *Dragonnades* of 1683–6, and had
revoked the Edict of Nantes (1598, giving toleration to Huguenots) in
1685, the result of which was several hundred thousand Huguenot
refugees. Treason and apostasy were thus brought together to form
one powerful indictment. Anti-Catholicism, in this period then,
cannot be understood as simple, one-dimensional religious intolerance without danger of misapprehension. Early modern English
anti-Catholicism was intensely political, embodying hopes and fears
for personal security and national liberty based upon the commonly
understood concrete evidence of European events. So dominant and
so palpably correct was this view to participants, that even when religious radicals abandoned Christianity, they retained much the same
political, anti-Catholic outlook. After John Toland had renounced

hope for reform of the Church in 1697, he gave sincere and energetic support for a free Protestant Europe against despotic and benighted Catholic hegemony.

For Toland and most Dissenters, the struggle against Catholic despotism was simultaneously a struggle against the quasi-papist religious oppression they faced – and viewed as inherent – in the Church–state relationship in England. In post-Restoration England, Anglican divines 'accepted without hesitation their role as servants of a regime of personal monarchy and as advocates of an authoritarian view of society'. Church courts still existed and were active, dealing with a range of matters which would now be considered civil, still exercising a wide control over the morals and religious life of the laity. Excommunication, traditionally a central arm in the arsenal of Catholic Church justice, was still used by the Anglican Church and could entail serious consequences. An excommunicate could not make a will or take an action to civil court, and was disqualified from public office by virtue of the requirements of the Test and Corporation Acts. In conjunction with secular authority, the Church could still have individuals imprisoned until they submitted to Anglican censure. Only when Catholic James II ruptured the alliance of Church and State by his 1687 Declaration of Indulgence, did the disciplinary powers of Church courts diminish somewhat.[23] Nevertheless, when it was felt necessary, state and Church could still act in oppressive harmony. In 1729 Thomas Woolston, a Cambridge academic, was imprisoned for one year for questioning the miracles of Jesus. He died there, unable to meet the fine levied upon him for his release.

In hundreds of eighteenth-century anti-Catholic publications (which, for Dissenters, of course contained many indictments more or less applicable to the Anglican Church), a central component of the subject matter was the historical and contemporary tyranny and chicane of the would-be priest-legislator. As the Nonjuror Laurence Howell noted, kings had been the dupes of ambitious popes:

> In short it has been their business [the popes'] to sow dissension in all parts of the Christian world, where they had not immediate power, that by their fatal division they might more easily devour; engaging kings in their quarrels against their subjects, and supporting children and subjects in most unnatural rebellions against their parents and sovereigns.

These were popes, 'who with an armed force ... often confronted their sovereigns'. For Howell the eleventh century was the most remarkable for the encroachments made on Church and state by Rome, principally by Pope Gregory VII. He was a usurper of crowns and 'the most insolent tyrant of the Christian world', and the prerogative of the papal chair had been placed above that of the imperial.[24] Howell's more hard-line fellow Nonjuror Jeremy Collier, iterated the same charge. Nonetheless, where he could – ever attentive to his Episcopalian aims – Collier exculpated the Anglo-Saxon Church in order to identify an independent Episcopal Church free from the corruptions of Rome.

In the thought of the Anglican writer George Gregory, the right of sanctuary in the seventh-century Church was abused and 'extended almost to the annihilation of the civil authority'. In the eighth century, 'the monks and superior clergy were invested with the rights and prerogatives of sovereign princes'. Kings so invested prelates because the church was found to be 'of the utmost efficacy in restraining the rebellions and the turbulent spirit of the nobles'. Royal largesse was also prompted because the influence of bishops 'was so extensive over the minds of the people'. This identification of secular and priestly collusion was not unusual in the works of eighteenth-century Protestants. Despite appearances, however, there was generally no intention to debase or demean the contemporary royal order. The intention was rather to graphically illustrate the ultimate venality of papacy and prelacy in a period when priestly power was enormous, insidiously corrupting and irresistible, even to kings and emperors. The apparent bond of religion between the Carolingian rulers, popes and prelates, Gregory continues, was really 'the political connection of mutual interest, not of religion'. In this manner, an 'alliance was formed between superstition and despotism [Church and state], which for the succeeding ages proved the scourge of mankind'.[25]

In seventeenth-century England, some Protestants believed there was a benign role for Christianity within the state in terms of social control. It was argued that some of the 'complexities' of religious life should not be made available to the masses in order to avoid the danger of religious confusion. Some Anglicans certainly wanted to avoid heterodoxy which might threaten Anglican religious domination. Yet others genuinely feared for social order if Protestantism was unable to provide and oversee an acceptable moral code – a form of benign priestcraft. This pragmatic view of Church–state relations was acknowledged and accepted amongst seventeenth- and eighteenth-century upper-class Protestants. It was acknowledged by the Cambridge Platonists Ralph Cudworth and Henry More, and by later thinkers such as Isaac Newton and Bishop William Warburton. English deists[26] and *philosophes* such as Voltaire also sometimes identified and accepted the need for a benign priestcraft, but both naturally condemned the corruption of religion by crafty priests for their own ends.

Protestants such as the Anglican Arthur Young (in 1734) certainly saw religion as 'the great Prop which upholds the Safety, Peace and Welfare of the publick.... 'Tis the Fear of God, not any worldly Consideration, which is sufficient to produce in us, at all Times ... Obedience to our Governours'.[27] The prospect of a benign state priestcraft was, however, unlikely to obtain unqualified approval by most plebeian lay Protestants. After all, benign priestcraft presupposed the wielding of religious knowledge by the rich and powerful for the general benefit of state and society. This was not a reassuring prospect for many relatively poor Dissenters, for whom class distinction and religious conflict had often chimed together since the Reformation in the form of the Anglican episcopate. As the Scot Brown opined, in the medieval period prelates had been enriched by the secular powers in order to enforce the 'tame subjection' of peoples.[28] Nevertheless, religion was still the 'great basis of civil happiness', even though '[b]efore the happy Reformation, the Popish clergy had reduced civil rulers into mere tools for executing their pleasure in religious matters'. He did not want to deny that to magistrates themselves, independently, 'belong a distinguished power in the *reformation* and *preservation* of religion'; but this prerogative had been 'too greedily embraced' by most protestant princes.[29]

Despite such reservations and fears, the overriding theme of Protestant historians remained the defence of kings against papal aggression. Thus, by way of condemnation, Thomas Gisborne told his readers the papal bulls *Ausculta fili* (1301) and *Unam sanctam* (1302) of Boniface VIII declared 'the successor of St Peter ruled the earth, by Divine right, with the temporal sword, no less than the church with the spiritual' and anyone who questioned this would be excluded from salvation.[30]

In the preface to a compilation of tracts edited by Thomas Bray, which (as the title notes) was *Design'd as Supplemental to the Book of Martyrs* (of Foxe), there is an unremittingly damning assessment of medieval royal comportment. Yet Bray was an Anglican and presumably, therefore, an Erastian. It is probably no coincidence Bray was writing the preface to his compilation in the last years of Queen Anne's reign (1702–14), when there was some fear for the Protestant succession. This circumstance seems to have prompted him to emphasize the nature of Catholic tyranny, the need for strong royal leadership, and the consequences of a lack of royal resolve. In the first volume of his compilation, entitled *Papal Usurpation and Tyranny ... with reference chiefly to Princes and States* (1712), he describes how medieval princes had been so obsequious towards the popes they had become 'beasts of burthen'. The first proof of the obsequiousness of the princes was their presence on the crusades, 'even tho' they knew these very Popes themselves would, in their Absence, be pilfering their Dominions from them'. Indeed, the 'Antichristian Tyranny and Usurpation' over the secular powers began with bringing the princes into formal vassalage to the Roman See. This was done because '[a]s well knowing, that these [princes] being brought to an Absolute Obedience, they would be affectual instruments of reducing others into the like submission to it'.[31]

At times even more so than Anglicans, Dissenters propounded an all-embracing, bitterly cynical tirade against papal trespass upon the secular state, although the analytical contours of their accounts do not substantially differ from those of Anglicans. 'Several Gentlemen' note that the introduction of auricular confession was artful: it was, besides other things, a 'politick picklock' designed to 'open the breasts of princes'. So great was the threat of the Church to the realm, King Richard II (1377–99) instituted a statute of Mortmain to halt the growth of ecclesiastical property. The monks and friars 'would have grasped all the land in England into their clutches, if timely provision had not been made against it'. Yet, despite the threat posed by the Church, the declining Roman Empire (the Carolingian emperors onwards) was glad to enter into a 'mutual league' with popery for its survival.[32] For John Angell, the situation had been even worse. In his considered opinion, from as early as the mid-fifth century, 'the bishop was almost entirely lost in the prince', and popes went on to contend with the greatest monarchs for temporal dominion. Popes such as Gregory VII, wanting to be 'sovereign monarch of the universe', did not refrain from fomenting wars to further or defend their power – a common Protestant indictment. On the subject of English monks and friars, Angell expresses an anti-monasticism very common in early modern Protestant and some anti-curial Catholic thought. It was then believed that for countless men and women to live idly in monasteries and convents was a serious drain on production and economic advance. The lack of such monastic dead-weight was often advanced as the reason for the relative

economic success of Britain and the Dutch Republic. Not surprisingly, therefore, Angell notes that 'both Church and commonwealth
groaned under the heavy burden of the abbey drones'. These drones
had become 'lords of very little less than one half of the temporalities
of the kingdom', and aimed at betraying the wealth and sovereignty
of the kingdom 'to the usurpation of a detestable foreign power'
(Rome).[33]

Joseph Priestley also damns the hierocratic pretensions of the
popes, illustrating, like Angell, that ecclesiastic encroachment on the
state started in the fifth century under Pope Gelasius (492–6). On
wealth and temporal power Priestley notes '[l]ike other politic
princes, the popes gained these advantages chiefly in consequence of
divisions in the families of the temporal powers'. By disposing of the
right to crown the Holy Roman Emperor, writes Priestley, the popes
were effectively able to lay claim to the empire itself. Like other
Protestants, Priestley believes the 'crusades contributed very much to
complete the power of the popes as temporal princes'. But the
'primary cause of the temporal power of the clergy was the wealth
which they acquired by the liberality of the laity'. Pious donations
were so copious that 'the utter extinction of all merely civil property'
was threatened. Several kings opposed this trend, but 'the superstition of the common people, and the situation of their affairs, made it
necessary for princes to give way'. Thus, the 'ground of ... [papal]
claims as the Vicars of Christ was never called in question', not least
because the civil and ecclesiastical power contributed 'in their turns
to advance each other'.[34]

Similarly, James Bicheno laments that 'tyranny and corruption,
idolatry and superstition universally prevailed, and all the kingdoms
of Europe ... gave their power to the beast'. The Church had became
a 'deformed and ravenous monster'. Even '[o]ur Henry the VIII, ...
was governed by no principle of religion; it was in resentment that he
threw off the supremacy of the pope, and assumed it himself'.[35] John
Wesley too tells readers that emperors and princes, prompted by
superstitious motives, enfeoffed the higher clergy; but they 'hoped
also to check the seditious spirits of their vassals by the influence of
the bishops'. Popes were also solicited for support by princes such as
Charles the Bald (823–77), who had need of the political power of the
papacy in times of war. Thus 'the power of the pontiffs, in civil affairs,
arose in a short time to an enormous height through the favour of the
princes'. The 'tyrannic ambition' of Pope Gregory VII aimed to
submit the universal Church, kings and emperors to 'the arbitrary

power of the pontiff alone ... and render their dominions tributary to the see of Rome'.[36]

Prompted by his desire to provide more focus on the supposed line of true, proto-Protestant piety uncontaminated by Romish corruptions, Joseph Milner claims too much has been written on Church and state. His selective parsimony, however, does not prevent him from depicting how, via territorial Donations the popes became temporal princes in the eighth century. By the twelfth century 'the emperors of Germany trembled under the rod' of papal power. For Milner too 'secular and ecclesiastical ambition [had] united to oppress the Churches of Christ'. He cites the example of the bloody thirteenth-century crusade against the Albigenses of France, in which the economic motives of the French crown and the needs of popes to destroy opponents of Rome were paramount.[37]

Scottish writers also participated in the avowal of a medieval priest-craft that gleefully trampled on the rights of princes and yet was, to a degree, in unholy alliance with them. For Nisbet, Roman emperors had 'converted the wealth and magnificence of the pagan priesthood and idolatry into ... a new channel' (the Church). Artfully, the popes had also propagated the idea that a division of power between the papacy and the emperor would promise greater security for the people. Ostensibly, this division was in order 'to retrench and moderate the power of the emperor, and prove a check to any tyrannical projects from that quarter'.

The fifth century saw ambitious prelates who were already 'exalted to a kind of princely power'. So 'elated with their vast power, opulence, and splendor, [they] began now to affect a kind of independent jurisdiction, and each to assume a lordly supremacy'. Many prelates had been created dukes and counts, something Gothic kings did from 'superstition and policy'. It was a ploy intended by them 'as a check upon the rising power of their own nobles', as well as on account of the 'commanding influence among the people' of such clerical nobility. By the ninth century, the popes, 'with a lordly air ... disposed of imperial thrones'; and from the thirteenth century, the mendicant friars 'governed Church and state with a commanding sway'.[38] Similarly, for the Scottish Secession Church member Brown, the popes 'greedily grasped at a supreme power of the civil kind', including temporal dominion. Such 'pontifical arrogance ... occasioned innumerable wars, rebellions and massacres'. Fiefs were awarded to prelates because 'their commands and spiritual thunders would infallibly keep the bulk of the laity in a tame subjection'.[39]

We should pause to note here that Nisbet's chronology of Roman priestcraft practised upon the realms and rights of kings, like that of Angell and Priestley, commenced in the fifth century. These claims constitute examples of the stretching of Luther's original chronology, which emphasized the assumption of papal supremacy in the early seventh century by Boniface III as the main point of departure on to the path of antichristianity. Since the Reformation, Protestant–Catholic polemical exigency had driven many Protestants, including some Anglicans, to tunnel farther back into Church history to more forcefully illustrate the deepseated historical malaise of the Roman Church. For Puritans and post Civil War Dissenters, proving the chronological extent and iniquitous depths of papal tyranny had become a matter of illustrating their own religious credentials against the popery of the Anglican Church. Anglican High Churchmen claimed legitimate descent for Anglicanism from the medieval Church: the bleaker the Puritan/Dissenter picture of Church history, the more potentially devastating was their comparison of Anglicanism with Catholicism.

High Churchmen faced a teasing quandary. If they were not seen to excoriate the history of popery, they remained more exposed to the charge of having sympathy with the Beast and being prepared to entertain the 'harlottes' of Rome. Yet if they did meaningfully contribute to dismantling the historical sacrality of Rome, they were only fashioning a rod for their own backs to be wielded in turn by their numerous and embittered critics. How High Churchmen negotiated these perilous straits depended on time, context and religious and personal inclination. We know that Field, in his *Of the Church*, pointed out that even in the primitive Church there were abuses and superstitions, albeit not yet decisively so. Thus, even in the thought of early seventeenth-century High Churchmen, it can be said, lay the grounds for the more radical assessment of Church history propagated by late seventeenth-century Dissenters.

Protestants who wished to tunnel deeper and farther into Roman corruption could also legitimately claim such tunnelling was not entirely without precedent. Luther himself had understood that papal tyranny in the form of the Antichrist had 'risen up and grown out of the Roman Empire'.[40] For Protestants, especially of the Presbyterian sort, the developmental chronology of Catholic priestcraft was therefore open to interpretation, as long as the purity of the simple apostolic Church was retained as the undefiled model of the Christian ministry. So, in his *Acta romanorum pontificum* (1558), Bishop John

Bale could note Pope Silvester I (314–35), although not the most wicked or corrupt, was the first pope to embark upon the antichristian road; and his pontificate of course encompassed the last years of the reign of Emperor Constantine.

The fourth century as the point of inception or consolidation of Roman priestcraft was an attractive chronology for Dissenters. Most Dissenters certainly felt no need to fight shy of the possible pejorative parallel of the Anglican Church–state reality with that of Emperor Constantine's. Predictably, as we shall see, the many decades of persecution and discrimination meted out by the Anglican state and Church against Puritans and Dissenters certainly prompted such parallels. Some dissenting Protestant thinkers, however, did not scruple to frankly indict the pre-Constantine primitive Church. In the anonymous *The Original of Popish Idolatrie*s (1624), the Puritan-minded author explained that, for four hundred years the bishops of Rome could not convert the Romans: 'For the Bishops of *Rome* were too busie in restoring the Iewish and heathen Ceremonies.'[41] It is not surprising this was an anonymous work, for its implicit comparative message was political and historical dynamite: the popery of Anglicanism had its root in a Church hierarchy corrupt since the demise of the apostles.

EDWARD GIBBON'S REITERATION OF PROTESTANT HISTORIOGRAPHY AND THE LIMITS OF ANTI-CATHOLICISM

Integral to enlightened historical thinking was a desire to demon-strate the historical fraud of all priests and their role in retarding the rational development of European society. Nevertheless, throughout the eighteenth century, Protestant and dissident Catholic writers continued energetically to proclaim most of Christian history little more than the history of priestcraft. An alarming tactical error? Perhaps, but the long history of religious disputes most frequently demonstrates a tendency of divided parties towards the absolute, in which there exists little or no middle ground in a dogged struggle to eclipse a competitor. Today's Christian ecumenicalism is indeed a very modern innovation.

There is no doubt that warring Christians helped to arm their Enlightened detractors. In Cosimo Amidei's *La Chiesa e la Repubblica dentro i loro limiti*, he relies on Giannone and Muratori when he describes how popes used fanaticism and superstition to induce princes to donate to them, even ceding their states to Rome in order to receive them back as subject vassals of the popes. For many anti-curial Catholics and all enlightened thinkers, Rome represented one of the major obstacles to breaking the obscurantist and essentially medieval hold of religion upon civil life.

In Britain, the Protestant defence of princely prerogative against historic Catholic design was in essence the same as that of the deists and later writers unsympathetic to Christianity, such as Edward Gibbon. The latter, in his account of the medieval Church, had borrowed very heavily from Protestant historiography. It is, therefore, not possible to claim that the contribution of Christianity to Gibbon's thought was 'modest and subterranean'.[42] The analysis of the medieval Church in Gibbon's *Decline and Fall* could be ascribed to any one of a number of Protestant (or indeed anti-curial Catholic) writers, as is evident in his comments on the Carolingian territorial donations and Pope Stephen II (752–7):

> Perhaps the humility of a Christian priest should have rejected an earthly kingdom ... [and] I will not absolve the pope from the reproach of treachery and falsehood ... The world beheld for the first time a Christian bishop invested with the prerogatives of a temporal prince.

On the subject of the forgery of the Pseudo-Isidorean Decretals and the Donation of Constantine – 'the two magic pillars of the spiritual and temporal monarchy of the popes' – Gibbon goes on to relate that some 'apostolical scribe' (curial) was responsible. He also adds that

> Fraud is the resource of weakness and cunning; and the strong, yet ignorant, barbarian was often entangled in the net of sacerdotal policy. The Vatican and the Lateran were an arsenal and manufacture which ... have produced or concealed a various collection of false or genuine, of corrupt or suspicious acts, as they tended to promote the interest of the Roman Church.... So deep was the ignorance and credulity of the times that the most absurd of fables was received with equal reverence in Greece and in France.[43]

Gibbon's description of Pope Gregory VII might also have come from any Protestant pen decades or even centuries before he wrote. He reveals the 'zeal and ambition of the haughty priest' Pope Gregory VII, that 'tyrant of the Church', whose ambition led to war in the Empire.[44] It cannot be denied that Gibbon certainly caused some furore with his *Decline and Fall*. A furore not on account of his portrayal of the medieval Church, however, but rather for his famous fifteenth and sixteenth chapters, which describe the rise of Christianity. In the 1770s to 1780s, thirty years after the decline of the English deists, the appearance of Gibbon's work might have caused heated indignation and a shower of pithy replies. But it could not produce the outrage amongst Anglicans as did deist and Dissenter historiography in the last decade of the seventeenth and the first decades of the eighteenth century.

In 1710–11, Convocation had signalled the dangerous link between an anti-Catholic historiography that condemned the greater part of Christian Church history, and the charges of priestcraft laid at the altar of the contemporary Church. Convocation was not alone in its views, for some Tories (usually High Churchmen) also felt that something should be done to 'restrain' the press and hinder the printing of seditious, schismatical, heretical, or anti-monarchical pamphlets.[45] New blasphemy laws had been introduced in 1697, with the consequence radical Dissenters and deist writers ran a greater risk of imprisonment. Nonetheless, such restraint was hardly as effective as many Anglicans would have wished. The deep divisions within Protestantism were hardly amenable to restraint, especially where pious outrage and class antagonism went in tandem, as they did in the thought of many Dissenters.

The Reformation had unleashed an irreversible historical revolution. The anti-Catholic genie had been let out of the bottle, but it proved to be a genie with chimera-like qualities. Anti-Catholic religious polemic had early developed in a political direction, identifying despotism with Catholicism. In the hands of those critical of the perceived tyranny of the Anglican confessional state and the failings of its Church, it was a formidable and versatile weapon, combining theological critique, historical evidence and concepts of just rule. Only at the end of the eighteenth century were there indications that some writers felt the need for a Protestant historiography that did not have anti-Catholicism as its primary theme and historical dynamic. Even though his own historiography represented little change, Joseph Milner condemned those 'who seem to think an indiscriminate aversion to the Church of Rome to be one of the principle excellencies of a Protestant historian'. Furthermore, 'the integrity of history may easily have suffered in particular instances through this aversion'.[46] Milner, and to some extent Joseph Priestley, were not simply proposing a more spiritual historiography. They were also signalling that

Protestant anti-Catholic historiography had reached its full polemical potential, and there was now need for a reassessment. In practice, however, that reassessment was left to another century.

5 Martyrs, Fanaticism and Empire Defended

The need for the Curia to defend the medieval *status quo* required orthodox polemicists to parry several of the Protestant polemical thrusts, including the development of Protestant martyrologies. Orthodox propagandists such as Rezka developed a new Catholic martyrology, constructed from the names of those who had suffered at the hands of the Protestant heretics. Rezka included a martyrology in his *De Atheismus et phalarismus evangelicorum* (1596), the title of which refers to the legendary cruelty of Phalaris, a Sicilian tyrant, intended as a byword for Protestant cruelty. Even in the eighteenth century, Vincenzo Gotti could include a martyrology in his *Veritas religionis Christianae* (1735–40).[1] But if the intention of Rezka and others had been to rival the work of the influential Protestant martyrologist John Foxe, they were to be disappointed. The innovation of a specifically Protestant martyrology fulfilled the religious needs of Protestants in a manner which new additions to the already long list of Catholic martyrs could not. Zealous Protestant martyrologists were also equipped with the weighty historical evidence and intermeshing contemporary reality of the supposed apostasy of Rome, something which – in propaganda terms – was very difficult for procurial propagandists to equal.

For the Curia, from the early Reformation, Calvin and Luther were of course the epitome of heretics: antichristian impostors leading the faithful into benighted error. It was important, therefore, to locate a place for them in the customary Catholic pantheon of heresies, and so deny reformers even the dubious distinction of heretical innovation. The epithet most usually chosen was Manichaeist, from the third-century heresy of Manes. As Bishop Francesco Panigarola expounded to the Duke of Savoy in 1584, the heretical protagonists of the Reformation were wolves in lambs clothes, serpents, robbers and tricksters who had at heart only ambition.[2] Similarly, Andrea Cardoini, in his *Relatione di Ginevra* (1619), depicted Calvin as the model of the universal heretic. Cardoini, Calvinist turned Catholic, chose to describe Geneva because it was of course the home and base from which Calvin developed and disseminated his theology. For

Cardoini, Calvin was ambitious, seditious and sexually profligate, and had withdrawn from obedience to the Church only in order to escape punishment for his own, mostly sexual, crimes. Calvin, he argued, soon realized the possibility of the political use of Lutheran ideas, and went on to develop and exploit them in his own manner, using them as a front for his political ambition.

Many other writers, drawing parallels with the supposed licentious nature of Islam (a feature of the medieval Christian canon on Islam), also stressed the unleashed, obscene lust of Protestant heretics, now lacking the most necessary moral guidance and restraint of the Church. For many Catholics, this was a degeneration confirmed by the marriage of Protestant priests. The claim that the heretic Luther was in favour of polygamy was common in the Counter-Reformation, as for example in Bozio's *De signis ecclesiae* (1591). In a period when there existed no acceptable moral code outside of the Church, this was a credible line of attack to very many ordinary orthodox Catholics who did not have first-hand experience of Protestantism. Such accusations were not, therefore – even from the point of view of many of the Catholic propagandists themselves – mere base insults in a propaganda war. Modern historians who dismiss all such polemic as mere hyperbole will not understand why these accusations persisted for so long and engaged the pens of some of the finest Catholic thinkers. The fact that Protestant heretics were outside of traditional Christendom, and thus not only bereft of moral guidance but also deprived of the benefits of Divine Grace and therefore prey to the will of the devil, became the theological foundation stone for Catholic anti-Protestant thought.

A century after Bozio's *De signis ecclesiae*, Paolo Segneri wrote his *L'Incredulo senza scusa*, which was but one of the numerous works that had continued the same genre of attack. As a pejorative comparison with the Protestant reformers, Segneri brought to his aid the early Christian sect of the Adamites, which aimed to return to primitive innocence by the practice of nudity. For another negative comparison Segneri then turned to the sixteenth-century Anabaptists (passing over the fact Luther and Calvin also condemned Anabaptists). He describes how the 'plurality of wives was amongst the first articles of their reform'. Consequently, as a law, 'every woman was obliged to subject herself to the lascivity of every man, and every man to satiate the libido of every woman'.[3] This genre of attack continued well in to the eighteenth century, as for example in the *Veritas religionis christianae* (1735–40) of Vincenzo Gotti. Gotti slurred the sexual morality of Luther, informing readers that Luther's wife had been an enticer, and already pregnant when she met him. He extended this attack by linking religious to sexual idolatry, relating how Luther and Calvin inspired idolatrous veneration of their own images, and how Protestant women had images of Calvin in their private chambers.[4]

The orthodox depiction of the fight against heresy was also linked to the intractable issues of religious and temporal jurisdiction. After all, the jurisdiction of Rome in temporals and spirituals was based on the divine legacy of the chief apostle of Christ, St Peter. Popes were thus in receipt of divine guidance which, in practice, conferred an infallibility in religious matters: heretics had to be mistaken and the papacy correct. Curialist historiography was therefore necessarily candid as regards the uncompromising attitude to be taken towards heresy. This was a stance exemplified by staunch defences of the Inquisition and its methods as, for example, found in Tommaso Vincenzo Pani's *Della Punizione degli eretici* (1789).[5] Pani defended corporal punishment for certain categories of heterodoxy, and argued that even the suspicion of heresy could be cause for punishment.

The Roman Inquisition had been founded in 1542 to combat the Protestant threat in Italy, and was more independent from the epis-copacy than the medieval inquisition. When the Protestant threat in the Italian peninsula had subsided (*c.* 1600), it was not abolished. As Giannone and others had learnt to their cost, the Inquisition remained a potent threat to religious dissent in eighteenth-century Italy, although conditions for its use were less propitious as the century progressed. The philosophical and doctrinal gap between the Curia and reformers on the issue of crime and punishment was at its widest after the 1760s. At the same time as Bishop Becchetti, Pani and others continued to advocate a medieval approach to the problem of heresy, Marquis Cesare Beccaria was writing his famous and widely influential *Dei Delitti e delle pene* (1764). Beccaria had been spurred to the pen by a shocked awareness of the inhumanity and arbitrary nature of criminal procedure and punishment in Italy and Europe as a whole.

On a subject with much potential for those wishing to illustrate the antichristian nature of the Catholic Church, some pro-curial propa-gandists were not always as diplomatic as Rome might have liked. One anonymous pro-curialist positively gloried in the 'cutting to pieces' of very large numbers of heretics in France – the Albigenses, a twelfth- and thirteenth-century offshoot of the Cathari, against which a crusade was called.[6] Bishop Becchetti also indulged in unlikely tales and less than palliative remarks, writing that various medieval pogroms and persecutions of Jews had been just punishments from God. In the context of the 1492 expulsion of the Jews from Spain, he narrates how the Jews crucified a boy and ripped his heart out in order to procure the diabolic death of some inquisitors. Of various heretical movements, such as the Waldenses, Patarini and Humiliati, Becchetti writes they 'were only so many branches of Manichaeism'.[7] The catch-all attribution of Manichaeism was common not only in pro-curial thought but also in some anti-curialist writings, such as those of Muratori and Giannone. On this point Muratori and Giannone were in the most august of company, for Edward Gibbon made substantially the same identification.

The depiction of the struggle against medieval heresy did not form a major component of Muratori's critique of the Church. This was partly because of his unwillingness to contradict Rome, observing a tactful silence on events that caused outrage in other critics of Rome. He also felt a horror of fanaticism almost as intense as some contemporary Protestants. He distinguished between innocent fanaticism, and the sort which can result in superstition, error, heresy and sedition. In his *Dissertazione* he declared the Inquisition was instituted with 'praiseworthy zeal', even if he did not agree with its excesses or most improper use as a defence of papal worldly interests. He was outraged that, in the fourteenth century, the Ghibelline princes (of whom his master, the Duke of Modena, was a geographical and political heir) were, for political reasons, turned into heretics through the declaration of crusades against them.[8]

Many seventeenth-century anti-curialists, such as Ferrante Pallavicino, were also outraged at the political use of the heresy charge. For Pallavicino, the historic use of the heresy charge by the Curia had been less a fight against the enemies of Christendom and more a major tactic in the defence of papal supremacy, power and worldly interests.[9] For Arconati, the tyrannical cruelty of the Inquisition 'had been generated in the most fecund womb of papal abuses', intended for action against anyone preaching the purity of the Holy Gospels. Once born, the Inquisition was found to be such a monstrous deformity that, in order not to terrify Christians, it had to pass its infancy concealed under the mantle of St Dominic (the Inquisition was usually staffed by Dominicans). The slaughter of the Albigensian Crusade provided the opportunity 'to condition the youngster to bath in the blood of innocent hearts'.[10] The historic misuse of the heresy accusation was, therefore, judged to be just one symptom amongst others verifying the fact of curial despotism, the same opinion expressed by anti-curialists of the eighteenth century.

For Giannone, the horribly bloody accounts of the historical struggle against heresy were yet more proof of the medieval barbarity of the Church. But it was also evidence of a systematic priestcraft. The heresy charge had been and still was, he thought, used by the Church to persecute political opponents and perpetuate a corrupt doctrine developed for its own political and economic ends. In sum, the Inquisition had been founded 'in order to better establish the monarchy of the popes'. This was a view – given his own tragic end – more prophetic than Giannone realized. In his opinion (and one correctly reflecting historical development), heresy had been rare from 800 to 1100. From then (as in Protestant accounts), in a religious reaction to the ostentation, scandals and lax religious life of ecclesiastics, numerous heretical sects flourished. They attacked the corrupt customs, despotism, power and wealth of the Church. Despite his historical sympathy for reaction to papal priestcraft, Giannone did not feel able to condone all heretical groups. Like Protestants, he thought some sects were 'full of superstition and error', although he added that brutal papal persecution had only served to confirm them in their errors.[11]

For Archbishop Capecelatro, heresy itself had been one of the factors in the growth of clerical influence over temporal dominion. The heresies of the 'early times' gave rise to disagreements between theologians, and 'the emperors and Christian princes took the highest interest in the disputes'. The result was that 'royal palaces were inundated by monks and prelates', which led to their undue influence over the princes.[12] In the north of the peninsula, Delle Piane also decried the barbarity and injustice of the Inquisition, and the fact that such 'unheard of barbarities, rather than exterminate heresy, had only served to maintain it'.[13] Rivarola too condemned the barbarism of heretic hunts, recalling how the label of heresy had been but a method to advance the interests of the papacy. This was an assessment not propounded only by a handful of reformers, it had wide currency. Archbishop Scipione de'Ricci, in his circular to his clergy on the Jansenist-inspired forthcoming Synod of Pistoia in Tuscany (1786), noted that the papacy had for centuries defended their superstition and ignorance by denouncing as heretical any attempt to revive the ancient discipline of the Church.[14]

In Luther's revision of the history of the Church, the Church of Rome was itself a medieval heresy: 'an obdurate errantry in respect to

Scripture'.[15] Popes and prelates were themselves heresiarchs who had consciously promoted and defended the Catholic heresy as a means to protect and further their own power and wealth. One of the most effective means used to protect the empire of the Church was the misuse of the heresy charge, by means of which the just opponents of the Church were transformed into enemies of Jesus Christ. True Christians who had suffered the final penalty at the hands of those heresiarchs on account of their opposition to the corruption of the Church formed the basis for Protestant martyrologies. One such was the *Catalogus Testium Veritatis* (1556) compiled by Matthias Flacius Illyricus. More importantly for this discussion, another was the very influential *Actes and Monuments* of John Foxe: *Actes and Monuments of these Latter and Perilous Days Touching Matters of the Church, wherein are Comprehended and Described the Great Persecutions & Horrible Troubles, that have bene Wrought and Practised by the Romishe Prelates*. For the readers of such works, precisely as intended by the authors, their contents were proof of the priestcraft behind the Catholic heresy charge.

As early as the 1540s, however, the unencumbered dichotomy of Protestant martyrdom and antichristian Roman despotism was beginning to dissolve. For Protestants such as William Turner, the English Reformation (formalized by the Act of Supremacy 1534) was incomplete. In accordance with the wishes of Henry VIII, that Catholic institution the episcopate remained; even though biblical authority for such hierarchical division in the preaching ministry did not exist. So, for some Protestant zealots popery – that is heresy – was still abroad in England. It was in alliance with the state, the state that brought heads to blocks and placed ropes around the necks of those Protestants and Catholics who criticized or opposed the Henrician settlement.

A bitter anti-episcopalianism, one of the pivotal elements that formed the nexus of the Puritan–Anglican split, formed the subject matter of William Turner's metaphorical *The Huntyng and Fyndyng out of the Romyshe Foxe, which more then seuen yeares hath bene hyd among the bisshoppes of Englonde, after that the Kynges Hygnes had commanded hym to be dryuen owt of hys Realme* (1543). Turner told his readers the problem had been that the hounds (bishops) the king had set upon the fox (popery) were in fact of the same lineage as the fox and so, according to natural law, would not harm the fox. In fact, the hounds protected the fox and pursued other hounds (Protestants), not of their own kind, to death. The logic of the collusion of the fox (popery) and hounds (bishops) and thus the failure to extirpate popery was that the bishops were of course guilty of heresy, but also – as Turner stated – of treason: 'If ye be no traytours proue in youre answere that ye wil sende me, that ye hold no doctryne of the pope contrarye to the worde of god'.[16]

For Foxe, Turner and other English Protestants, sheltering on the continent from the heresy trials and subsequent burning of leading Protestants brought about by Catholic Queen Mary (1553–8), the political use of the heresy charge and the inhumanity of Catholic priestcraft palpably continued in England. Under Protestant Queen Elizabeth the persecution of Protestants mostly abated, although she remained implacably opposed to Puritanism. The English monarch continued, however, to be the head of the Anglican Church and, for Puritans, its doctrine was still visibly tied to the imperatives of the English state. Indeed, determined and overt dissent from the Anglican Church could still be considered treasonous. The perception of the growing numbers of disaffected Puritans that the Anglican Church was continuing Catholic-style tyrannical policies against its spiritual enemies is reflected, for example, in Job Throckmorton's *A Dialogue. Wherein is Plainly Laide open, the Tyrannicall Dealing of L. Bishopps Against God's Children* (1589). For Throckmorton, Anglican bishops more readily tolerated papists than Puritans and – in the Protestant tradition of attacking the perceived moral outrages of popery – he revealed that the bishop of St Davids in Wales had two wives.[17]

In the seventeenth century, repression and discrimination against non-conforming Protestants continued and worsened as the relatively tolerant religious regime of James I (1603–25) gave way to the more intolerant policies of Charles I. After the Restoration (1660), religious discrimination and persecution continued and various punitive acts were passed. These included the Corporation Act (1661), the Act of Uniformity (1662), the Conventicle Act (1664), and the Five Mile Act (1665). It is true the Toleration Act of 1689 afforded some limited toleration of Dissenting worship, but the Anglican Church remained dominant as the Church of the state. Thus Dissenters still faced religious, political and economic disadvantages. Catholics too suffered, for even most Dissenters agreed Catholicism should not be tolerated, and twenty-four Catholics were hung, drawn and quartered in the period 1678–1681. For Dissenters, one means of replying to persecution was to compare state-Church persecution in England with that of Roman Catholic priest-kings and of ancient

Rome. One very popular tract exploiting this type of comparison was Thomas Delaune's *A plea for the Non-Conformists, giving the true state of the dissenters case. And how far the conformists separation from the Church of Rome ... justifies the non-conformists separation from them. ... To which is added, a parallel Scheme of the Pagan, Papal and Christian Rites and Ceremonies* (1684). In the early eighteenth century, the equation of Anglicanism with religious tyranny aimed at protecting the power and wealth of the clergy was verified in the minds of Dissenters by the hard-line pronouncements of High Churchmen such as Henry Sacheverell. In 1709, in a sermon simultaneously drawing support from many Anglicans and condemnation from Dissenters, Sacheverell argued 'whoever, presumes to innovate, alter, or misrepresent any point in the articles of faith or our Church ought to be arraigned as a traitor to our state'.[18]

The Dissenter identification of religious persecution with the cunning of papal priestcraft continued to be a common theme later in the eighteenth century, as portrayed, for instance, in the anonymous *The Book of Martyrs, or The History of Paganism and Popery* (1764), a work consciously modelled on Foxe's martyrology. Anti-Catholicism was, therefore, as potent a force as ever in England, as testified by the bloody toll of the anti-Catholic Gordon Riots of 1780 which left 285 dead. Neither were the Gordon riots an aberration of an otherwise tolerant religious outlook, for religious division remained a potent source of prejudice. There were anti-Jewish riots in 1753 and Church and King riots against Dissenters (in which Joseph Priestley was one target) in 1791.

So it was, then, that John Brown could write and publish a pamphlet in 1780 entitled *The Absurdity and Perfidy of all Authoritative Toleration of Gross Heresy, Blasphemy, Idolatry, Popery, in Britain*. As a pious Protestant, however, Brown naturally condemned the horrendous persecution of certain medieval heretical sects, especially those considered to be the spiritual forebears of Protestants, such as the Albigenses and especially the Waldenses. For Reformation propagandists, the Waldensians – isolated from papal corruption in their Piedmont valleys – were considered to have retained a pure Christianity free from Roman corruptions. Protestants were thus able to answer the simple yet disarmingly effective Catholic jibe: where was your Church before Luther? The need to render as firm a reply as possible ensured that eighteenth-century Protestants continued to manufacture and propagate the most unlikely and unsupported claims for the apostolic origins and therefore impeccable credentials of the twelfth-century Waldenses.

Jeremy Collier, like anti-curial Catholics and other Protestants, argued that executing heretics was not consistent with the sentiments of the ancient Church Fathers. On the contrary, the doctrine of the Fathers was that disbelief in religion was no ground for the forfeiture of life. Hence Collier declared: '[t]his roasting Men to Orthodoxy, and enlightening them with Fire and Faggot, was a discipline not understood in these early Ages.' Similarly, at the end of the century, Milner opined that the 'burning of heretics had only 'increased the compassion of the people for the sufferers'. Such persecution had 'roused a spirit of inquiry and opposition to the existing hierarchy, which, at length ... proved fatal both to papal corruptions of sound doctrine, and also to papal usurpation of dominion'.[19] It was a Protestant commonplace that 'under the pretence of heresy' the popes continued to 'suppress orthodox truths, and establish heresy in the Church by law'.[20] Under cover of the same pretence, popes had preached crusades 'against such princes as incurred their displeasure'.[21]

The Inquisition itself was naturally a prime Protestant target, and in 1699 one writer revealed that even in the seventeenth century the 'Inquisitors have at several times made use of all the Cruelties that Hell itself could invent' against the Waldenses.[22] A century later Thomas Gisborne informed his readers that 'in every quarter the inquisitors chased their victims with fury alike a stranger to mercy and to weariness'.[23] This was no surprise to most Protestants, for it was commonly thought that the Inquisition was founded as 'a project of the court of Rome to establish their usurped supremacy'.[24] Brown thought it important to warn his readers – and he was not alone in this kind of vicious rhetoric – that the inquisitors have 'sixty, seventy or more' women in common who are 'probably murdered' along with their children when their houses are full. The surrounding clergy also make use of the threat of the inquisition to extort sexual favours, forcing women to submit to 'their unbridled lust'.[25]

In most Protestant thought, the phenomenal growth of heretical sects in the thirteenth century was primarily considered by Rome to have been a threat to its worldly empire rather than to fundamental Christian principles. These heretical sects, declaimed George Gregory, railed 'against the power, the opulence, and the vices of the popes and the clergy'. Such complaints 'were extremely agreeable to many princes and civil magistrates, who groaned under the usurpations of the sacred order'. The fear of unity between aristocracy and heresy, of losing Church empire, was then the underlying rationale for the merciless persecution of heresy by the papacy. The quasi-genocidal Albigensian 'crusade', stated John Wesley, 'was highly profitable both to the kings of France and to the Roman pontiffs' in terms of land acquisition by the Crown and 'peace offerings' to the Roman See. For Priestley, such persecution had to an extent succeeded in its aim, for after the trauma of the Albigensian Crusade, 'the great dread of heresy ... prevented discussions of the greatest consequence within the precincts of the Catholic Church'.[26]

Humanitarian outrage aside, like anti-curial Catholics, eighteenth-century Protestants did not unconditionally support all medieval heresies on the principle that an enemy of the papacy was therefore an ally. Some High Churchmen wished to identify at least a strain of right religion amidst the superstitious corruption and vice of the medieval Church. But this strain was not to be found in most heretical sects, which were duly condemned as the aberrations of religious fanatics. Amongst dissenting Protestants, medieval sects that did not possess the semblance of Protestant forebears were summarily dismissed in a similar manner. All Protestants, therefore, could agree to one extent or another, that one lamentable product of the corruption and superstition of the Church was a sizeable crop of fanatics seized by 'enthusiasm'. Inevitably, such fanatics were often even more heretical than the Catholicism that had spawned them.

Enthusiasm, as opposed to the rational and informed theology of Protestants, was one of the purported products of the superstitious ignorance of the medieval Church. John Calvin, when discussing fanaticism in his *Institutes of the Christian Religion* (1536), had already noted Christians who abandon Scripture 'must be considered as not so much misled by error as actuated by frenzy'.[27] The antithesis and antidote to frenzy or enthusiasm is of course rational reflection, the use of human reason. In this sense the role of the practical demands and conclusions of religious polemic has been underestimated as a factor in the rehabilitation of reason in Protestant thought. It is sufficient cause to begin to reconsider the originality of some of the rationalist thinking of such seventeenth-century figures as Herbert of Cherbury (whose work will be touched upon in the following chapter).

In the eighteenth-century then, when the editors of the *History of Popery* apply adjectives such as 'rational and historical, plain and scriptural' to their historical account, the claims should be understood more as the traditional excoriation of enthusiasm and superstition, than as an innovative proclamation of credibility against the rationalist polemic of deists and sceptics. The heterogeneity of English Protestantism, however, ensured disagreement on the choice of medieval targets for vilification as enthusiasts. Most Protestants praised the anti-Rome Church reformer John Wycliffe (*c.* 1329–84) and his followers the Lollards, while some episcopalians condemned them because they had been too anti-episcopal in outlook. Those who condemned them still expressed the general Protestant attitude to medieval sects of which they did not approve. Collier, for instance, pointed out that, although the Lollards may have been correct as regards some of the errors of the Roman Church, '[t]o take them at their best, they seem to have had more Heat than Light, and to have been govern'd by a Spirit of Enthusiasme'.[28]

Wesley, even though he thought medieval heretics and their tenets had been unfairly represented, also expressed the opinion that would-be Church reformers had not been equal to their task. They failed because they were 'involved in the general ignorance of the times' and, as a consequence, they fell into the errors of 'enthusiasm'.[29] The appellations of enthusiast or fanatic were not reserved only for medieval heretics. Such terms were also generally applied by Protestants to orthodox facets of medieval piety, such as monastic life. Patrick Nisbet was of course far from unusual in exempting the revered Waldensian heretics from the label of enthusiasm. He also wrote, however, how others of those who opposed the corruption of the medieval Church were 'tinctured with the prejudices of the times, their zeal was not always tempered with prudence ... [and] they some-times degenerated into enthusiasm'. These sects struck out on their own 'onto some new path of religion' urged on by the 'false doctrines, the absurd ceremonies and superstitions and the intolerable tyranny of popery'.[30]

In much anti-curial Catholic and Protestant thought, the history of the crusades – generally considered to be the worst example of super-stitious enthusiasm – provided more irrefutable evidence of the bloody lengths which the craft of the papacy was prepared to sanc-tion in its search for power and wealth. For Giannone, the crusades were against the will of God and the tenets of Jesus Christ. The barbaric military struggle against the infidel had been used as a pretext for advancing the economic and political aims of the papacy. He related his amazement at how the minds of the masses were lit by the idea of the crusade. In the call to the crusade, a desperately perilous enterprise, the popes took advantage of the 'superstition of people' (by which he means the concept of pilgrimage itself). Popes had encouraged the kings and emperors to go on crusade, 'because, occupied in ... those dangerous expeditions, they would not pay any attention to their domestic affairs'. Monarchs had even 'abandoned their states and kingdoms to the care of the pope' whilst away on those brutal expeditions. Rome was thus provided with the possibility of more easily exerting its dire influence in their realms, and, as a consequence, the power of kings and emperors was weakened and that of the popes augmented.[31]

In northern Italy, in the anonymous *Istoria del pontificate* and other works, the crusades – initiated at the behest of Rome – were depicted as the bloodiest wars mentioned in world annals. These were wars in which 'the Sepulchre of Jesus Christ served as a pretext for usurpation, violence and murders'. As a result 'Europe remained almost deserted', and the loss to agriculture and the arts was incalculable.[32] Delle Piane too condemned the 'infinite robbery and murders' of the crusades as deeds against the will of God and the pacific teachings of Jesus. The popes, realizing the potency of this new and bloody form of religious endeavour, then went on to use it against supposed heretics in Europe. Europe was consequently exposed to the horrific spectacle of the Church eating its own children. The crusades also offered the papacy the prospect of elevating religious fraud to new levels in the form of the award of crusading indulgences. The spurious efficacy of indulgences (the remission of temporal penalty for forgiven sin) 'was believed by the ignorant and incautious because of the powerful authority and claimed infallibility of the popes who dispensed them'.[33]

For Rivarola, the plenary indulgences awarded to crusade fighters brought infinite wealth to the popes, and procured armies of 'fanatics' to extend the geographical boundaries of their claimed 'divine plenipotence' without expense. Another objective of the popes was to increase clerical power in the domains princes left behind. But despite this hint of regalism, Rivarola's republicanism does not allow kings any respite. The 'art and bloody politics of kings' used the crusades to occupy the attention of their warring noble vassals in order to distract them from the many wars that were an obstacle to royal 'usurpation and pillage'. But worse, the popes erected themselves as 'despots of despots', in so far as they arbitrated over the dissensions in and between the new crusader kingdoms.[34]

The attitude of the various Protestant tendencies to the crusades was substantially the same as that of anti-curial Catholics: that in most respects, the crusades had been yet another, particularly brutal, facet of Roman priestcraft. Exceptions to this rule were rare indeed, and when concessions were made, as for example by John Wesley, they were usually minor. Wesley rejected the explanation advanced by 'several learned men' (most likely the Several Gentlemen of the *History of Popery*), that the crusades were recommended by the popes solely to rid themselves of their more powerful vassals and seize their possessions. Instead, he argued the crusades were at first a question of superstition, but by experience the pontiffs learnt crusades could increase their opulence and extend their authority.[35]

Thomas Bray's account of the crusades, however, as those of most other Protestants is mercilessly damning, and his description provides a neat summary of their thought. The 'great *Arcanum* of the *Roman Conclave*' locked up the Holy Scriptures and obscured the light of the Gospel so that darkness, ignorance and superstition spread over the earth. This benighted climate was cultivated so that princes and people would be induced to 'slavishly undertake any Enterprises ... for the Grandeur and Interest of the See of *Rome*'. The first test of cringing princes was – as we have already seen – to send princes on crusade even knowing popes intended to benefit from their absence by 'pilfering their dominions'. Worse, having made princes 'beasts of burthen', they were also turned into *'Beasts of Prey'*, and Rome 'put them upon worrying and devouring, each of them their own people'. The crusades turned from the infidels and rounded 'upon the true believers in Jesus', the Albigenses, and a million Christians were cruelly slain.[36]

RATIONALITY, ENTHUSIASM AND GIBBON ON THE CRUSADES

For dissenting Protestants and anti-curial Catholics, the spectacle of the self-serving use of the heresy charge by Roman priest-kings and, for Protestants, that of the Anglican Church and state confirmed the priestcraft of the medieval and contemporary established Churches. The evident priestly guile and superstitious corruptions of the medieval Church had also driven many into the errors of enthusiasm and heresy. But Protestants had proclaimed a distinction between scriptural/rational and fanatical/enthusiastic sects, and fanaticism was itself a response to the heretically corrupt nature of the medieval Church. The Protestant emphasis upon the use of reason against enthusiasm was, therefore, as much or more a product of practical polemical necessity as it was of the inherent theological implications of rational – that is to say individual – study of the Bible. To focus solely upon theological developments in tracing the rehabilitation and growing use of reason in Protestant thought, as has often been the case, serves to de-contextualize the early stages in the development of Protestant thought. It is to dislocate the important place of reason in simple but most effective polemical counterpositions of right and wrong religion.

The consequence of downplaying the role of widespread polemic and elevating that of relatively elite theological enquiries is that it has, to an extent, facilitated the view that the burgeoning rationalism in Protestant thought was solely or mostly a product of mid-seventeenth-century theological enquiry – as for example that of the Cambridge Platonists (1633–68). This attribution has prompted some modern historians to regard the growing emphasis on the use of reason in religious thought as part of the rational religious preamble of the English and European Enlightenment, rather than as a practical development of post-Reformation polemic. The supposed connection between Herbert of Cherbury's (1582–1648) proposal of an implicitly rational core of beliefs on which all Christians could agree (on which see Chapter 6) and the rise of English deism in the last decades of the seventeenth century is mostly the wishful thinking of historians. There is little proof of such a connection. It is instructive to remember that the widespread counterposing of Catholic irrationality to Protestant rationality continued unabated even while some radical Protestants began to defect towards deistic thought in the late seventeenth century.

There is evidence that radical Protestants, on the verge of embracing deism, drew upon the traditional Protestant distinction between enthusiasm and rationalism. As Toland noted in his *Christianity not Mysterious,* when discussing the early development of superstitious ceremony, there is no degree of '*Enthusiasm* higher than placing Religion in such Fooleries'.[37] The horrendous reality of religious intolerance, and the contemporary and historic use of the heresy charge as a defence of priestcraft, were proofs for some Dissenters that the established Christian ministries were incurably infected with the aggressive bacillus of priestcraft. The fortunes of the Huguenots had been closely monitored in England since the reign of Elizabeth, though official support for them had ceased with the accession of Charles I. The arrival of tens of thousands of Huguenot refugees in England and publication of accounts of their persecution as well as

that of the Waldenses in the Duchy of Savoy[38] constituted fresh
evidence (if it was needed) of the prostitution of the heresy charge
by kings and their antichristian priestly advisers. Everywhere, past or
present, religious intolerance seemed to be a means to a political
end. It was the same in France, Scotland, Ireland, England, Piedmont
or the states of Germany, whether the victims were the Waldenses,
Calvinists, Lutherans, Catholics, Scottish Presbyterians, Puritans,
Quakers or Unitarians. For enlightened thinkers, Protestant
accounts of the cynical use of the crusades and the long-standing
abuse of the heresy charge formed a ready-made critical package. It
was a package providing a neat and implicit parallel to contemporary
barbarities, one which could be easily adopted and inserted into the
Enlightenment critique of Church history.

The Protestant rationale of the cause, progress and practical
outcome of the crusades, was equal to and, at times, exceeded the
descriptive venom of Gibbon in his *Decline and Fall of the Roman
Empire*. There is, therefore, little originality in Gibbon's account –
except for his razor-sharp irony. Even Roy Porter, in his otherwise
glowing account of the *Decline and Fall*, admits Gibbon did not go far
beyond the prejudices of traditional Protestant historiography on the
subject of the medieval Church.[39] Protestant writers – even Anglicans
– could, therefore, happily adopt whole sections of Gibbon's account
of the crusades in order to make good use of his irony and masterly
prose style. Citing Gibbon, the Anglican George Gregory describes
Peter the Hermit's pious preaching (in 1095) for the first crusade as a
monstrous example of priestcraft, noting how the hermit carried with
him a letter written in heaven and how he had conversed with the
saints and angels of paradise. The crusade column, led by a divinely
inspired goose and goat, was composed of 'the most stupid and savage
refuse of the people, who mingled with their devotion a brutal licence
of rapine, prostitution and drunkenness'. Like other Protestant
accounts, Gregory also describes how the crusades increased the
wealth of the Church and the power of the popes.[40]

Gibbon's description of the crusades is, in some respects, actually
less critical than some anti-curial or Protestant accounts. In Chapter
60 of the *Decline and Fall*, Gibbon defends the morality of the
crusaders of the Fourth Crusade, who stormed and sacked
Constantinople in 1204, against the indictment of the incumbent
Pope Innocent III. Innocent, Gibbon tells us, accuses the sacking
crusaders

of respecting in their lust, neither age, nor sex, nor religious profession; and bitterly laments that the deeds of darkness, fornication, adultery and incest, were perpetrated in open day; and that noble matrons and holy nuns were polluted by the grooms and peasants of the Catholic camp.

But, Gibbon reminds his readers, in Constantinople there was certainly 'a stock of venal or willing beauty sufficient to satiate the desires' of the crusaders. He goes on to add that the noble French leaders of this crusade were patrons 'of discipline and decency' and mirrors of chastity, 'for we are no longer describing an irruption of the northern savages'. It is true the crusaders gave free vent to their avarice, but 'time, policy and religion had civilised the manners of the French and still more of the Italians'.[41]

Even partial defences of the deeds of the crusaders such as Gibbon's were indeed most uncommon in Protestant thought. For most, the crusades represented some of the lowest depths reached in the medieval period, both in terms of the inherent priestcraft of popes and prelates and of the moral decadence and barbarity of the actual expeditions themselves. About fifty years before the publication of Gibbon's *Decline and Fall*, the editors of the *History of Popery* explained that the common people were lured into military action by the offer of plenary indulgences, a licence to sin:

> This free and plenary absolution from all their sins, without any kind of penance, was a rare bait in that impure and dark age, wherewith to win and allure the simple people to that war. For what greater excitement could there be to men who were to invade a country, wherein all things were left to the lust of the soldier to commit all manner of wickedness whatsoever?[42]

Brown, also several years before the appearance of the *Decline and Fall*, reminded fellow Protestants that the crusades 'ruined millions of families', and by means of these expeditions, Europe was

> drained of her rulers, her inhabitants and wealth. Murders, rapes, and robberies of the most infernal nature were every where committed with impunity by these pretended armies of Christ. For about two hundred years they rendered the west of Asia and sometimes Egypt a scene of blood, and everything horrid.

Exasperated at the thought of such grisly spectacles, Brown concludes that the crusaders were more wicked than infidels.[43]

For modern historians living and writing in a predominantly secular society, the study of the medieval treatment of heresy is a simple historical proposition. To early modern Protestants, however, the subject was brimming with historical proof of priestcraft. In the view of many Catholic anti-curialists and Protestant Dissenters, those spectacles of chicane and bloodlust presented parallels with contemporary religion. One may or may not agree with the Protestant view of the crusades, the exploitation of the heresy charge or the nature of heretical movements. It is, nevertheless, clear that enlightened historians such as Gibbon – hardly known for his sympathy towards Christian history – thought the general Protestant approach to the subject eminently suitable for his own pen. This was a compliment repaid by the later Protestant use of his own incisive style.

There is one important point yet to reaffirm in this chapter, that of the tension between Reformation theology and the practical spiritual and polemical needs of Protestants. Both Luther and Calvin pointedly denigrated the place of reason in religious thought. Reason, it was thought, had been an important component of the disastrous medieval theological outlook, in which it had been considered an aid to spiritual understanding. Yet the Fall clearly demonstrated human reason was corrupt and not at all to be considered a reliable aid in religious thought. In order to counter the superstition and (to use Calvin's term) frenzy of Catholicism, it was necessary to embrace the Word, the Word of God contained in the Bible. Deviation from the Word, the use of human faculties to construct theological systems, had been the root of deplorable heresies, including Catholicism itself.

We already know, following the lead of Luther, that Reformation protagonists early struck out on the path of explicit comparative religious history. This practice, although much neglected and hitherto not properly studied or awarded its just role in early modern religious and intellectual development, was only the tip of the Protestant comparative iceberg. In a period of acute religious conflict, whether Protestants consciously perceived it or not, reading the Bible was most often more than pure spiritual study. For embattled Protestants (and most were – against Catholics or Protestant opponents) reading the Bible was to take part in a comparative religious exercise. It was to reflect upon and compare the heretical failings of Catholicism or other quasi-papists to the true, simple and unadulterated spiritual prescriptions of Scripture. It was this implicit comparative dimension – integral to a Europe divided by long-term religious ferment – that goaded Protestants into a *de facto* process of rehabilitating reason, smoothing the intellectual path for the Enlightenment use of reason against priestcraft. Catholicism, it was seen, promoted frenzy, superstition and heresy rather than the reflective, that is to say rational, study of the Bible and simple Christian worship.

Almost as soon as Luther and later Calvin declaimed against the place of reason in religious enquiry, the exigencies of the harsh religious environment began to promote the opposite tendency. The Cambridge Platonists, it can be said, were only reflecting and developing everyday Protestant practice and experience. As long as the practical use of reason as a prime tool against perceived Christian deviants remained informal and, in theological terms, not explicitly formulated, there was no reason to condemn the use of it as contrary to Reformation theological principles. Those Protestants such as the Cambridge Platonists who had the temerity to notice that everyday fact, and overtly proceed from it as a given in their writings, unavoidably faced substantial theological inertia and opposition. It was, however, given the reality of early modern religious struggle, most unlikely that seventeenth-century advocates of the role of reason could have been silenced or forgotten. This discussion begs another question, that of the importance of reason to Enlightenment anticlericalism, for discussion of reason in Enlightenment studies has frequently been allotted greater prominence than I have here allowed. Reason was one of the primary conceptual tools with which the enlightened attacked the *ancien régime*. Reason in itself, however, did not constitute Enlightenment anticlericalism: the emancipation of reason was the *result* of anticlericalism not its cause.

6 The Book of Priestcraft Open: Fraud and Idolatry

We have already seen that Protestants and Catholic anti-curialists denounced the miracles of the Catholic Church as priestly craft, and orthodox Catholic propagandists similarly those attributed to Protestants. In order, however, to be effective in the battle of the confessions, the assault upon the doctrine and religious practice of opponents needed to be broadened. The most efficacious polemical and analytical form suited to general denunciations of religious opponents was comparative religious history, a technique quickly developed during and shortly after the Reformation. Catholic, Protestant, Moslem, Judaeo-Christian and other religions were compared to one another in order to demonstrate that religious opponents – whether Catholics or Protestants – were infected with various degrees of paganism. In early modern mentality, the term pagan could not be separated from, and was virtually synonymous with, the presumed gross priestly guile of the ancient priests. Thus, for dissenting Protestants, anti-curialists, Enlightened deists, sceptics and atheists of the eighteenth century, the conclusion that the heathen and much of the Christian priesthood had practised long-term religious fraud upon state and subjects was old news. All such thinkers had at their disposal a large and varied corpus of ready-made comparative and sociological analyses with which to inform their own historical comparisons.

The potency of the Reformation historical revolution was its ability not only to scrutinize, theorize and reinvent a thousand or more years of history, but its ability to simultaneously explain the present condition of Christianity. A decidedly analytical and comparative mode of historical thinking on the one hand, and an analysis of contemporary religion on the other constituted a Protestant sociology of religion. There was thus an evolutionary interaction, a dialectic of change, between the evidence of the present and the evidence of past religions. The perceived scandals of contemporary Catholicism were translated and transported into an historiographical context, becoming a *de facto* confirmation of historical accounts. At the same time, history informed the reader of the 'true' historical nature of contemporary

Catholicism behind the clerical masks. So Henoch Clapham, in his *Chronological Discourse touching, the Church; Christ; Anti-Christ; Gog and Magog* (1609), advanced that the popes and Muhammad were impostors. The proof of the claim was his historical methodology itself: by comparing the history of different religions against the model of Protestantism and with each other, the believer was armed to discriminate between priestcraft and real religion. That historical proof was then subjected to and verified by other comparative/socio-logical tests in the present. So Clapham, for example, surmounting the problem that religious images were forbidden to Muslims (a potential difficulty in the comparison of idolatrous Catholicism and Islam), compared the idolatrous images used by papists with the veneration of the 'Mahumetistes' for the picture of a Rose.[1]

This socio-historical technique was common amongst English Protestants. At the heart of the attack was an accusation of idolatry. The equation of popery with paganism referred to the Catholic use of images, statues and the invocation of saints, but also to the idol of the Mass because the priest who performed the Mass was held to recreate Jesus himself. Following the bleak lapsarian view of human nature delineated by Luther and Calvin, the 'disease' of idolatry was held to be the Fall's most pernicious outcome.[2] The Fall had resulted in a corruption of human nature, including human reason. This mortal weakness was enshrined in the Westminster Confession of 1643, which asserted Adam and Eve 'being the root of all mankind', a corrupt human nature was 'conveyed to all their posterity, descending from them by ordinary generation'.[3] The posterity of Adam and Eve were thus prone to the greatest of religious errors, that of worshipping a false god.

For Luther, all non-Protestant religions shared similarities: the dubious foundation of a natural knowledge of God, discovered by corrupt human reason. Worship based on the discoveries of reason was not true worship of God, but rather of an illusory god. Hence such worship was idolatrous, as was Catholicism with its cults of saints and chapels devoted to their images. Bishop John Bale in *The Actes of Englysh Votaryes* (1546) railed against such antichristian superstition and idolatry. Robert Crowley could write in 1566 that papists are in a 'darke dungeon of ignorance, superstition and errour'.[4] Henry More, in his *Antidote Against Idolatry* (1669), succinctly stated the problem, noting the souls of men 'in this lapsed state, are naturally prone to so mischievous a Disease [idolatry], as both History and daily Experience do abundantly witness'.[5]

The theological potency of the idolatry accusation – that is to say the paganism charge – was profound. Crafty ancient priests, it was claimed, had created and perpetuated a series of fake demigods in order to bewilder the laity into abject spiritual and political subjection to the high priest, as well as to excite more pious donations than would be possible with only one god. For Protestants, there was a veritable pantheon of gods to be found in Catholic churches. Catholics gave these open idolatrous veneration, and were encouraged to do so by their priesthood as an integral part of their faith. For more than a thousand years the Catholic clergy had used pagan idols to entrap the laity into a false worship concocted only for the worldly benefit of the priests. The paganism charge was the summit of all the anticlerical attacks by Protestants upon the Catholic Church. It was the baseline by which was measured the level of Catholic deviance from the simple precepts of Jesus, and by which could also be measured the purity of other non-Catholic, even Protestant, Churches: once created, such a formidable anticlerical weapon was not neglected when conflicts between Protestants erupted.

In the mid-sixteenth century, Bale and Crowley had written from the vantage point of the reformed, those who had recognized the existence of idolatry in Christendom. Paradoxically – given that flawed human reason was held to be the root of religious corruption – these Protestants were using the human mental faculty of reason and the Word of God, the Bible, to be on their guard against idolatry. From Bale onwards, then, the practical requisites of Protestant theology and the polemic against enthusiasm had already begun to manufacture an implicit antidote for the theological pessimism of Luther and Calvin. But the remaining gestation period for the theologically explicit emergence of reason in Protestant thought was to be several decades, found in the thought of Herbert of Cherbury and in that of the Cambridge Platonists.[6] In his *De veritate* (1624), Cherbury established five simple tenets (i.e. springing from human reason) of Christianity around which warring Christian confessions and factions might unite.[7] Nevertheless, as we have seen, in historico-polemical terms – rather than purely theological – Protestant rationalism had already proceeded apace. From the Reformation itself, propagandists and historians of the Church had increasingly striven to isolate and depict the secondary, human roots of historical causation. This was an enquiry in which human reason and empirical knowledge were combined to form an increasingly rational historio-graphical account. An historical account which, in its day-to-day, year-by-year chronology was rooted in recognizably human activity susceptible to all the usual methods of historical enquiry.

Not long after the Reformation, the comparative indictment of paganism became the prevalent paradigm in European Catholic–Protestant polemic. Polemicists often constructed a comparison at least partly based on the medieval canon that had characterized Christendom's main religious opponent, Islam, as a fraudulent and licentious religion, craftily concocted to suit the weaknesses of the flesh.[8] Traditional anti-Semitism was also brought to bear in comparative polemics, and Martin Luther's own anti-clerical polemic had compared Papism, Mahometanism and Judaism in an attempt to illustrate that they coincided in their fundamentals. This wide, no-holds-barred comparative technique was used by scores of English Protestants who were following, for example, the mid-sixteenth-century lead of John Bale. Bale had declared the pronounced licentious nature of Catholicism – 'that carnall Synagoge' – was linked to idolatrous paganism. Similarly, John Foxe pronounced the superstition of the Roman Church to be the same as that of the Jews.[9] The same sweeping and poisonous salvoes criss-crossed other parts of Europe as part of the mainstream Catholic–Protestant polemic. The reply of the Dean of Exeter, Matthew Sutcliffe, to the Catholic *Calvino-Turcismus* (1597) – which compared Calvinism to Islam – written by the priest William Rainolds and the Archbishop of Rheims William Gifford, was naturally framed in terms of a comparative polemic. In his *De turcopapismo* (1599), Sutcliffe argued that Islam and Catholicism were the same in their moral and religious essentials, ascribing to each 'intemperance and excess'. Thus both 'equally oppose the Church and doctrine of Christ'.[10]

In 1601 William Perkins's *A Warning against the Idolatrie of the Last Times,* attacked the hideous problem of the idolatrous nature of the transubstantial Eucharist, in which holy bread became an idol representing Jesus himself. Perkins explained that, as heathens cut trees to make idols and to provide firewood for cooking, so the Romish Church reaps corn for bread, of which one part 'they make Christ, their Breaden God. The Gentiles builded houses and Temples to their gods: so doe Papists to Saints and consecrated altars to the honour of their idols: so doe Papists to Saints and Angels'.[11] In 1606, the Anglican Oliver Ormerod (c. 1580–1626) of Emmanuel College Cambridge published the first edition of what was to become one archetype of the paganism charge: *Pagano-Papismus: wherein is proved by irrefragable demonstrations, that papisme is flat paganisme: and that the papists doe resemble the very pagans, in above sevenscore severall things.* Ormerod, with a stress on idolatry, systematically compared ancient pagan religious beliefs and practices with those of Catholicism. Even nuns did not escape his glare, for nuns were only remodelled vestal virgins (virgin priestesses of the Temple of Vesta).[12] But 'sevenscore', apparently, was not the final tally, for in the last pages of Ormerod's *Pagano-Papismus* is a list of seventeen items in which the papacy went beyond the errors of the pagans.

Ormerod's views were hardly unusual in the early seventeenth century. In 1611, for example, the first of several editions of Henry Ainsworth's (1571– *c.* 1621) widely read *An Arrow against Idolatry* appeared. For Ainsworth, Catholicism was a counterfeit religion. Religious corruption had begun when King Jeroboam of Israel (the *Book of Kings*) introduced idolatrous practices. The popes, 'as the Heathens had their Gods and Goddesses of divers ranks, supreme, inferiour and middle', had proceeded in imitation of the heathen model. These inferior deities were thought of as 'mediators and inter-cessors', and via them the heathens 'thought men's desires and merits did come unto *God*'. In this way, Roman Catholic priests became *'mediators between God and men'*. Thus the 'whore-mother' Rome revived the idolatrous practices of Israel, and '[o]f the Jewes she hath received one high Priest, ... to be the chiefe Governour and Monarch Ecclesiastical': the pope. In this unholy mixture of the spiritual and secular, the priest-kings of Christian Rome had imitated ancient Egypt, where they had mixed the 'Kingdome and the Priesthood; the Civil Magistracie, and the Ecclesiastical Ministery in one person; and would have all their Kings to be also Priests'. Yet, unlike the popes, even the pagan priests of ancient Rome were not permitted to have any magistracy. Romish idolatry is 'so fast retained' even amongst some (by which Ainsworth meant Anglicans) who hate the Whore because from Rome they received their ministers, their provincial and national Churches, liturgies, angels and saints days, and even Churches formerly built and dedicated to the 'Heathen Divels'.

The idolatry of Catholicism was worse than that of the ancient heathens, for the *'Idolatry of these* [present] *times, farre exceed*[s] *Ieroboams'*. Ainsworth firmly records that some heathens even forbade the worshipping of images: that is to say heathens, using only corrupt human reason, had managed to avoid the excesses of the Catholic Church, which had even been granted the inestimable benefit of the revelation of God's Son.[13] It is not such a large step from this point to a rehabilitation of the use of reason in Protestant thought, and it certainly constitutes a significant yet so far unnoticed marker in its gestation. In important respects, even though Ainsworth's language register is Puritan, his analysis is similar to that of Cherbury. The pejorative contrast of Catholicism with a rudimentary, mistaken, yet not altogether virtueless ancient pagan religion is also present in Cherbury's work. Thus Cherbury's may have been a cogent account of the origins of priestcraft, but was less than original in conception. In his *De religione gentilium* (1663) Cherbury contends the religion of ancient heathens was not so absurd or stupid as imagined, received as it was for 'so many ages' by the greatest and best magistrates and most valiant of heroes. But there sprang up a race of crafty priests, who added inferior gods to that of the supreme deity. This was designed to 'embarass the minds of the people' with a plurality of gods, so holding them in ignorant and superstitious awe. The priests 'also expected to reap more Profit, and have larger Stipends from the various *Rites, Ceremonies* and Sacred *Mysteries,* that they contrived and divulg'd'. Thus all these religious corruptions redounded to their 'own Private and Particular *advantage'*.[14]

Despite fundamental similarities, Ainsworth's analysis is in one very important respect more politically incisive and radical than that of Cherbury: when discussing the origin of religious corruption, Ainsworth places emphasis upon the priest-legislator. That a Puritan should expound an historical example of Church–state inspired priestcraft while contending simultaneously against both the priest-legislator at Rome, and the perceived quasi-Catholicism of the head of Church and state (James I), should be no surprise. This was, of course, the same James who went on to confirm the worst suspicions of Puritans by reversing Queen Elizabeth's anti-Catholic foreign policy by drawing close to Catholic Spain, the major military threat to England and Protestant Europe. As we shall see, given Anglican hostility to Dissent, Ainsworth's prudent technique of tacit – but well-understood and effective – comparative polemic was necessarily common.

Evidently Oliver Ormerod realized the pagan accusation was the litmus test for right religion, but not just a test to be applied to papists. One year before the publication of the *Pagano-Papismus*, he published *The Picture of a Puritane ... Whereunto is annexed a short treatise, entituled, Puritano-papismus: or a Discoverie of Puritan-papisme* (1605). Besides linking Puritans to the much criticized

Anabaptists, in this tract Ormerod provided a typology comparing puritans to various medieval heretical sects, but also to the biblical Pharisees. Using the ancient Fathers as his authority, Puritans were decried as pagan idolaters because they worshipped their own opinions, conceits and fancies. In fact, stated Ormerod, to worship one's own religious opinions is worse than the pagan worship of the sun, stars and moon. This type of Anglican critique of Puritanism/Dissent continued throughout the seventeenth and in to the eighteenth century.[15]

Ormerod's use of the pagan accusation in Protestant infighting was of a kind characteristic of faction fighting since at least 1534. In Turner's anti-episcopal *The Huntyng of the Romyshe Foxe*, it is explained that the worshipping of the cross is a Romish practice and there should be no kneeling and bowing before images or idols because the Scriptures forbid idolatry. In the Vestiarian Controversy, in such works as the anonymous *Fortresse of Fathers* (1566), some Protestants criticized others for failing to reform thoroughly the Anglican Church, allowing the survival of idolatrous (Catholic) forms and ceremonies – including priestly vestments. The embittered and destructive tenor of the Puritan anti-Anglican critique is evident in the title of Ainsworth's *Certayne Questions* (1605), one of which addressed the subject of those Anglican *Idol Temples commonly called Churches*. Such deep religious enmity was not likely to evaporate easily, and the Puritan/Dissenter critique of the Anglican Church continued in various works during the seventeenth century.[16] Evidently, then, the deployment of the comparative paradigm of paganism in English thought is not to be dated from 1675 and Joshua Stopford's *Pagano-Papismus: Or, an Exact Parallel between Rome-Pagan and Rome-Christian* as has been suggested by some.

In the eighteenth century,[17] the canon that popery, or religions likened to it, were pagan continued to be both an important polemical tool and a comparative historiographical proposition. Protestants continued to vilify religious opponents with the pagan allegation regardless of the rise and fall (*c.* 1740) of English deism, with its programme of hostility to all Churches and its most pejorative comparison of pagan and Christian priestcraft. Neither were Protestant writers always overly concerned to maintain a sense of balance in their writings, such was the continued Protestant kudos of exemplary anti-Catholicism. William Brown's *Impiety, and Superstition expos'd: a Poetical essay* (1710), for instance, sported a 36-page preface on the historical development of Catholic paganism.

The only more or less consistent exception to the ubiquity of the paganism reproach is to be found in the narrow ranks of High Churchmen. For Jeremy Collier, for instance, to have sported the indictment that the medieval Church had been irretrievably corrupted by paganism would have detracted from his glowing portrayal of the Anglo-Saxon episcopate. For very many or most Protestant writers, it seems, there were no such restrictions on the choice of polemical weapons, and most naturally chose the most destructive ones available. The only division of any note amongst these writers was the choice of target: Catholicism; or Catholicism and Anglicanism. The choice of targets naturally entailed a great difference in the intended significance of the allegation. The target chosen in some works, however, even if the allegation itself was crystal clear, has been the subject of some confusion.

For Nisbet, the nations that conquered the Romans had always been 'accustomed to look up to their augurs and their druids as almost exalted above the human species ... [they] paid them a kind of implicit obedience, and were regulated by them in peace and war'. A common theme amongst Protestants was that pagan converts to Christianity transferred this veneration with 'superstitious reverence' to the pope, whom they considered to be the 'great arch-druid'. Early-medieval excommunication was therefore thought effective against the peoples of the northern nations because they 'considered it as of equal horror with all the dreadful interdicts of their druids'. The pagans also brought their religious practices with them, therefore many of the excessively ostentatious medieval ceremonies 'derive their origin directly from paganism'.[18] The Editors of *The History of Popery* informed their readers '[t]he truth is, this saint and angel worship is a piece of revived paganism'. Just as the heathens attributed the role of mediation between God and man to demons, so Catholics did to saints and angels. In the first six hundred years of the Church '[y]ou may see how our Catholic Romans have renewed these idolatrous laws of their heathen ancestors ... the popish hierarchy, with all their unscriptural orders of priests, monks, etc., is no other than the old pagan hierarchy revived'. Image worship was responsible for all manner of evils, such as 'irreligion, polytheism and atheism', a doctrine 'maintain'd only for filthy lucre'. On the subject of the transubstantial Eucharist, the Editors also illuminated the fact that 'Mahometanism' was less absurd and unreasonable in its tenets and more religiously tolerant than Catholicism.[19]

Similarly, in Brown's *General History* it is noted that medieval Church ceremonies were 'mostly of pagan and partly priestly invention'. The focus on this type of explanation for the perceived gaudy ostentation and pretended mystery of medieval ceremony – mere external, superficial religion – was very common and ardently argued. Protestants believed exaggerated and mysterious ceremonial pomp to be a popish sacerdotal tactic developed in order to promote the legitimacy of Romish doctrine, especially the cult of saints. Thus the Church 'took care to amuse the people with pompous ceremonies, images, altars, churches, festivals and processions, consecrated to their [the saints'] honour'. As John Wesley bitterly lamented, 'the people were sunk in the grossest superstition, and employed their zeal in the worship of images and relics and in the performance of a trifling round of ceremonies, which were imposed upon them by a despotic priesthood'.[20] Not unexpectedly, the pagano-papism characterization was also used by Italian Protestants such as Giacomo Picenino in his *Apologia per I Riformatori* (1706), which compares altar worship and processions with the idolatrous, polytheistic practices of the Gentiles (i.e. pagans).

Despite the importance of the pagano-papism critique which trained its barbs mostly upon the evils of idolatry, the heart of the Protestant and to a significant degree Catholic anti-curial attack against Rome contained another, closely interrelated and fundamental criticism of the Catholic religion: the claimed intercessory role of the Church. The assertion that the Catholic Church was able to intervene in spiritual realms beyond worldly existence on behalf of humanity was deemed by Protestants palpable proof of the priestly decision to retain the simple and genuine Christian truths solely for the priesthood. In the stead of scriptural truths, they peddled a false esoteric theology in order to maintain a monopoly over religion and persuade or frighten the laity into enriching the Church. Rome even contended Catholic priests had the power to re-create the body of Christ via communion. Priests had persuaded the laity to accept the notion that saints could intervene in this world on their behalf; and the catastrophic consequence was idolatrous worship of them. The Church also benefited in terms of religious authority and wealth from the oblations made by pilgrims to tombs, other supposedly holy places and relics of saints.

Christians, it seemed, had also been duped into accepting the existence of purgatory, where final penance for worldly sin was served and which was infinitely more painful than any earthly punishment. This was a hellish realm, but one in which popes could intervene by the granting of an indulgence reducing the timespan of punishment

served there. Deep fear of such torment had been assiduously inculcated from the pulpit and via terrifying fresco depictions. The result
was vast numbers of pious donations to the Church given in the hope
of escaping such torment and the ultimately corrupt practice of the
sale of indulgences. A papal campaign to encourage the purchase of
indulgences was the occasion of the 95 theses Luther drew up in 1517
and pinned to the door of the Schlosskirche at Wittenberg. Whether
he intended it to be so or not, his protest at the sale of indulgences was
a public accusation of priestcraft. In 1520 Luther wrote that the
Roman Church 'has become the most licentious den of thieves, the
most shameless of all brothels, the kingdom of sin, death and hell'.[21]
When Calvin condemned Catholic idolatry and the various claims of
intercession in his *Institutes of Church History*, he did not pose the
issue as one of a long-term doctrinal error, but similarly, one of deliberate fraud by a devious and venal priesthood.

Religious errors of all types could be expected from the baneful
effects of the Fall on the faculty of human reason. Thus some corruption of Christianity by pagan belief might be expected, or would at
least be unsurprising. But in most of the reformed camp it was
accepted that the corruption of Catholic doctrine had in fact been the
result of deliberate sacerdotal policy. Relatively soon after the
Reformation this had been explained by many 'ordinary' Protestants
(whose works now lie mostly unread), and later by better known
figures such as Cherbury and later in Charles Blount's *The First Two
Books of Philostratus* (1680). As Robert Howard explained in his *The
history of Religion. As it has been manag'd by priestcraft* (1694), the
'Idolatry of Bread-Worship' is more 'impudent' than anything of the
Gentiles, who never claimed that they could transubstantiate their
images into demons. Purgatory, that old '*Hades* and *Elysium* of the
Gentiles [has] ... now been improved into Gain ... 'Tis most clear,
that Mystery and dark Notions vented in hard Words, are not studied
or maintein'd for the sake of Religion, but for the Priests' particular
interest and Power.'[22]

Edward Aspinwall's *Preservative against Popery* (1715) was typical
when it tilted at the religious mysteries represented by the 'three great
points' of Catholic Doctrine, spelled out on its title page: 'I. Prayers
to Saints and Angels. II. Purgatory and Prayers for the Dead. III. Real
Presence and Transubstantiation'. The creation of such religious
mysteries, Protestants observed, had also contributed to the execrable
pomp of ceremonies, rites and processions. Such esoteric ostentation
served to confirm the exclusive power of the priestly caste to mediate

between Heaven and Earth. As George Gregory put it at the end of the eighteenth century, the doctrines of the Church were 'obscured by superstition, and rendered ludicrous by a ceremonious and pompous worship'.[23] For John Wesley, the multitude had been sunk 'into the most opprobrious ignorance and superstition ... and a stupid zeal for a senseless round of ridiculous rites and ceremonies'.[24]

The iniquity of Catholic priestcraft seemed to know no bounds in Protestant thought. Laurence Howell averred 'the better to promote the worshipping of images ... the second commandment, which forbids the worshipping of graven images, [was] ... taken out of the Decalogue,' and the ninth [was] ... subdivided to make ten. The laity was forbidden Holy Scripture in the vulgar tongue, 'that they might the less understand' it, and the Church was enveloped in a 'labrynth of errors and superstition'. Medieval theological thinking and canon law were developed in order to defend the 'encroachments and usurpations of the court and Bishop of Rome'.[25] For George Gregory, the theologians 'instead of explaining the doctrines of the gospel, mined them by degrees, and sunk divine truth under the ruins of a captious philosophy'. As iniquitous was the fact that '[t]he same impostors who peopled the celestial regions with fictitious saints employed also their fruitful inventions in embellishing [saints] with false miracles'. Thus 'all the resources of forgery and fable were consequently exhausted to celebrate exploits which had never existed'. Some had been 'excited to this by the seductions of a false devotion', others by the 'prospect of gain and the ambitious desire of being reverenced by the multitude'.[26] For John Wesley, the 'arts of a rapacious priesthood were practised upon the ignorant devotion of the simple'. There was a 'horrible cloud' of superstition and new saints were created to calm the multitude'.[27]

For the Editors of the *History of Popery*, Pope Gregory the Great had 'hatch'd' indulgences 'to allure the people ... to visit the chief temples of the city of Rome', for on certain days they might receive a plenary remission of their sins. But, in reality, the design of the Roman Church was to 'empty her children's purses', expected, as they were, to give pious donations to the Churches of Rome. The Editors also castigated the motives for the introduction of auricular confession with a sectarian zeal not outdone by the hottest Protestant or enlightened thinker. They asked,

to what end was it advanc'd? Meerly, like most of their other superstitions and rogueries, to enslave the poor people, and to increase the wealth and power of the priest. By this politick picklock they open the breasts of princes, and sift out every man's inclination and interest, and learn how to suit themselves to his humour for their best advantage.

The papacy had bolstered its claim to superiority by various forgeries, false claims and deceits. In the guise of canon law, these falsehoods were obtruded upon the world as 'Divine prescriptions ... [a]ll these being carefully registered, each former usurpation serv'd as a precedent to justify a greater afterwards'. These were traditional accusations. No wonder some decades earlier radical Protestants such as Charles Blount had doubted religious truths could ever be obtained from the written record of the Church. Indeed, the Editors explained how Rome had deliberately chosen the first, corrupt version of St Jerome's translation of the Bible – for 'we know that St. Jerome made two translations and confesseth that the first was corrupt'.[28]

The Scot John Brown described how the clergy had striven 'to perplex and darken the truth ... to sink the people into the most shameful ignorance and superstition'. Their 'fundamental doctrines related to the worship of images and saints, the fire of purgatory,... old heathen rites, a little changed, for the salvation of men, [and] the power of reliques to heal the diseases of the body and mind'. Scripture was made to 'support the most delirious stuff that could be invented ... Hence the pure and peaceable wisdom of the gospel was perverted into a science of deceitful chicane.'[29] But, as usual, Brown and earlier Protestants had not had any monopoly of the revelation that fraudulent priests had perverted the doctrine of Christ for very terrestrial ends. Claims of the same ilk were present in the writings of pro-Rome polemicists.

Catholic propagandists claimed Protestants had deliberately falsified and perverted scripture to reinforce and ensure the success of their clerical imposture. In 1544, in his *Compendio d'errori, et inganni luterani,* the Dominican Lancelotto Politi expounded how reformers claimed only they understood the Bible, so 'deceiving the poor and unlearned with perversions of Scripture'. In the development of the comparative religious technique, orthodox propagandists too drew upon comparisons between ancient Judaism and the medieval canon on Islam. Thus Politi also added that the perversions of scripture made by the reformers were of design pleasing to the flesh.[30] Muhammad was depicted as a religious fraud, bandit, schemer and lecher, and the Reformed faith was compared to Islam and Judaism in such works as Bozio*'s De signis ecclesiae* and Segneri's *L'Incredulo senza scusa*. As we have seen, outside Italy the Catholic authors of the *Calvino-Turcismus* also developed the comparative technique.

Counter-Reformation propagandists, in defending papal infallibility and the popes' role as defenders of orthodoxy and guardians of ecclesiastical discipline, also accused Protestants of idolatry. This was a charge of paganism but, although it endured until the mid-eighteenth century, it was hardly even a pale shadow of its Protestant counterpart. From the beginning it was seriously disadvantaged in not having what seemed to ordinary Protestants the obvious evidence of the everyday use of a plethora of images and various Catholic cults which were available to Protestant propagandists. As a consequence, the Catholic paganism reproach could not benefit from the valuable fact of a popular consciousness increasingly permeated with a common-sense understanding of the idolatrous practice of its religious opponents. But one should not assume the efforts of Catholic propagandists such as Jacopo Moronessa were necessarily any less adroit, only disadvantaged. In his *Il Modello di Martino Lutero* Moronessa purported that Luther – in the same way as the pagans had idols created by the devil – had been an idol sent with the task of seducing Christians into a false worship. A similar theme is to be found in Rezka's *De atheismus et phalarismus*, in which he pointed out that ancient pagans had sported a panoply of greater and lesser gods or prophets, and Luther formed just one of the Gods of the new pagan (Protestant) pantheon.

Much of the same copious evidence of Church corruption long identified by Protestants also formed the core of the anti-curial attack upon Rome. Like Protestants, eighteenth-century Catholic critics of Roman Catholic doctrine usually concentrated upon the orthodox Church's claimed mediatory role between humanity and divinity. It is on this subject that dissident Catholics considered they were identifying some of the worst superstitious excess, doctrinal corruption, and economic fraud which supported the papal empire upon the ruins of Christian doctrine. Their examples were, as in Protestant works, saint worship, purgatory and indulgences, although the balance varied from one writer to another. The anti-curial assertion that some or all of the claimed powers of intercession beyond this world were fraudulent was not, however, a development of eighteenth-century Italian thought. The concept of purgatory was denied by some medieval heretical sects such as the Waldenses, and of course by Luther and Calvin, as well as some heterodox Renaissance thinkers. Identifying historical precedents such as these is, unfortunately, of no or very limited use to the historian. Indicating the mere historical existence of anti-curial or even sceptical ideas does not explain their renewed upsurge or the degree of public and institutional acquiescence or resistance to them. It is primarily the context in which ideas exist that determines the degree of their attraction, acceptance and efficacy.

In a radically new context, an old idea can become so infused with new meaning it hardly resembles its original form, even if its constituent elements remain unchanged. The scandal of Reformation and Counter-Reformation propaganda battles, and the exploitation of the flag of religion in political and military alliances, had served to imbue old anticlerical ideas with a much greater social resonance. Such shifts in the perception of the content or power of old ideas constituted the usually undeclared rationale of Rome in effectively ignoring or tolerating some heretical notions for decades or centuries, only to viciously condemn the same ideas as an inherent threat to the Church at a later date. In the renewed orthodox vigour of the Tridentine revival of the 1680s, supporters of the ancient theory of atomism were considered a threat to Catholic fundamentals such as the Real Presence in the Eucharist. This perception, in a period of declining papal influence, the growth of philosophical enquiry and of a continuing Protestant denial of the Transubstantial Eucharist, was probably not mistaken.

A more ostensibly curious example is the fortune of Copernican ideas. There is evidence to demonstrate that in 1616 – the very year the Curia finally proscribed Copernican ideas – Rome had correctly assessed there was still little support for Copernicus's ideas of 1543. Galileo's name was not mentioned in the 1616 rulings of the Inquisition or the Congregation of the Index, even though he had published his support for Copernican ideas in 1610. If the papacy wished to prevent the spread of Copernican ideas, why did it not publicly indict Galileo as an overt warning to others? The question remains, then, as to why the ruling of 1616 came about?

In the first years of the Reformation, a twinge or more of fear for the future of Roman Catholicism was naturally present in the Curia, but the harsh longer-term reality was yet to impose itself. More than three decades were to elapse after Luther's defiance before Rome began to compile the Indexes of Forbidden Books in 1549. Two more decades of hard experience were necessary to prompt the Curia to establish the Congregation of the Index in 1571 as a formal agency of the Curia. But these dates only more or less mark a prologue in the formation of a corpus of detailed Protestant accounts overtly aimed at demonstrating the forgery and fraud of Rome. Around the year 1600, it can be argued, protestant polemic began to come of age. It was a maturation typified in such publications as William Crashaw's *Falsificationum romanarum* (1606). The 'evidence' compiled by Crashaw was used by subsequent scholars and polemicists into the eighteenth century. From this vantage point, the proscription of 1616 is more intelligible. Rome was forced into defensive action not on account of any scientific threat, but by the needs of its overall strategy to combat the growing threat to Roman orthodoxy and biblical doctrine posed by the widespread and far-reaching anti-Rome polemic of Protestants.

As Sella has explained, if the Bible were not to be considered literally true in its account of the universe, 'it might lend credence to Protestant charges that the Catholic Church took liberties with the sacred text. Accordingly, they fell back, defensively, on uncompromising, literalist exegetical standards'.[31] Biblical views of the universe had to be seen to be defended. Copernican ideas had to be seen to be condemned; but accompanied by a damage limitation exercise that refrained from a public confrontation with Galileo and ignored his published support for Copernican ideas.

Orthodoxy was of course also under threat in Italy itself. The Reformation schism could not but give confidence to anti-curial Catholics: did not millions of Christians (mostly Protestants) now accept Rome was guilty of long-term priestcraft? Writers such as Gregorio Leti and Gerolamo Arconati criticized the popes for opening heaven and hell at their whim (or at least claiming to be able to do so), and for deliberately distorting Scripture to support the 'impiety of Papism'.[32] Inevitably, given the destructive potential of the technique, some anti-curialists also utilized comparative religion. Paolo Sarpi too deplored the superstition and abuses he identified in the Church, and comparative ideas were never far away. Thus he thought it apt to compare the enforced Roman extraction of the tithe with the tenets of Mosaic law and the actions of the rabbis. He bitterly recorded that in *c.* 1170 Pope Alexander III had used excommunication to enforce payment of the tithe, and in 1195 Pope Celestine III even decreed that prostitutes should pay the tithe.[33]

In the eighteenth century, attacks upon orthodox doctrine became more concerted, supported by well-considered historical evidence – an avenue into which even the conservative Muratori was prepared to tread. Muratori illustrated how penance for confessed sins had been

slowly reduced to the giving of donations. What had been a laudable
process of penance was thus turned into a font of immense wealth, the
experience of which produced 'ambition, interest and incontinence' in
secular and monastic clergy. The survival of superstitious and pagan
practices into the eighth century, rather than being eradicated, flow-
ered and became rife by the tenth century. Superstition and paganism
infected commoners and nobles because both had 'participated in the
same ignorance'.[34] Ignorance and depravity, declared Muratori, had
meant religion became material and without spirit. Forgeries and
falsifications, used to support various outrageous papal claims (he
especially noted the Pseudo-Isidorean Decretals and the Donation of
Constantine), had been common. But, unfortunately, the learned had
'lacked criticism, that is the manner in which to discover fables', and
such naivety was the reason why the laity had welcomed forgeries with
'open arms', as they did false miracles and the fantastic lives of saints.

For Giannone, especially prominent in the exposition of Mosaic
law in his *Triregno*,[35] Christian doctrine had been perverted and
exploited as a facade for secular ends, and his main example of that
process was the papal creation of purgatory. To demonstrate his claim
he provided a 'scientific demonstration' of the impossibility of the
resurrection of souls without the resurrection of the body. He argued
'the resurrection of the body is absolutely necessary in order to be
introduced in to the heavenly kingdom, since the sole alone is not
capable of any action or emotion'. Thus, before the Resurrection, the
concept of purgatory as a region and intercession within it by the
Church on behalf of souls would be impossible. If the soul is separated from the body 'our soul will remain in perpetual inaction and in
a most profound sleep': inactive and non-sentient – a state termed
psychopannychy.[36] He related that it was in Egypt that the concept of
the soul was tainted and then even more so by the Greeks and the
Romans, filling the world with fables, until it finally entered Christian
doctrine. Giannone's notion of the corporeality of the soul, however,
had earlier roots in Anabaptism, libertinism and popular culture.
More directly, his Christian materialism was first arrived at via his
master Domenico Aulisio, although other sources were Descartes,
Gassendi, Toland and Newton.[37]

Most early modern English Protestants, like Catholics, held to the
Aquinian conception of the soul, in which the separate, sentient existence of the soul from the body after death was accepted, and the
notion of psychopannychy rejected. Some more radical Protestant
thinkers argued for the corporeality of the soul, and consequently the

impossibility of a sentient existence for it without the body, as did John Toland in his *Letters to Serena* (1704). It is not true, however, that the only dissent from the Aquinian concept of the soul was to hail from deists and other radicals. Some Anglicans, such as the Master of the Charterhouse, Thomas Burnet, sought a compromise position. In his *De statu mortuorum et resurgentium liber* (1720), Burnet argued souls were sentient after death, but that pleasure and pain were not possible because of their incorporeality. Joseph Priestley, in his *Inquiry into the Knowledge of the Antient Hebrews, concerning a Future State* (1801), argued that the concept of a sentient, spiritual soul surviving death was a doctrinal corruption introduced by heathens: a notion 'really inconsistent with the doctrine of a resurrection'.[38] The views of Burnet and Priestley are clearly examples of the ability of Christianity to absorb materialist ideas, as were the views of Giannone. To hold materialist views, then, did not mean abandoning Christianity, or the Resurrection, as the intense piety of Sir Isaac Newton demonstrated.

Giannone's attack on the immaterialism of the soul was of course not intended as an abstract theological debate; rather he wished to demonstrate the priestcraft of the papacy. From the eleventh century, averred Giannone, the fruit of avaricious motives, the new mine of purgatory, was established, in which was to be found a door to heaven for the credulous, and inexhaustible riches for the papacy. Such riches, when combined with temporal dominion, meant popes and bishops 'thought with greater promptness to things temporal, than to those divine and sacred'. The acceptance of fantastic ideas such as purgatory and intercession within it were the result of a 'long ignorance that could not produce any other effect than an unheard of superstition and idiocy'. The use of images was a return to pagan practices and the popes, despite opposition, had tenaciously defended the practice of image worship, because they knew it 'would furnish them with immense riches'. Sanctuaries for these images arose and, 'as a consequence pilgrimages, which resulted in unprecedented and prodigious riches', sufficient 'to establish and conserve a new kingdom', the temporal kingdom of the popes. The cult of the saints and their fantastic lives was invented and preached by monks in order to influence people to offer riches to monasteries. The development of canon law merely had the aim of competing with secular law and establishing 'pontifical greatness'. Most importantly, via the establishment of scholastic doctrines in the twelfth and thirteenth centuries, ecclesiastical history was forgotten and replaced by 'abstract and useless questions and disputes full of ... obscurity'. In this manner, the Achilles heel of the papacy – the history of its antichristian search for wealth and power – was left unexamined.[39] Archbishop Capecelatro was to make the same point half a century later when he argued it was necessary to forge a new Church history.

As already seen, Capecelatro effectively compared the medieval papacy to the priesthood of the druids and the scourge of the Saracens; a period in which existed 'an infinite dose of superstition and ignorance'. He denied the Church's role as intercessor in purgatorial punishment and condemned the consequent fraud of indulgences. He also considered that the doctrine of clerical celibacy was introduced in order 'to usurp the goods of clerics when they died', something impossible if 'they left behind them wives and children'. From the introduction of this unnatural law 'began a series of [moral] disorders, and the clerical state fell continuously in the opinion of the people'.[40] In the anonymous *Istoria del pontificate romane*, less cynical yet more dramatic conclusions are drawn from the introduction of the doctrine of celibacy. It is explained that the practice of celibacy and the withdrawal to the cloister resulted in a scarcity of agricultural labour, on account of which Europe became under-cultivated. Rivarola too concurred with Capecelatro's explanation of the motive behind the introduction of celibacy, but also argued that it had been, in effect, part of the clerical attack upon the state. He asked whether it was not true that the law of celibacy was part of the process of 'obtaining the exclusive right and independent power of the pope to enact laws on marriage and, as a consequence, rendered himself adjudicator of all civil authority?'[41]

In the *Monarchia* of Capecelatro's fellow Neapolitan, Eusebio Scotti, there is the usual concentration upon the self-serving debasement of doctrine by Rome. For Scotti, Church history was characterized by Pharisaism. Rome had 'reduced religion to an external apparatus' of ostentation in order to increase its attraction. Consequently, profiting from the ignorance of the people and princes, 'the result was that [Rome] was held in greater repute and esteem', and attracted rich donations. The popes gave the same distorted biblical interpretations as the Pharisees had given to the Old Testament. From Pope Stephen II (752), Rome became the workshop of falsity and imposture. The considerable forging skills of the monks and clerics were thus learnt 'from the new maxims of the Pharisaical Gospel of Rome become carnal', the new Sanhedrin of Christendom. Canon law was born of the avarice and ambition of the 'Universal

Judaic Monarchy', created in order to obscure divine scripture and 'to sanction the claim of the papal universal monarchy'. Canon law, was, in a word, the 'Talmud' of the popes.[42]

In the north of the peninsula, anti-curialists also denounced doctrinal corruption and ignorance, as did Delle Piane, in his *Storia cronologica de' Papi*. Compared to the unmitigated bile of Rivarola, however, Delle Piane's critique, although trenchant in itself, was relatively restrained. As English Protestants had done in the seventeenth century,[43] Rivarola harnessed both the gravamen of Pharisaism and the generic epithet of pagan as terms of deprecation. For Rivarola, beginning in the pontificate of Gregory the Great, divine service had been corrupted partly to the pagan and partly to the Hebrew model. For him this mutation had been easily achieved because the language of the northern peoples had slowly changed (the decline of Latin as a spoken language), so much so that the laity 'did not understand any more what was being done or said in the Church'. Later the veneration of images became dogma, and popes lit 'the imaginary fire of purgatory' which, via oblations and indulgences, produced unimaginable riches for the Church. Cunningly, a 'vast field of illusion' was produced, and theological disputes were but a screen for the pretensions of popes, who finally managed to renew all the 'madnesses of paganism'. Rivarola also overtly attacked the transubstantial Eucharist: that belief which is 'so contrary to reason' and does not have 'any foundation in antiquity'. In sum, Rome managed 'to submerge entire nations into the gloom of ignorance and the darkness of superstition'.[44]

CHRONOLOGY AND BOUNDARIES OF DOCTRINAL CORRUPTION

It is most important to remind ourselves that, at about the same time as Giannone was writing the *Triregno* and comparing medieval Catholicism to paganism, the Dominican Lodovico Gotti was writing his *Veritas religionis Christianae*. Gotti directed substantially the same comparative charge of paganism and idolatry at the Protestant reformers as used by Protestants and anti-curialists to assail Rome – spicing his arguments with all the usual accusations of venality, iniquity and lascivious behaviour. Historians who search for the origins of Enlightenment anticlerical polemic in any one writer are unlikely to be successful. The cut and thrust of seventeenth- and eighteenth-century religious polemic and historical analysis took place within a long-standing and deeply-entrenched European culture of comparative religion. Virtually all combatants wielded the weapon of comparative analysis, simply because it possessed the potential – a telling combination of the blunderbuss and rapier – to effect the most devastating assault upon the religiosity of opponents. It is necessary to emphasize the adjective European, because we know the comparative method was put to very effective use by writers elsewhere in Europe in the sixteenth and seventeenth centuries. This was the case, for example, on both sides of the confessional divide in France: as in the Catholic *Calvino-Turcismus* of Rainolds and Archbishop Gifford; and the *Mystére d'iniquité* of the Huguenot du Plessis-Mornay. In using comparative analysis in their historical accounts, however, writers were constantly tilling a fertile critical soil for use by later Enlightenment thinkers who also greatly valued the power of the comparative technique, but were very much less well disposed towards Christianity.

For Protestants, there was abundant historical and contemporary proof of systematic doctrinal corruption – even of the Bible itself – by Catholics. In addition, the Anglican Church had failed to purge itself properly of its Catholic hierarchy and the popish legacy of superstitious mystery. It was quite logical, therefore, that some radical Protestants such as Charles Blount began to despair of ever locating religious truths in the written tradition of the Christian Church. In 1680, in his *First Two Books of Philostratus,* Blount also trod the well-worn path of comparative religion, espousing all the common-or-garden elements of the priestcraft allegation. He condemned the religious fraud of Islam and the fraudulent and idolatrous religion of Catholics, who could justly plead for the antiquity of their Church because they had appropriated image worship from the 'old Heathen Religion'. Contrary to the view put by some that Blount was a sceptic, he did not deny revelation and noted that Christ 'really was the only legitimate Son of God'. He also believed in the immortality of the soul and quoted the Bible against atheists.

The problem for Blount was that the contents of the Bible, Christian doctrine and accounts of miracles had been transmitted to the present by fallible human tradition – although of course rebellion against the use of some corrupt elements of the human tradition was the very hallmark of Protestantism. This was a plea for toleration, for, he asserted, given the well-known frauds of the priests, it was hardly surprising that some doubted the doctrine of the Church was true

Christian doctrine. Because faith is insufficient to detect priestly chicanery, it was requisite to use the light of reason as the final arbiter in religious enquiry. In the light of the overwhelming corruption of the written record, revelations such as miracles needed to be seen to be proven conclusively. It followed, therefore, that while it should certainly not be encouraged, disbelief of the Gospels should not be punished,[45] because it was a justifiable, if lamentable, reaction to the intractable problem of more than a thousand years of adroit priestly fraud. It was Blount's explicit recommendation of the use of reason as the final judge, of course, which was the nub of the furore Blount excited in Anglicans.

Like John Locke (in his *Essay Concerning Human Understanding*, 1690), Blount was advocating that human reason should be employed to judge the written tradition of the past and present Church. This was an implicit threat to traditional hierarchical Churches such as that of Rome, but also to Anglicanism, in which the laity were also given no choice by the Church hierarchy but to unquestioningly accept the Anglican creed. Blount's arguments were implicit, yet boomed out with the force of cannons in the ears of Anglican prelates. His call to reason was correctly perceived as the thin end of the wedge with which to break the Anglican state-Church monopoly over theological enquiry – although it was most unlikely that many intelligent Anglicans would so frame their objections. Far more effective to have Blount condemned as a scurrilous sceptic.

Anglican prelates had – despite the possible misgivings of some – no choice but to accept and utilize some of the written traditions of the Church; for otherwise there would have been little upon which to base Anglican thought and justify its quasi-Catholic hierarchy. In effect, Blount was advocating that Protestants should take the many decades of their exhaustive critique of medieval and contemporary popish fraud and forgery at face value and be most sceptical of the written record and doctrines of the established Christian Church as a whole – including Anglicanism. Protestants should draw the appropriate conclusions from, for example, Crashaw's *Falsificationum romanarum* and numerous subsequent texts with the same concern.

This, as we shall see, was Toland's view in his *Christianity not Mysterious* – written while he was still a Dissenter – for he justified his priestcraft accusation by boldly stating he was continuing the critical polemical and historiographical tradition of Luther, Calvin and Ulrich Zwingli (a leading Swiss reformer). For most Dissenters, frank statements of the corruption of the Catholic written tradition, and the

use of reason as an aid in what was perceived as a maze of falsifications, were welcomed more than frowned upon. Most Dissenters
adhered to a Presbyterian model of Church government. There was,
therefore, no need to defend the legitimacy and prerogatives of an
elite (Anglican) hierarchy from the reasoned thought of Protestants.
Indeed, the frank anti-hierarchical appraisal of Blount formed part of
the very *raison d'être* of the Dissenter project.

Blount and Toland were considered to have overstepped the mark,
yet the fear of going beyond the Protestant pale and effectively aiding
deists and sceptics in their efforts to reveal the gross adulteration of
Christianity's written record never seemed to hinder many ardent
eighteenth-century polemicists, including Anglicans. Such noncha-
lance is evident, for example, in Reverend Bull's uncompromising
Corruptions of the Church of Rome (1714), and much later Priestley's
History of the Corruptions of Christianity (1782).[46] But what were the
dissenting editors of the *History of Popery* (1735) doing? For, as we
have seen, they warned readers Rome had deliberately chosen a
corrupt version of the most vital Christian document, the Bible. Yet
no rocky Anglican avalanche descended upon these Editors. Clearly
they were perceived to be within the pale, on account of overtly
directing their barbs only at Rome (and presumably for implicitly
acknowledging the existence and acceptability of the Protestant
Authorized Version (1611) of the Bible).

For other more radical Christian thinkers – those who had abandoned all affiliations to institutional Christianity – there was no mark
to overstep. Their freedom of action, however, resulted in remarkably
little in terms of their historical analyses. In *A Succint History of
Priesthood* (1737), the exiled Italian and self-confessed freethinker
Alberto Radicati stated: 'We may ... with very good Reason reproach
the *Popish* Priesthood with their using pious frauds ... they have
corrupted and altered the Gospel, that they might the easier impose
their Trumpery on [Christians].'[47] This sort of declamation was of
course hardly original, having been a commonplace for more than a
hundred and fifty years. Similarly, several decades after Radicati's
pronouncement, Edward Gibbon's account of the priestly corruption
of medieval doctrine was also quite unexceptional, as were accounts
by other radical, or so-called deistic writers, including Matthew
Tindal (1657–1733) and Anthony Collins (1676–1729). Gibbon
accepted the 'genuine revelation' of Jesus Christ, which ousted superstitious polytheism and inspired 'the most rational esteem and
conviction'. But subsequently, this rational esteem and conviction

'was adorned with all that could attract the curiosity, the wonder and the veneration of the people'. Later, the Christian priesthood revived pagan polytheism: 'between the reign of [Emperor] Constantine and the Reformation of Luther, the worship of saints and relics corrupted the pure and perfect simplicity of the Christian model'. We may also remember Gibbon proclaimed that Rome was 'an arsenal and manufacture ... of false or genuine, of corrupt or suspicious acts, as they tended to promote the interest of the Roman Church'; and the peddling of its spurious products was aided by the deep 'ignorance and the credulity of the times'.[48]

Gibbon and Radicati were typical of much dissenting Protestant and anti-curial Catholic thought, in which, until Emperor Constantine, the Church was not usually considered to have been completely and irrevocably corrupt, and sometimes not until the fifth or sixth century. Already, in the late seventeenth and early eighteenth century, however, some dissenting Protestants had increasingly begun explicitly to darken the reputation of those earliest centuries of the Church, more nearly condemning them in one with the lost cause of the rest of papal history. The same Dissenters, as we have seen, had long ago broken with the Anglican Church because it had palpably failed to purge itself of priestcraft – exemplified by its retention of a powerful Church hierarchy, the episcopate, and the tyranny it exerted over its just critics. Once both the Anglican and the early Church had – like the medieval and Catholic Church – also been convicted of priestly guile, the road to denying the legitimacy of all traditional hierarchical priesthoods was open. To impatient Dissenters still suffering discrimination, this step represented a natural progression from the venerable Protestant tradition of laying bare the various corruptions of the Christian faith by hierarchies of venal priests. It also represented the final maturation of Puritan historiography.

In what has been considered one of the earliest deist works, *Christianity not Mysterious*, John Toland's starting point was the struggle against 'superstition and idolatry', which was also the dominant theme of his *Letters to Serena* (1704). Toland's point, like those of Protestants before and after him, was to demonstrate how '*Christianity became mysterious,* and how so divine an Institution did, through the Craft and Ambition of the *Priests* and *Philosophers,* degenerate into mere paganism'.[49] The difference between Toland's historiography and that of other less radical Protestants is not, however, revealed in terms of its polemical character or religious tone, but rather in its chronology of priestcraft. Toland, under dissenting (Presbyterian) patronage at the time of writing *Christianity not Mysterious*, wished to point out not only the priestcraft of Catholicism, but above all that of the popish Anglican Church. In order to mount the most effective indictment and demonstrate the profound depth of the Anglican priesthood's malaise, Toland pointed out it was suffering from the same malady to which the hierarchical Christian ministry had been subject since relatively soon after the natural expiration of the apostolic Church. His strategy, in attacking Anglicanism then, was to illustrate how Church doctrine had been corrupted by priestcraft earlier and more profoundly than Protestants had hitherto argued or had been prepared to admit publicly. Toland was hardly alone or first in the application of this strategy, as will be seen in the next chapter.

For Toland and like minds, without the concept of a relatively undefiled and enduring early Church after the demise of the apostolic Church, the claim of Christian hierarchies – whether Anglican or Catholic – of succession from a once pristine hierarchical priesthood was no longer tenable. Rather there was a more or less *de facto* continuum between the frauds of ancient heathen priests and those of traditional Christian hierarchies past and present. The furore of the Anglican Church against Toland was, therefore, not primarily against the historical charge of priestcraft itself, for that was a Protestant given. The real bone of contention was the extension of that accusation to encompass the very early Church, his failure to exempt the Anglican Church from his indictment of religious fraud and – like Blount – his explicit exposition of the necessary role of reason in religious matters. Naturally, for a Dissenter, Toland's arguments for the use of reason were buttressed with frequent biblical references. In *Christianity not Mysterious* the message was simple, if implicit: if collective Christian worship was to be rescued and to remain viable, hierarchical ministries had to be replaced by collectives based on the Presbyterian, that is to say, apostolic model.

7 The Birthpangs of 'Deist' Historiography

In late seventeenth-century England, Presbyterian ideals of Church government were diffuse amongst the several Nonconformist tendencies resulting from the splintering of Puritanism in the Civil War and Interregnum period. The breakup of Puritanism has been understood as a diminution in the influence of their religious ideas. This was the case to some extent, but it was not so with their opposition to traditional hierarchical forms of Church government. As anti-Catholicism was the one feature uniting most Protestants, so the Presbyterian ideal of a simple non-hierarchical Christian ministry served to unite the very numerous and varied army of Dissenters. The influence of Presbyterian thought upon conceptions of Church history in the post-Restoration period has thus been considerably underestimated. Presbyterian ideals provided a powerful theological paradigm from within which to launch devastating attacks on all established Church hierarchies. Another reason for the endurance of the Presbyterian ideal was its ability to express political opposition – in good part class-orientated – to the perceived oppressive state-Church *status quo*.

For most Dissenters, the corruption of right religion was embodied – and so presupposed – in the very concept of an established hierarchical sacerdotal caste. As regards their critiques of Church history, however, the dividing line between Dissenters and so-called deists can seem unclear, and has resulted in some confusion. This is especially so because historians still encounter significant difficulties in their attempts to define deism. Samuel Clarke, in *A Discourse Concerning the Unchangeable Obligations of Natural Religion* (1706), early signalled this problem by providing his readers with a typology of four types of deism or natural religion. David Pailin, in 'The confused and confusing story of natural religion' (1994), notes that in the seventeenth and eighteenth century there were eleven varieties or gradations of what has been termed natural religion, some of which have 'significant sub-divisions'. Consequently, he warns, to ask if a writer was a deist is not a precise or even a fruitful question.[1]

Uncritical acceptance of the term deist, or attempts to construct a simple user-friendly definition of it, have served only to compound past errors and obscure the very real difficulty of definition. Similar confusion has also been apparent in the work of modern Italian scholars. Pietro Giannone has at times been deemed a deist, principally on the evidence of his *Triregno*. Giannone finished his *Triregno* in 1733, yet he went on to write a history of Church in the pontificate of Pope Gregory I *(La Chiesa sotto il pontificato di Gregorio il Grande)*, which he finished in 1742. Therein, Giannone praises Gregory's initiative of Augustine's mission to England and refers to Pope Gregory as learned and pious. For Giannone, Gregory's thought was free of the pernicious errors and heresies that were later to infest the Church. Is this really the historical thought of a deist who thought all Christian ministries innately corrupt? If one still wishes to classify Giannone as a deist, it seems the application of the term has been so broad as to render it hopelessly imprecise and misleading.

There is no reason to suppose a term coined as a religious insult should possess precise significance and, as Pailin notes, the term radical today represents a similar case: its meaning depends on the person who is using it. For Pailin, the term deist 'typically connotes those whom the user considers to be too restricted in what they believe as a result of their understanding of the demands of reason, rather than the adherents of a specifiable set of doctrines'.[2] The term 'religion of nature', often understood as signifying an otherwise unknowable God whose existence was proven by the Creation, therefore, does not necessarily correspond to the views of all those accused of deism. It was not uncommon for so-called deists – such as Blount and Toland – to declare a sincere belief in the revelation of God in the form of Jesus Christ. This is to go beyond rational proof of God's existence by the act of Creation and by observation of nature itself, even if such men were considered by Anglicans as still so woefully restricted in their beliefs by the demands of reason as to be antichristian.

Hence, in practice, if it is possible to use the term deist in any meaningful sense at all in this present discussion, it is perhaps only in the most narrow sense: a rejection of the history of the Christian ministry as but one example of the corrupting influence of all priesthoods. This may well be a working definition only of significant utility within the parameters of this book – the task of delineating the Enlightenment view of Christian history and its origins. Unfortunately, in some accounts of Church history, the distinction between those who rejected the very concept of the Christian ministry *in toto*, and those dissenting Christians instead wishing for a dismemberment of traditional Church hierarchies and the formation of a simple apostolic-style Church government, can seem less than obvious.

It is now generally accepted that late seventeenth- and early eighteenth-century English deist historiography and polemic influenced the radical anticlerical outlook of some protagonists of the French Enlightenment – the intellectual engine of High Enlightenment Europe. It is, therefore, important to understand the origins of English deism. Within the last decade or so, there have been attempts to explain the origins of the English Enlightenment as a product of the intense scrutiny of the political and social power of the Anglican Church by writers such as Charles Blount and John Toland.[3] This is certainly an advance, for, as Dale Van Kley noted in 1987, '[t]he notion that a movement so secular as the French Enlightenment might have had other than purely secular origins would have until recently raised scholarly eyebrows'. More traditionally, it has also been considered a commonplace that the Reformation established the conditions that led to the secularization of society and consequently to the growth of secular (deistic) views of religion.[4]

It is true that Protestant and anti-curial Catholic historical accounts – under the weighty hammer of religious polemic – became in practice increasingly reliant on secondary, that is to say secular, human causality. But at the same time Protestants (and to some extent orthodox Catholics) developed vague metaphysical historical analyses via the use of biblical prophecy. Similarly, are we also to say the bloody sixteenth- and seventeenth-century European witch-crazes in pursuit of the devil, or indeed the belief in the imminence of the Millennium, were congruent with a general process of secularization? Clearly, this overly simplistic commonplace on the secularizing role of the Reformation is one to be rejected, as it manifestly fails to capture the complexity of the period. We may remember this complexity was exemplified in the thought of Isaac Newton, in which, far from a conflict between providentialism and science, there was an unprecedented harmony between scientific advance and metaphysical enquiry.

In accounts concerning the origin of deist historiography, one source of anticlerical influence acting upon writers such as Charles Blount and John Toland has been identified as clandestine irreligious texts, such as the enigmatic *Tribus Impostoribus* (namely Jesus, Moses and Muhammad).[5] There is, however, little proof of such influence; and the claim that Herbert of Cherbury is the father of deism is similarly without evidence. Such claims are perhaps best understood as the desire of some historians to chart a reassuring progress towards the modernity of the Enlightenment. We know Cherbury believed in both providence and acts of divine revelation. Furthermore, as Pailin has noted: 'Apart from Charles Blount the so-called deists hardly mention Herbert'.[6] It can also be confidently said that most of the late seventeenth-century thinkers discussed in this chapter would have been horrified at the prospect of equating Jesus with Muhammad and Moses, and condemning all three as religious impostors.

So dominant has been this argument for secular, external influence, that writers such as Peter Gay – who did at least note some Enlightenment links with Liberal Anglicanism – nevertheless failed to explore or forge any links between deist and Christian historiography. Once sceptical thought has been identified as at least a partial catalyst for intellectual change leading to the Enlightenment, one is naturally obliged to search for its source, its possible antecedents. Thus the sources of the Enlightenment have been 'sought in those thinkers of prior generations who most resembled *philosophes, Aufklärers* and the "modern" minds of the mid- to late eighteenth century'. The end point of this regression has been Classical Antiquity or, more often, that great author, the Renaissance. But merely pointing to the historical existence of sceptics and sceptical systems of thought does not establish influence. The problem of locating the influence of Christian historical schemes within deist thought is also compounded by the deists' own failure to acknowledge Christian influences. Such a lack of attribution was common:

> Because Enlightenment authors themselves sought to contra-distinguish their epoch categorically from the 'orthodox' past, acknowledging as a source of their ideas only, for the most part, what was new in the seventeenth century, scholars often have begun with a similar assumption about influence. What was not part of the 'new philosophy' of the seventeenth century was somehow ... without 'positive' influence.[7]

There is, however, some indication available of the positive influence of Christian historiography and anti-Catholic polemic. It has already been seen that the Convocation of Canterbury thought the 'Frauds of *Pagan* and *Popish Priests* have been display'd, in order to ... draw Infamy upon the *Priesthood* in general'.[8] They were, of course, correct in their assessment. We also know the anti-Catholic *Mystére d'iniquité* written by the Huguenot Philippe du Plessis-Mornay was chosen as anti-Church propaganda by French Jacobins; and the anti-Catholic polemic of Pierre Bayle was misunderstood. On Bayle Elizabeth Labrousse writes,

> in Paris, these attacks were perpetually understood as if they had been directed against Christianity itself, for indeed, Roman Catholicism was practically the only form of Christianity with which Frenchmen were familiar. In other words, what had been written as anti-Catholic controversy was read as anti-Christian polemics ... Bayle's scepticism was deemed to have been the source of his horror for superstition; no one stopped to consider that in the son of a Calvinist pastor and in a persecuted Huguenot, the feeling of horror for fanaticism and superstition very well could spring from religious motives.[9]

This brings us once again to the problem of distinguishing between radical Protestant and deist historical writings in England. This discussion, we must remind ourselves, is crucial if we wish to understand under what circumstances Christian religious and historiographical traditions were able to form the basis for Enlightenment anticlerical thought, unarguably one of the most characteristic traits of the Enlightenment. Robert Howard's *History of Religion* (1694) provides an instructive example with which to commence. In this work Howard (1626–98), ex-Royalist, Privy Councillor and Whig MP, illustrates how the Church was corrupted almost from the beginning by priestcraft. But, as other Protestants, he emphasizes how the state adoption of Christianity by Emperor Constantine was a turning point: 'Yet they [Roman Christians] were no sooner freed from those Miseries [of state oppression], but they practis'd upon others all the Mischiefs and Crimes which themselves had suffer'd, and had inveigh'd against.' This was a weighty, if implicit, parallel with the contemporary Anglican state–Church treatment of Dissenters, and must have struck a very loud chord in his audience. After discussing the craft of Roman pagan priests, Howard confirms he has endeavoured to show how these pagan practices and powers were retained and even exceeded by the Church of Rome. He contends that popes took their 'Pattern from the Heathen Priests':

> This same Method of Priest-Craft is continu'd in the Church of *Rome*: the Romish Saints and Angels answer to the Demons and Heroes, Deify'd by the Heathen Priests; and their Idol of Bread, Divinity infus'd into crosses Images, *Agnus Dei's* and Relicks, correspond to the Pillars, Statues and Images consecrated by Pagan Priests.[10]

It has been argued that Howard's work is deist in orientation and that he projects the priestcraft charge against all priesthoods;[11] but what is meant by 'priesthoods'? If the term is used to denote clerical hierarchies typified by the Anglican or Catholic clergy, its usage in relation to Howard's analysis is correct. But this is not the same as abandoning the concept of the Christian ministry. As we know, prevalent amongst Dissenters was a very different concept of the Christian ministry, and Howard was a Dissenter.

For those historians not familiar with the nature of Protestant allegations of priestly fraud, it is all too easy to underestimate the polemical power of an historical critique that assumes the truth of those allegations. When encountering a strident example of such accusations in the work of a Protestant like Howard, it is possible to assume it to be, on account of its virility and comparative form, a deistic work. Howard, like many thousands of other Protestants, was enraged at the evident popish chicanery of the Anglican Church and wished implicitly to jibe at Anglicanism. Howard argued the Christian Church could be considered the heir to the priests of pagan Roman, and even 'among the most Reform'd Christians ... Methods of Priestcraft' were pursued. He was, however, apologetic on behalf of the Church fathers, and left readers in no doubt as to his Protestantism. He also wrote, in typical Protestant fashion, that the Church of Christ was to be found in believers, and cited the Latitudinarian Archbishop of Canterbury John Tillotson (1630–94) as the model of a 'plain and certain way to Salvation'. None of these points suffice to indicate that Howard was a sceptic or a deist. On the contrary, there is manifest proof in his work that he was an anti-Trinitarian Dissenter, a Unitarian.[12] Hence Howard wrote his *History of Religion* anonymously, for anti-Trinitarian thought had not been included in the 1689 Toleration Act and was still proscribed. John Toland published his *Christianity not Mysterious* in 1696, two years after Howard's *History of Religion*; and he was then still a Dissenter.

For sceptics, Howard's analysis could be construed as a wonderful free gift. For many Anglican prelates it could be understood as antichristian sectarian ravings; or proof of sceptical thought (as it has been for some modern historians truffle-hunting for deists). High Churchmen and other staunch Anglicans were, of course, solicitous to misconstrue and misrepresent the work of Howard, Toland's *Christianity not Mysterious* and others as calls to deism. In their attempt to stem the reaches of the dissenting tide, how better to discredit Dissent than bracket it with the vague catch-all, but ultimately anti-Church, label of deism? By so doing, the Anglican Church could credibly be seen to act as a defender of the faith and so perhaps bolster its position amongst its flock. To tar all opponents with the same brush was not an unusual tactic for an established Church facing competition, for we know that Abbot Bencini used the same tactic in Italy. For some twentieth-century historians – rather too concerned to head-hunt for modernity – the conflation of Dissenters and more radical thinkers has at times meant the search for what might be termed 'modern attitudes' became a little easier; simply because the hunters were able to identify more heads to pursue. Only in anti-Catholic and overtly pro-Protestant accounts of priestcraft, such as Henry Care's periodical *A Pacquet of Advice from Rome* (1678–83), was there no possibility of such 'confusion'.

So the problem of audience – the conceptual and material circumstances and indeed motives of a readership – has rarely been of such pivotal importance as it was in the last decade of the seventeenth and first decades of the eighteenth century. But we must not exaggerate the problem in numerical terms. Howard's considerable dissenting audience would have understood his ecclesiological position without difficulty – if not from elsewhere in his book, then from his deliberately unguarded anti-Trinitarian comments.[13]

In the opinion of Howard, and in those of most late seventeenth-century and early eighteenth-century Dissenters, the established hierarchical priesthood had begun to decay very early on and had been confirmed in its decadence by Emperor Constantine. This did not mean the ministry of the apostolic period and that of very shortly after was also condemned in the same breath. Since the Reformation most dissenting Protestants had constantly aspired to the principles and practice of the apostolic Church – that simple congregation of equals with little or no formal hierarchy – for a renewal of Christianity. Indeed, we know Protestants had long gone to great lengths to manufacture spurious apostolic origins for their imputed forebears, the revered Waldenses. Howard and other Dissenters could sometimes also seem to have their cake and eat it. They might give faint praise to some progressive elements of the Church, as with Howard's compliment to Archbishop Tillotson, yet otherwise mercilessly damn the established European priesthood in general.

In *Priestcraft distinguished from Christianity* (1715) written by the critic, playwright and polemicist John Dennis (1675–1734), there is also the possibility of 'misapprehension'. His lengthy pious arguments and language register are clearly those of a dissenting Protestant and go far beyond any dissimulation or platitudinous comments necessary to placate or mislead a censor. He believes Satan has inflamed the heart of humanity with 'self-love' and destroyed 'the Empire which Heaven had set up in his soul, which was an empire of Reason and Law'. Thus some Christian 'Teachers' do 'contaminate the Doctrine of Christ by their own Inventions, and the Doctrines of Devils'. These antichristians have 'opposed [themselves] to the Lord's Anointed, i.e. to Christ'. Dennis states his attack is not upon the 'Pious, Learned and Numerous body, who are truly Christian Priests of the Church of England'. But this censor-orientated encomium is accompanied by an overview in some respects more radical than Howard's. Dennis describes how there was more 'virtue' in the times of ancient paganism than since the coming of the Saviour, excepting the first and primitive times of Christianity, 'when the Supreme Magistrate was not as yet Christian [i.e. pre-Emperor Constantine], and the Christian Priests were yet undebauch'd by worldly Power and Greatness'.[14]

Just as Puritans had earlier demonstrated their Calvinist, Presbyterian credentials by publicly appearing the most consistent and implacable opposition to Rome and Anglicanism, so now did Howard, Dennis and others demonstrate their hostility to the traditional hierarchical Christian ministry in general. Times and circumstances had changed; it was only to be expected that the historiographical strategy of dissenting Protestants would reflect those changes.

In *The Natural History of Superstition* (1709), written by the Whig MP John Trenchard (1662–1723), is as radical an indictment of the Christian ministry as one is likely to find. The title alone has led some historians to consider it an undoubtedly deist work. This is not the case, for Trenchard's defence of revelation and providence, his condemnation of papists, and other comments inform us he was of the dissenting type. He relates how the frauds of priests, visions of enthusiasts, impostures of pretended prophets, forgeries of papists, and the follies of 'some who call themselves Protestants ... have so far prevailed over genuine Christianity.'[15] It has also been noted he was certainly not a deist. He was so labelled by his opponents on account of his 'unsparing attacks' on the 'high-church party'.[16] Given the dissenting orientation of the works of Trenchard, Dennis and Howard, it is difficult to accept that their intention 'was to fragment the narrow Christocentric view of the past'.[17] On the contrary, these men wished to cleanse the Christian priesthood by a return to an original Christocentric and apostolic form of Church government embodied in the Presbyterian model. But what of the epithet 'anticlerical', much used in relation to these and other supposed deist writers? It has been suggested that 'anticlerical' writers such as Blount, Howard and others drew substantially on the anticlerical thought of earlier writers such as Cherbury.

It has already been seen that Cherbury's analysis of the craft of ancient priests and its implicit analogy to the perceived nature of the medieval, Catholic and Anglican Church was hardly original. His account would not have seemed out of place to a Puritan wishing to point out the profound corruption of the traditional Christian ministry, as indeed Ainsworth had done in the first years of the seventeenth century. Cherbury's lack of historiographical originality (aside from his bold, rationalizing five principles for Christian unity) also helps to explain why Cherbury's work failed to become a general model for late seventeenth-century Dissenters. Thus, even if Cherbury's influence on Toland could be proven, it would be to say little or nothing of any worth. It would be no more than to observe the fact that, as we have seen, comparative anticlerical polemic was a pervasive feature of Protestant (and Catholic) thought.[18]

In the politico-ecclesiastical tension of 1680s and 1690s England, some Dissenters, caught in a vice between Catholicism and Anglicanism, were prepared to state the maximum case for the historical corruption of the established Christian ministry. The traditional pre-Constantinian point of demarcation for a not entirely corrupt and sometimes salvageable Christian hierarchy was abandoned by some, and all but abandoned by others as antichristian. Little or nothing was thus left of the hierarchical priesthood's historical legitimacy. This was perhaps not such a large step as some historians have imagined, for, we may remember, in 1606 even the High Church Richard Field admitted there were 'superstitions and abuses' in the primitive Church, but that this 'defection' (such as tomb worship) was then still opposed.[19] Other Protestants naturally went further, as did of course Ainsworth and Cherbury, who implicitly included all the established Churches in their scathing analysis. Cherbury's clear Protestant – that is to say dissenting – rationalism caused him to rationalize away the need for hierarchical ministries with his five principles for Christian unity. In 1675, the Dissenter William Allen published his *Mystery of Iniquity unfolded, Or The False Apostles and the Authors of Popery compared.* Allen argued that, in order to avoid persecution, the 'false apostles' of the primitive (i.e. Pre-Constantinian) Church diluted Christianity with pagan belief to make it less antagonistic to the pagans. This led to an outward religion, which inevitably gave way to the self-indulging ordinances of a powerful church hierarchy and the iniquities of Catholicism and also (stated the unwritten coda) to those of Anglicanism.

In the 1690s, boldly stating the maximum case in print provided a provocative and attention-grabbing analysis designed to unequivocally manifest the need for a root-and-branch reform of the Christian ministry. Presbyterianism had, as a coherent challenge to Anglicanism, finally been defeated in and shortly after 1660. Nonetheless, its propagandists were still very much alive and embittered. The double irony, then, is this: only in defeat did Presbyterian-minded propagandists bring Puritan historiography to maturity; but the end product was the illegitimate birth of the Enlightenment view of Church history. Illegitimate because, although sceptics and Dissenters came to share the same historical analysis, they did so with diametrically opposed intentions.

Peter Gay has stressed that 'Liberal Anglicanism' and deist thought 'were connected by a thousand threads'. But he did not draw in those threads to link Protestant historiography with deist historical conceptions. One might ask why should he? After all, deism was more than an historical view of the Church. But this rather facile truism only begs the question of how central deist historiography was to the development of deist thought and to the Enlightenment. For those deists who believed that, after the Creation or alternatively after the revelation of Jesus, God had not intervened and would not in the future intervene in human affairs, institutional religion – even of the Presbyterian type – was not necessary. Rather it was a tangible menace to the development of a rational, progressive civilization. If institutional Christianity could be shown to have been divinely guided, the archetypal deist project would prove to be mistaken. It was essential to the deist project, then, to demonstrate the historical fallacy of all ministries of religion.

For Gay, rational Anglicanism and deists 'saw the universe as rational ... both despised enthusiasm and mysticism, both were critical of the written tradition ... Yet they were separated by a chasm as impassable as it was narrow'.[20] If liberal Anglicanism is taken to be Latitudinarianism (a trend in seventeenth-century Anglican thought which attached relatively little importance to matters of dogmatic proof and liturgical practice), then Gay's assessment is unsustainable. Yes, they were divided by a chasm, but far from a narrow one: even Latitudinarian Anglicans viewed the Anglican Church as legitimate.

In recent reassessments of the role of Unitarian polemic in the

1690s, some writers have concluded the Unitarian (Socinian) polemic of the 1690s was a more significant, indeed crucial, factor than formerly realized in the development of the Enlightenment notion of religion. It has been proposed that, on to the comparative and hyper-critical study of religion, men like Toland 'grafted the classical idea of civil religion'. In addition, the origin of the polemical use of Islamic religion is to be found in the Unitarian attack on the Anglican Church–state relationship in the 1690s.[21] We already know, however, that the polemical use of other religions, including Islam, by Anglicans, Catholics, Protestant Dissenters and anti-curial Catholics against their respective religious opponents dates from the sixteenth rather than the late seventeenth century. One need only call to mind the Catholic Bozio*'s De signis ecclesiae*, or the Anglican Sutcliffe's *De turcopapismo*.

The writings of John Dennis and John Trenchard demonstrate that one did not need to be a Unitarian to write radical accounts of Christianity capable, without careful consideration, of being mistaken for deistic works. Similarly, John Toland, at the time of writing *Christianity not Mysterious*, was not a Unitarian but rather a Presbyterian, writing under the patronage of London Presbyterians from 1690 to 1696.[22] As for grafting classical civil religion on to the comparative critique of religion, this assumes what needs to be demonstrated in the writings of Trenchard, Dennis, Howard and, in the *Christianity not Mysterious*, of Toland: a deist historiography that rejected the Christian ministry in all its possible forms. The critique of these writers represented a clarion call for a purge and renewal of the Christian ministry rather than an archetypal deist blast equating the very concept of the Christian ministry with priestcraft. We know Toland would go on to dismiss the concept of or cease to believe in the reformability of the Christian ministry, as did other radicals such as Matthew Tindal and Anthony Collins; but in 1696 those developments were yet to take place.

For Unitarians, Trinitarianism was a priestly corruption that had triumphed within the Church at the Council of Nicea (325), summoned by Emperor Constantine. Unsurprisingly, then, the Unitarian Howard, like many Trinitarians, also stressed the reign of Emperor Constantine in the further decline of the priesthood. This was a chronology of corruption very similar to that of Isaac Newton. Newton, although having been raised with a Puritanical stamp, was outwardly a conforming and pious churchman but, from about 1674, he had been a secret Unitarian. In his vehemence against the

medieval Church and the corruption of Christianity, he was at one
with Howard. Newton, who spent a great deal of time analysing biblical prophecy, wrote in his *Observations upon the Prophecies of Daniel
and the Apocalypse of St. John* (1733) that it had been foretold there
would 'be a falling away among the Christians, soon after the days of
the Apostles'.[23] 'Soon' is never properly defined, although, from his
exegetical chronology, it is clear that the fourth century, the century
of Constantine, marked another significant moment in his chronology
of corruption. Unitarian historiography was, therefore, only a most
recognizable version – congruent in all its fundamentals – of the traditional Puritan/Dissenter priestcraft theory, applied both to Rome
and to Anglican Trinitarian popery.

We have traced the origin of Enlightenment anticlerical historiography. It is now necessary to discuss the factors in the final defection
of Dissenters such as Toland to deism. To shed some light on this
process it would be useful to examine some kind of parallel, and there
is one available in the socio-religious turmoil of the Civil War and
Protectorate period (1642–60). There is abundant evidence in
Christopher Hill's *The World Turned Upside Down* (1972) and other
studies that, during this period, there existed popular and politically
radical deistic and pantheistic tendencies. Many of the participants of
these sects laid great stress on the use of reason in religion, and forcefully advanced the criticism that the Bible only represented human,
that is to say fallible, tradition. In the religious upheaval and social
freedom of that period, many Protestants were alienated from religion by contending claims for religious truth amongst numerous
religious sects. Some were also repelled by the moral and religious
rigour of the Puritan 'godly elect' and the putative popery of
Laudianism (High Churchism). Sects such as the Seekers and early
Quakers rejected institutional religion. Others were further disaffected, and not only rejected institutional religion but also espoused
an inchoate pantheism.

The competition between Protestant factions and with the
Anglican Church did not end with the Restoration. After 1660 the
possibility of religious alienation or exhaustion remained inherent in
the competition and conflict between, for example, Baptists, Quakers,
Presbyterians and Anglicans. The hope for a reformation or dissolution of Anglicanism could also seem very, very distant, if not
impossible, when confronted with the spectacle of renewed Anglican
Church and state persecution of Dissent. Persecution was often need-
lessly bloody and cruel, as in Scotland; and we should remember that

before 1689 over four hundred Quakers are known to have died in prison. With the apostasy of James II, a Catholic when he acceded to the throne in 1685, his blatant favouring of Catholics, and the still limited toleration remaining after the great hopes placed in the Protestant succession of William and Mary in 1689, it was impossible that some Dissenters should not be at least troubled by the reality of religious life. One possibility was that former acolytes would become disheartened. Some others would certainly feel increasingly enraged at the impotence of Dissent in relation to persecution, the failure of 1689 to herald real religious change, and the manifest popery of Anglicanism. For the latter type, it was clear that new tactics in the attack on Anglicanism were necessary.

By 1690 supporters of the Presbyterian cause had been struggling against Church and state for a hundred years. This was a fact very much alive in the minds of all active Presbyterians who – as we have seen – never overlooked history in their struggles with each other or with Church and state. It was time for sharp polemics indeed. It was necessary to state uncompromisingly the historical failure of hier-archical Churches.

The debate as to how practically free or comparatively repressive was the English state-Church regime in the 1680s and 1690s I shall pass over with but one comment. The debate itself is somewhat of a red herring, for the crux of the matter is the perception of the period by the participants themselves. From their copious writings, we know very many certainly considered religious tyranny to exist still, and that very pressing religious matters needed resolution. John Locke (1632–1704), in his *Letter Concerning Toleration* (1689), wrote that kings and queens of post-Reformation England had been 'of such different minds in points of religion, and enjoined thereupon such different things', that no 'sincere and upright worshipper of God could, with a safe conscience, obey their several decrees'.[24] Bennett has also commented that, after 1688, 'it was clear even to the most detached observer that ... [the] clergy and laity were involved in a radical reappraisal of the whole role of the national Church in English society'.[25]

An important factor in the practical reality of that reappraisal was much greater press freedom after 1694, when England's became one of the freest presses in Europe. As we have seen with the publication of Toland's *Christianity not Mysterious*, however, the reaction of Church and state could at times still be a cause for caution. Nevertheless, the relative press freedom enabled Dissenters to wage a more public campaign against the established Church. Although greater press freedom was to be welcomed, it did not signify to Dissenters a relaxation of intolerance, rather the chance to publicly air grievances. We know the *de facto* press freedom of the Civil War period served to heighten doubts over the legitimacy of the Christian ministry in general. The spectacle of a variety of sects large and small each publicly claiming to represent true Christianity or at least the Word of God did little to enhance the concept of the Christian ministry.

The political and religious turmoil of the 1690s was not on the same scale as that of the 1640s. The political and social disruption was insufficient to generate radical and footloose popular movements as there had been in the Civil War period. Nevertheless, the strife and bitterness was such that it still provided the essential ingredients for a degree of religious alienation. The religious response of the 1690s and the first years of the next century was thus narrower in terms of social class, less politically radical (one searches in vain for Diggers) and dominated by well-educated men. As a result, the polemical expression of political and religious dissatisfaction was less diverse. Yet it was expressed in a polemic theoretically and historiographically much more well-founded, and of an intellectual depth also appealing to frustrated scholarly minds. Engaging such scholars, the response was, therefore, potentially most damaging to the legitimacy of the established Church as much amongst the well-off as amongst the large number of relatively poor but attentive and educated Anglicans.

For some, the scandal of renewed religious turmoil was the cause of disaffection from Christianity towards deism. Even Whigs, in defiance of the progress-saturated historiography they bequeathed to posterity, were still able to note what was, in essence, a dialectical turn in history. As has already been seen (and its relevance justifies repetition), in 1696 William Stephens wrote: '[having seen] that *Popery* in all its Branches was only a device of the *Priesthood*, to carry on a particular Interest of their own', some gentlemen, 'could not forebear to see that these *Protestant* parties [Anglicans and Dissenters], under the pretence of Religion, were only grasping at *Power*'. As a consequence, some gentlemen refused to countenance both parties.

In the work of a writer identified only as D. E., there is a very similar analysis. D. E.'s work, *The Prodigious Appearance of Deism in this Age Modestly Accounted for in a Letter from a Deist to his Friend* (1710), stresses that the divided nature of British Protestantism is incompatible with Christian truth. He laments how each sect justifies its own case by the perversion of scripture and 'tricks and subterfuges'. He condemns their self-interest and the prostitution of religion in order 'to palliate the most enormous pretences'. The 'inveterate Spite and Malice' of religious disputes of the various tendencies, 'openly blazed and published', are to him proof that all Protestant parties are guilty of bringing Christianity into disrepute.[26] At the end of the eighteenth century, the same explanation for the rise of deism is encountered in John Coward's *Deism Traced to one of its Principal Sources* (1796). It seems the lessons of the late seventeenth century, in terms of the self-destructive behaviour of Protestant tendencies, were not lost until at least after the first years of this present century. Thus, the Rev. Arthur Powell, in *The Sources of Eighteenth-Century Deism* (1902) catalogues the 'catena' of events that led to deism. He notes the

> reforms and repressions and upheavals, with revolution and dynastic change, with Acts of Parliament authorising and reauthorising and anon abrogating certain religious official books and duties, with ceaseless developments, political, moral and religious.

By 1662, he states, there was not one religious body in England, but six (Anglicans, Catholics, Presbyterians, Independents, Baptists and Quakers); and Catholic King James II went on to render England even more bitter with religious feuds.[27]

John Toland, the son of a Catholic priest, converted to Protestantism at the age of sixteen and in 1688–9 went to Scotland to study. There he witnessed the 'Bloody Persecution of the Church of Scotland, and must have been an eyewitness of many tyrannical and relentless scenes'.[28] Following his relocation to London, espousing the Presbyterian cause, he could not see why 'men who were sound Protestants on both sides, should barbarously cut one another's throats'.[29] Nevertheless, like most Dissenting Protestants, he was not about to offer toleration to all and sundry – not to atheists, deists, and above all not to Catholics. In his anti-Catholicism, Toland was in very good liberal company. As a typical reforming Protestant, John Locke (who championed toleration as a natural right) also excluded Catholics from his pleas for toleration, as did a whole range of eminent men from poets to bishops. In politics, Catholicism was inseparable from the threat of Catholic absolutism, the sort it had been feared James II wanted to introduce and which was then perceived to exist in the France of Louis XIV. Catholicism could only be tolerated in private. Toland's anti-Catholic views, like those of most other Protestants, were based upon a mixture of religious conviction and a widely shared understanding of the – real or received – Catholic threat to life and liberty. Catholic rulers were either subject to the priestcraft of the Catholic Church or, as in France, were perceived to be in cahoots with popery. This politico-religious stance was also promoted for nationalistic ends, something hardly surprising given that King Louis declared war on England in 1689, a war which endured until 1697. This was the bleak and often fearful outlook which enabled Protestants to detect no contradiction between the suppression of Catholicism on the one hand, and earnest pleas for religious toleration on the other. Naturally, this ostensible contradiction can seem inexplicably backward to modern minds if its political rationale is not appreciated.

Toland was a Whig and therefore in favour of a limited monarchy, that is to say a monarch whose actions were limited by parliament. Yet Toland has been described by some historians as a radical republican. For much of his active intellectual career, however, he was patently not a republican in the usual twentieth-century sense of the word, which pits monarchism diametrically against republicanism. In 1697, one year after the publication of his *Christianity not Mysterious*, Toland broke publicly with the cause of Dissent. That that shift did not indicate a political shift towards republicanism in the modern sense of the word is evident. It is difficult to see how a radical republican could write a such a work as *The Memorial of the State of England, in Vindication of the Queen, the Church, and the Administration* (1705).[30] If Toland became a radical republican in the modern sense, it seems it was after 1705. As Herbert Butterfield has noted, the search for 'progress' in history can lead one to identify movements and individuals as 'much more modern than they really were', and 'divert our attention from what is the real historical process'.[31] This is exactly the case with Toland.

Throughout his life Toland was concerned to promote and ensure the Protestant succession in England as a counter to the threat of a benighted European Catholic hegemony. The heart of Whig history, at that time synonymous with the general Protestant scheme, depicted Europe's fall from the glory of Rome to the superstition and tyranny of the medieval Catholic Church.[32] The Reformation had partly broken the Church's stranglehold on European culture and political life. But Catholicism was not yet fully defeated, and had to some extent revived in the Counter-Reformation. Thus, for most

Protestants, the future for religious toleration and political freedom in Europe was manifestly not yet assured. Despite Dissenter hostility to the Anglican Church and its relationship with the state, the principle of advocating a Protestant succession – free Christian Europe against antichristian tyranny, light against darkness – was a principle then almost inviolable.

Six years after his break with Dissent, Toland leaves his readers in no doubt as to his Protestant, anti-Catholic orientation. In his *Vindicius liberius* (1702), he can still reply to accusations of heterodoxy by stating he considers himself a member of the *'establisht Religion'*; and, although it is not perfect, it is the best Religion in the world. He does not adhere to any particular 'society', but has joined with all Protestants against the superstition, idolatry and tyranny of 'Popery'. He is a *'true Christian'* and as such cites his 'conformity to the public Worship', which proves him a *'good Church man'*.[33] Toland, no longer tied to the Presbyterian cause, can of course now pay lip service to the *'establisht Religion'* while earnestly advancing the Protestant (and Whig) political cause.

Most Protestants and especially Whig Dissenters heaved a sigh of political and religious relief at the Protestant succession of William and Mary in 1688–9. Yet some High Church Anglicans – who became the Nonjurors – still felt bound to honour publicly their allegiance to James II. This was hardly a stance calculated to endear Anglicanism to Dissenters. For most, however, gone was apostate King James II and the immediate threat to Protestant liberty. As a consequence, Protestants hoped to be able to forget the various post-Restoration acts that had continued to enshrine religious discrimination and persecution. In the event, Dissenters such as Toland were very soon to be considerably disappointed. After the Toleration Act (1689) the Anglican Church still remained officially dominant and Dissenting worship remained significantly restricted. Perhaps the most anachronistic factor to survive the settlement, one reeking of Church–state collusion, was the continued obligation to pay the tithe for the upkeep of the Anglican Clergy. It was clear to Dissenters that the Anglican Church was content to retain much of its privileged position and would continue to defend its relationship with the state. This was no empty fear, for the Occasional Conformity Act of 1711 (repealed 1719) restrained Dissenters from qualifying for government posts by receiving the Sacrament in the Anglican Church.

The Anglican Church had survived the vicissitudes of the Civil War, the execution of its head (Charles I), the Protectorate years, the

Restoration, and then the nefarious behaviour of King James. Anglican prelates were certainly not now about to wave the white flag of surrender or peace. Church reform increasingly seemed but a utopian project. Clearly the defence of Protestant liberty against Catholic despotism had to be retained, yet this was no reason not to spell out the seemingly intractable problem of Anglican priestcraft. Dissenting propagandists did not shy away from their self-appointed task, least of all John Toland. His *Christianity not Mysterious*, there-fore, is reforming in character.[34] Yet it is as unmitigating in its hostility to the history of the Christian hierarchy as – aside from his discussion of reason in religion – it is unoriginal in its historical critique and anti-Catholic point of departure. In his preface, Toland wrote that he was raised in the 'grossest superstition and idolatry'. Contrary to the often repeated claim (or sometimes assumption) that *Christianity not Mysterious* categorically rejected revelation, Toland also explained how the instructions of Jesus Christ were clear and convincing. He contrasted Jesus' simple clarity with the intricate and ineffectual declamations of the scribes. His aim was to show how '*Christianity became mysterious*, and how so divine an Institution did, through the Craft and Ambition of the *Priests* and *Philosophers,* degenerate into mere paganism'. It was the '*Contradictions* and *Mysteries*' charged to Christianity which caused so many Christians to become deists and Atheists. Then, wishing to emphatically underline his reformist stance, he observed that he was only doing that which the Reformation had set out to achieve, namely laying bare priestcraft.[35]

Yet, as in the works of Trenchard, Dennis and Howard, in Toland's work there is little or no analysis specifically targeted at the papacy and the medieval Church. This should be no surprise, but has been one of the factors that has led some historians to consider *Christianity not Mysterious* a work of deist inspiration, that is to say attacking the very concept of the Christian ministry. Dissenters felt no need to reiterate the common-or-garden critique of the medieval or contemporary Catholic Church. It was one of the few facets of English Protestant thought which were not accompanied by widespread and damaging dissent. Catholic priestcraft was an uncontentious subject, a given, something safely relegated to the conceptual anti-Catholic evidence supplied by the Protestant readership. When polemicists had other, more pressing exigencies, why devote valuable space to an argument that had already, long ago, achieved hegemony. Indeed, this 'omission' was not a novelty of the 1690s. In Cherbury's *De religione gentilium*, and in Charles Blount's *First Two Books of Philostratus*, there is, for the same reason, little or no specific targeting of their analysis at the medieval Church. When the frauds of pagan priests were described, the comparison with the medieval Church and Catholicism was understood.

More pertinent for this discussion, is that dissenting writers often failed to exempt the Anglican Church from the devastation of their priestcraft allegations, or gave only a polite nod to the difference between Catholicism and Anglicanism. The less the explicit exemption of Anglicanism, the more the worst horrors of priestcraft – without loss of critical credibility – could be tacitly attributed to Anglicanism. This tactic of guilt by implicit association was early exploited by Ainsworth, Cherbury, and many subsequent Dissenters; and was a tactic too efficacious in the battle for true Christianity to be easily abandoned. In Angell's *The History of Religion* (1764), the same tactic is deployed. Angell claims to have been impartial in his treatment of history; indeed, an 'Impartial Hand' was his pseudonym (effective until this century). Nevertheless, he laments that rational religion does not prevail, and relates at length all the usual enormities of Catholicism. He also points out '[t]here is scarce any Church in Christendom that does not obtrude many false hoods';[36] and he does not exempt the Anglican Church from his coverall indictment.

Seventy years before Angell, Toland did not exempt Anglicanism from the blistering invective of his *Christianity not Mysterious*, allowing its scourge to be applied implicitly in full measure to the Anglican Church. Convocation was, therefore, absolutely correct when it noted in 1711 that 'Priests without Distinction ... [had been] traduc'd, as Imposers on the Credulity of Mankind'.[37] The bonus of this tacit comparative technique was that the burden of contemporary proof (including space) for charges against Anglicanism was avoided. In addition, and certainly most importantly, the possibility of arousing the public ire of Church and state was reduced. Even when it was aroused, specific and official charges were made more difficult to formulate and prosecute if the indictment of Anglicanism was understood rather than explicit.

In *Christianity not Mysterious*, therefore, the indictment he formulated against the primitive Church was meant to be fully applied to the Anglican Church by his readers. He argued it was the motive of 'their own Advantage ... that put the Primitive *Clergy* upon reviving *Mysteries* [and] they quickly erected themselves into a separate Body'. Utilizing the language of piety appropriate to his religious outlook, he then related how soon distinctions of rank and orders in the clergy and other usurpations made their way 'under pretence of *Labourers in the Lord's Vineyard'*. These priests ornamented ceremony and rite with 'Extravagancies of Heathen Original'. Thus, the Eucharist was 'absolutely perverted and destroyed' and is 'not yet fully restor'd by the purest Reformations in *Christendom'*. Matters became worse, almost incurable, when Emperor Constantine endorsed Christianity. As a result the multitudes flocked to Christianity from 'politick considerations', and the Christian priesthood was enriched with the endowments and benefices of the pagan Priests, Flamens and Augurs.

When philosophers became Christians, a further degeneration was set in train. The erroneous opinions of philosophers entered Christianity, and the simple precepts of Christ became intelligible only to the learned. He explained how

> Decrees or Constitutions concerning *Ceremonies* and *Discipline*, to increase the Splendor of [the clergy] ... did strangely affect or stupify the Minds of the ignorant People; and made them believe they were in good earnest Mediators between God and Men, that could fix Sanctity to certain Times, Places, Persons or Actions. By this means the *Clergy* were able to do anything; they engross'd at length the sole Right of interpreting *Scripture,* and with it claim'd *Infallibility,* to their Body.[38]

Because Toland's *Christianity not Mysterious* represents but one more resolute attempt of Dissent to cleanse the Augean Stables of priest-craft, the terminology, chronology and methodology of his historical analysis is hardly original in its feel or content.

In the life and works of Toland, the transition from a crisis of the Church to a crisis of faith is manifest. The same forces that brought Puritan/Dissenter historiography to maturity also propelled Toland towards deism. In the years after 1697 Toland drew away from his reforming stance. Even after abandoning his Presbyterian ideals and with them the practical concept of the Christian ministry, Toland, of course, had no need to retract or regret almost anything contained in his reforming *Christianity not Mysterious.* His Dissenter histori-ography continued to serve his deist aims very well indeed, and is something that has helped to produce or reinforce the impression that Toland was a deist in 1696: one historiography, two very differ-ent aims and rationales. He and others went on to form a variegated and relatively small collection of writers termed deists. Writers such as Tindal and Collins used the same historical critique as that of Toland, Dennis, Howard and other Dissenters as the historical and sociological foundation for their various religious, philosophical and political attacks upon the Anglican and Christian Church in general.

A specific form of Christian anticlerical thought had been adopted in a natural, 'organic' intellectual development. Enlightenment anticlerical sociology and historiography had emerged from the cauldron of Christian conflict. In the first three decades of the eighteenth century deists intensified the attack upon the Christian ministry. English deists led Enlightenment Europe in the attempt to harmonize natural and revealed truths in religious understanding and, in doing so, completed the process of readmitting the role of reason in religious thought begun more than a century before by English Protestants. By the 1730s, in the works of Tindal, Collins and Toland, English deist thought was fully developed, and the cutting edge of Enlightenment anticlerical thought was to pass to French thinkers.

English deism, already waning because its programme had met unyielding opposition in Church and state, and further weakened by Bishop Butler's attack upon it in his incisive *Analogy of Religion* (1736), was virtually defunct by the 1740s. Its career of less than fifty years constituted a relatively short deviation in the more than 250-year career of the Christian priestcraft theory, which continued with its vigour intact into the nineteenth century. In the eighteenth century, the searching glare emitted by the priestcraft paradigm continued to highlight the failure of the Christian priesthood in Italy and elsewhere. In 1760s France, Voltaire initiated his campaign against the Church and, as other *philosophes,* drew upon the writings of English deists. English deists constituted a somewhat precocious development of Enlightenment thought, one arising from the specific circumstances of English political and religious life. Nevertheless, the religious trajectory of Toland and that of other like-minded thinkers, from dissent to deism or from a crisis of the Church to a crisis of belief, was not uniquely an English phenomenon.

We know the Italian radical exile Alberto Radicati began his unconventional career as a pious anti-curialist, declaiming against the jurisdiction and worldly nature of the Roman Church. In 1725-6 he was supported in his views by Victor Amadeus II (1684–1730), sovereign of his native Piedmont. Subsequently, Radicati fell prey to one of the frequent changes in relationship between Italian sovereigns and the Curia, and was ultimately forced to flee to England. That experience, combined with exposure to radical critiques of Catholicism and Anglicanism encountered in England, drove Radicati to become a deist (or freethinker, as he termed himself in his *Succint History of*

Priesthood ... inscrib'd to the Ever-illustrious, and most Celebrated sect of FREE THINKERS (1737, trans. from French)). Little change in historical outlook was necessary to adapt his anti-curial critique of the Church to the more radical view of thinkers such as Toland – whom he praised. Predictably, Radicati's historical scheme is remarkably similar in chronology and content to that of English Dissenters and deists.

Italian enlightened thinkers, unlike their English cousins, were not permitted the luxury of being able to accept as established the priest-craft of the medieval Church, so enabling them to concentrate their critical efforts elsewhere. For enlightened Italians, the medieval Church was still present and very much alive in the form of the Papal States, forming a most tangible, obscurantist obstacle to Enlightenment ideals. There was, for all Italians to see, a *de facto* chronological continuum between the medieval and the contemporary Church, both in spiritual and material terms. For this reason the problem of locating the 'positive' influence of Christian historiography does not raise itself in their critical output. This is because the anti-curial priestcraft analysis was, of necessity, used by the Italian *philosophes* against the target for which it was first developed, the Roman Church. Hence, Amidei, in his *La Chiesa e la Repubblica dentro i loro limiti* (1768), outlines the medieval imposture of the popes. In the chapter *Delle Cause della forza della potestà ecclesiastica ne'governi temporali*, he relies upon the historiography of Giannone and Muratori. The consequence of the manifest inclusion of the papacy in critiques such as Amidei's, is that these accounts appear more Protestant than those of English Dissenters such as Howard, Dennis or Toland, in which anti-Romanism was often tacitly understood.

In 1789, the French Revolution's strong anticlerical ideology was also directed at the Catholic Church and state. In practice, French *philosophes*, who had earlier been influenced by English deists, supplied the Revolution's anti-Church critique. It is not justifiable, however, to jump from that fact to the assumption that the *philosophes* were the principal purveyors of anticlericalism, and therefore responsible for the anticlericalism of the revolutionary masses. Yet it is an implicit assumption sometimes encountered. There certainly was a pre-Enlightenment French anticlerical culture, as there was in all European countries. In the French case this was one directed at Catholic priestcraft by Huguenots, by Catholics at Protestants, and by many nominal or dissenting Catholics at the wealthy Catholic hierarchy itself. The tenor of the anticlerical critique accompanying the revolution of 1789 which swept away Louis XVI and his Catholic regime was essentially the same as that of contemporary and past Huguenots and English Protestants. This is only to reaffirm that, as elsewhere in Europe, anticlericalism was also an efficient vehicle with which to express economic and political grievances.

Huguenots, who had suffered greatly in the Wars of Religion and subsequent bloody persecutions (we should remind ourselves Huguenots were not free to worship as they wished until 1787 and the last Huguenot galley-slaves were only liberated in 1775), had as much if not more reason to formulate an anti-Catholic priestcraft theory than English Protestants. The *Mystére d'iniquité* (1611) of the Huguenot du Plessis-Mornay is an example of just that theory (or, rather intended as historical proof of that theory). Mornay wrote from the product of his own experience and his own historical understanding. Much of both was confirmed in the massacre by Catholic nobles of thousands of Huguenots on St Bartholomew's Day in 1572, the year in which the Fourth Religious War in France began. Not surprisingly, Mornay was also the author of the *Vindiciae contra tyrannos* (1579), which argued that Catholic tyranny and religious persecution by Church and state had to be militarily opposed if necessary, indeed, it was a Christian duty to do so.

In the hands of Huguenots, Calvinism could become a source of revolutionary ideology, for an ideology that justifies armed resistance also sanctions civil war. But ideological justification rarely adequately explains the causes of major conflicts, as illustrated by the English Civil War, the roots of which lay in economics, politics, social class and religion, even if its expression was often religious in tone. We may remember the Neapolitan jurisdictionalist Allesandro Riccardi stated in 1708 that, if necessary, Naples would seek the rights of its Church by the sword. Riccardi was expressing the desire for the sovereign of Naples, his nobles, and his jurisdictionalist supporters to be free of Roman interference in the richly endowed Neapolitan Church. This was, of course, more an economic and political conflict than a purely religious one. Even what is usually considered the most secular event of the century, the French Revolution of 1789, could not escape the intimacy of political and economic conflict and religion – a subject which forms part of the next chapter.

8 Conclusion: the Spiritual Politics of Social Class

If one were to assess accounts of eighteenth-century Europe written since the 1950s, one would find there has been a tendency amongst some writers to exhibit a division of labour: those who have focused on the Enlightenment, and those who have taken the eighteenth-century itself as their subject matter. The latter type of account has tended towards a more empirical and descriptive approach, and the former to the problem of intellectual change sometimes relatively isolated from its broader societal context. The aim of this present work has been to locate the historical thinking of the defenders and detractors of the two great confessions and their subdivisions into the wider European politico-religious framework. In doing so I hope to have taken a tiny step towards drawing together the two traditional approaches, the intellectual and the empirical. One of the issues addressed in this book has been the misapprehension resulting from an over-concentration on the narrow band of Enlightenment thinkers at the expense of 'non-enlightened' thinkers. The idea that the little family (as Peter Gay has expressed it) of *philosophes* grew, matured and wrote without receiving any significant influence at all from the Christian society into which they were born – from the comparatively vast numbers of Christian historians, philosophers, theologians, politicians and social critics – is one most historians will dismiss.

The historian wishing to reconstruct something of the thought of eighteenth-century individuals, must define the cultural legacy of previous generations. It is essential to understand how eighteenth-century participants viewed their past, and how contemporary events concerted either to continue or change their historical perceptions, their view of the past social, religious and political configuration. The limitations of my attempt to fulfil this goal should be relatively obvious. The lack of any systematic account of the development of Christian anticlerical thought in pre-Enlightenment Europe has obliged me to present more than two hundred and fifty years of historiographical development. Despite what may seem to some an over-ambitious project, only by this route can the historical attitudes of the early Enlightenment be understood as part of the overwhelmingly

Christian cultural context enlightened thinkers inherited. There has, however, been a price attached to the need to present a very wide overview: I have been able only to provide sufficient focus on the anti-clerical historiography of the early Enlightenment in England and, to some extent, that of Italy in the later eighteenth century.

The need to concentrate on the task of reconstructing the historical outlook of early modern thinkers in order to facilitate our under-standing of their views of their own period also poses the danger of assembling (by default) an idealistic view of historical causality. As we have seen, the problem with the idealist approach is that the same ideas (form) can, if the context in which the idea is found differs from that of an earlier period, have very different implications (content). The ideas in the heads of early modern thinkers, clerical or secular, were not the product of a study of history in an objective or value-free context. Neither did the ideas of the great minds of the period on their own shape the development of eighteenth-century Europe. The ideas – the outlook and allegiances of such individuals – and the smaller or larger events and developments caused by the combined actions of social groups or classes, were all products of an amalgam of social, political, religious and economic factors. This is a simple and fundamental point, but a truism not now fashionable amongst some historians. There has been a trend to downplay and even denigrate economic factors in historical causality. Changing attitudes towards the nature and cause of the English Civil War exemplify this trend. The leading exponent of the understanding that the causes of the Civil War contained a strong economic or class dynamic has been Christopher Hill.[1] Hill's contribution to our understanding of the reciprocal interplay between economics, class, politics and religion has been of central importance to our understanding of the events and attitudes of seventeenth-century England.

Perhaps one of the best-known revisionists on the origins of the Civil War is Conrad Russel. In his work *The Origin of the Civil War* (1990), Russel's project was to re-emphasize religion, politics and the financial problems of the monarchy, effectively downplaying the wider economic and class aspects of Hill's account. His work, although weak in its understanding of the interaction between the economic, religious and political consciousness of individuals and classes, nevertheless contains some useful insights into the problems of royal rule of three kingdoms (Ireland, Scotland and England). However, theories of early modern historical causality have at times become more distant from the material realities of history. This shift was reinforced in some by the odd perception that the decline of the Eastern Bloc meant an end to the need for an awareness of economic and class causality in history. Some post-modernists have even declared it is no longer fruitful to search for general causes of historical development. It has been noted that Whig and Marxist historical accounts are 'parochial' in outlook (that is to say were focused on national developments rather than European), and the idealist view of history has been considered a third way between Whiggism and Marxism. Thus, it has been hoped, the imputed errors of economic and teleological determinism in accounts of historical development might be avoided.[2]

For the most part, these developments in the philosophy of history have been barren and have led to a curious phenomenon. Palpable and undeniable changes in the structure of European society (agents of historical change) have been sidelined or even forgotten. It is well documented that post-Reformation Europe saw a large rise in literacy levels, combined with the numerical growth – and therefore economic and political weight – of what had traditionally been regarded as part of the top echelon of the third estate: the trading, manufacturing and intellectual-professional sections of society. Until the 1980s many historians had rightly debated the importance of these changes. The gradual restructuring of facets of political, intellectual and economic life could not but exert a significant causal role in the development of Europe. Historical accounts lacking recognition of these factors, and the undeniable facts of recurring economic crises, periods of great hunger and hardship, and the glaring disparities of wealth under the *ancien régime*, make strange reading indeed. To discuss the intellectual developments of the decades prior to the French Revolution of 1789, without exploring or even giving a curt nod to material circumstances and cultural change, is to write of a Europe that never existed. It is to float in the air balloon of idealist historiography over an eighteenth-century landscape that would have been unrecognizable to the vast bulk of its population – intellectuals and peasants alike.

This discussion raises the general question of the relationship of religious and historical outlooks to economic and political perspectives and class antagonism.

Max Weber, a German economist of the early twentieth century, produced a now famous argument that the spirit of capitalism in Europe was above all to be found amongst Protestants, especially amongst those with Calvinist inclinations.[3] He did not necessarily intend it, but many historians understood his work to demonstrate the further point that capitalism was the fruit of the Protestant work ethic. Such conclusions have rightly been demonstrated to be without any basis. The important point to be taken from his work, however, is that in England, as elsewhere, godly Calvinists were often disproportionately concentrated in what has been termed the 'middling sort' – the growing middle class. This fact has, correctly, gone uncontested. The question as to why and how this significant class-religion parallel came about is undoubtedly important, although (for the sake of brevity) I will here simply accept the fact of it.

In practice, this correlation meant religious differences could and at times did embody more or less implicit or explicit political and economic dissent. This was especially so in a period when a challenge to the established Church also signified a challenge to the state. When, in the 1590s, Queen Elizabeth suppressed the growing Puritan separatist Church, she and her Anglican-dominated advisers were well aware of the dangers to the state of losing control of the Church, and the implicit benefits of social control accruing from effective control of the pulpit. Supporters of the separatist Church reflected the usual disproportionality of social class amongst English Calvinists. It was a movement with a pronounced leavening of the middling sort and, therefore, represented a potential challenge not only to the relationship of Church and state, but potentially also to royal and aristocratic prerogatives. This was hardly a fear to be expressed publicly, but we may remember that in 1601 the House of Commons broke the Queen's prerogative on the granting of monopolies. The coincidence of religious and politico-economic views was, of course, not unique to England.

As we have seen, although in some respects a very different phenomenon, many anti-curial Italian Catholics combined politics and economics in their religious critique of Rome. If this general lesson is forgotten – one as relevant in the English Civil War as in the French Revolution – then it is quite possible to construct a false dichotomy between economic/class and religious factors in historical development. To do so would reduce our potential to understand the complexity of historical causality and, ultimately, history itself.

We have seen how English Puritans, in competition with the Anglican Church, vied to appear the most hard and consistent opponents of Rome in order to demonstrate their spiritual credentials. Yet we know Puritan/Dissenter opposition to Anglicanism was frequently or even mostly conveyed in anti-Catholic terms, expressing antagonism directed at episcopacy and aristocracy who were seen to lord it over the relatively poor and powerless laity. When confronted with Catholic King James II, the same Puritan/Dissenter anti-Catholic critique, with its no less sharp anti-Anglican political and religious content, became a much more powerful yet dangerous weapon. State and Church had – in the thought of very many Protestants – allowed the accession of an apostate king. To have named the king as an antichristian supporter of the priest-king at Rome would, however, have been to court the wrath of the state. James forbade preaching against Catholicism, allowed pro-Catholic tracts to be published, promoted Catholics in the army and universities, and had renewed the persecution of the Scottish Covenanters. It was not possible to exempt Parliament from the indictment of aiding Catholicism, for their treachery was seen to be compounded when the Commons had agreed a grant to James of two million pounds and had enacted more severe penalties against treason. Their definition of treason could not but be seen to include the traditional accusation that Catholic kings led their realms into the thrall of an antichristian power (Rome). As we know, anti-Catholicism was commonly understood to represent a challenge to the perceived status quo of Catholic Europe, where kings – exemplified by Louis XIV – were in league with the priest-king at Rome to ensure that Christianity was prostituted to self-gain and the oppression of the poor.

To talk, then, of religious dissent in the seventeenth and eighteenth centuries is to talk of a great deal more than religion: of power, of politics, of class, of conceptions of kingly rule and of rational truth against superstition. We may remember the public proclamation of Sacheverell in 1709 which, despite engendering great controversy, had considerable support amongst Tories, Anglicans, the wealthy and the powerful, and was certainly not an anachronism: 'whoever, presumes to innovate, alter, or misrepresent any point in the articles of faith or our Church ought to be arraigned as a traitor to our state.' Dissenters naturally condemned Sacheverell, but above all they were condemning the ugly reality expressed in his statement. An assault upon the popery of Anglicanism could thus never be solely theological, to do so was to assail the vitals of state and established society. An historical challenge to the ancient priest-kings whom papacy and prelacy had emulated, and whose corrupt hierarchy Anglicanism perpetuated, constituted an implicit attack upon an Anglican Church–state settlement understood to have been conceived under the rubric of a false religion.

Since the Restoration, Dissenters had been the subject of various repressive and punitive acts, including a bar from municipal office and posts at national universities. In 1673 the Test Act – requiring all holders of Crown offices to take the Oath of Supremacy and receive the Eucharist according to Anglican usage – effectively rendered Dissenters ineligible for civil or military offices. The Occasional Conformity Act of 1711 reaffirmed the bar from governmental posts by stringent measures against practising Dissenters who took the Anglican Eucharist only in order to qualify for government posts. A significant section of the intelligentsia – those many well-educated Dissenters who aspired to academic and public posts – were thus deprived of important avenues of economic and professional advancement. Instead, they found those posts in the hands of Anglicans, supporters of the Church-state alliance. This was an economic and political relationship exemplified by the Spiritual Lords, the Anglican bishops who continued to sit in the House of Lords. That the Anglican prelacy were taking part in an unholy alliance with the rich and powerful was evident, for who else sat in the House of Lords?

Even in what some historians have considered to be the high point of the Enlightenment, the revolution of 1789,[4] fundamental aspects of social class and economic and political life could still be expressed in terms of religious adherence or opposition. It is undoubtedly true that amongst the French *philosophes* were found many of the leading European advocates of a secular society. Naturally, therefore, the French Enlightenment has been the subject of a plethora of accounts. Most of these accounts have, correctly, placed the small group of elite *philosophes* on centre stage. The unfortunate consequence, however, has been that the vast background of the masses and the various strata of Christian writers have often been relegated to little more than a very distant blur. Only a very few writers have tried to redress this imbalance – notably Alan Kors. The momentous outbreak of revolution, however, brought the masses unavoidably to the limelight.

Although economic crisis and class conflict (including the action of the nobility to preserve its parasitic privileges) constituted causal factors and catalysts of the first order, the role of religion before and during the revolution should not be underestimated. Attitudes to the Church were fundamental components in the mobilization and legitimation of mass revolutionary action. The famous slogan Liberty, Equality and Fraternity undoubtedly expressed opposition to the nobility and their feudal exactions, as well as other fundamental criticisms of the *ancien régime*. One part of that oppressive regime was perceived to be the ecclesiastical nobility, the landed bishops: important supporters of the king, and ostentatious repositories of wealth amidst plebeian squalor. We know the Huguenot critique of the Catholic Church, exemplified by that of Bayle (or indeed the earlier work of du Plessis-Mornay), was similar to that of English Protestants; and that the critique of the Church by *philosophes* was substantially the same. In the years of revolution it was, therefore, to be expected that the Church would be vilified as the epitome of the *ancien régime* by peasants and elite intellectuals alike.

In November 1789 Church lands were nationalized. In November 1790 it was decreed the clergy should swear loyalty to the Civil Constitution. In October-November 1793 the De-Christianization movement began; and in May 1794 Robespierre instituted the Cult of the Supreme Being. The Church in France had been cowed. Churches were closed and the Christian calendar and Sabbath were abolished. The Goddess of Reason was enshrined in Notre Dame cathedral, and in many cities Temples of Reason had been established. Some historians have seen the initiation of this cult as the pinnacle of the deist programme. One point of agreement uniting the otherwise often disparate phenomenon of deism was, of course, antagonism to institutional worship. What need was there for a temple to the Supreme Being? The answer to this question is to be found in the character of the cult itself, and its relationship to the aspirations of the Revolution.

In Châlons-sur-Marne in 1794 there was a civic festival held to inaugurate a Temple to the Supreme Being. The evening before, and early on the day itself, the festival was announced, and the news was accompanied with drummers and trumpeters. In what had been the sanctuary of the former Church of Notre Dame a pedestal supporting the symbolic statue of Reason had been erected. It was flanked by two columns, upon which were antique bronze perfume boxes which – in typical Catholic style – would emit incense during the whole ceremony. In front of the columns, at the foot of three steps, had been placed an altar of antique form to receive symbolic offerings. The pillars of the sanctuary were to be adorned with busts of contemporary and ancient republicans. At nine o'clock in the morning the military and civic procession assembled. On the pennants of the cavalry was the slogan Reason Guides Us And Enlightens Us; and the cannoneers had a banner inscribed Death To The Tyrants. Behind these was a cart with prisoners of war and wounded in the process of being cared for, with banners stating Humanity Is A Republican

Virtue. On the banners of the troops was written We Will Exterminate The Last Of The Despots.

All the community were represented in the procession. Children carried fruit and flowers, and women citizens marched under the banner of Austere Morals Will Strengthen The Republic. One couple were seated on a plough under the slogans Honour The Plough and Respect Conjugal Love. Four women, appropriately adorned, represented the four seasons, and old citizens sported the slogan The Republic Honours Loyalty, Courage, Old Age, Filial Piety and Misfortune. Another cart carried emblems of feudalism such as armorial bearings, and various emblems of superstition. In the same cart stood a man dressed as the pope with two cardinals for acolytes, the scene was accompanied by billboards declaring Prejudices Will Pass Away, and Reason Is Eternal. There was patriotic singing en route, and outside the city hall the papal cart was ceremonially assaulted and pope and acolytes chained to the Chariot of Liberty and its goddess. At the Temple of Reason musicians gathered behind the altar and the organ blared. Evidently, beyond the *philosophes* and the much maligned Jacobins, the plebeian experience of the years of revolution was more rich and complex than some accounts have depicted.

That this procession and others like it were celebrations and inculcations of laudable civic virtue and its victory over superstition and feudal reaction is clear. It was also a momentous step in philosophical and political thought, for it represented the first practical attempt to substitute a secular moral code for that of Christianity. Equally obvious in the minds of the participants and municipal organizers of the procession was the impossibility of extricating the Church from questions of state power and class, something vividly portrayed by the papal cart and its fortunes. But the cult and Temple of the Supreme Being was another matter. Amidst music and incense, the ceremonial arrival of the procession at the altar of the Supreme Being encapsulated the need of the revolution's leaders to harness secular republican virtues to a quasi-deistic concept of a God who had given his/her blessing to the Revolution. Clearly, those deists who believed God no longer intervened in human history, and that the fruit of collective institutional worship could only be superstition and a brake upon society's rational development, had lost or were losing the debate.

We may remember, however, that deists and radicals had not only condemned the religious fraud of the Church. Along with large numbers of Catholics and Protestants, many had also recognized the role of Christian doctrine in the successful government of the masses by providing a divinely sanctioned and widely acceptable code of social conduct – termed by some the rule of the wise. The cult of the Supreme Being was being used by the revolutionary leaders to legit-imize an acceptable framework of social norms to facilitate an ordered society. Despite the secular 'modernity' of the most thoroughgoing of national Enlightenments, the concept of a univer-sally accepted secular code of social norms and morality was still, at most, in its very early infancy. The altar of the Supreme Being provided, paradoxically, the spiritual cement for the construction of a society based on reason. Expressed in other terms, the cult was the expression of the anti-aristocratic and anti-Church economic, political and class aspirations of the revolutionary regime and large sections of the masses. In the 1790s, therefore, to talk of religion was still to talk of politics, social class and the distribution of wealth and power.

Notes

CHAPTER 1 INTRODUCTION: ANTICLERICALISM AND HISTORICAL REVOLUTIONS

1. John Pocock, in O. Ramum (ed.), *National Consciousness, History, and Political Culture in Early Modern Europe* (Baltimore, 1975), p. 97.
2. On the importance of the historical views of past ages in historical research, see for instance the comments of Christopher Dawson, in Laird Okie's *Augustan Historical Writing: Histories of England in the English Enlightenment* (London and New York, 1991), p. iii.
3. T. Hulme, quoted in J. Harrison's *Late Victorian Britain* (London, 1990), p. 95.
4. See for instance Anthony Milton's *Catholic and Reformed. The Roman and Protestant Churches in English Protestant Thought 1600–1640* (Cambridge, 1995), p. 188.
5. F.J. Levy, *Tudor Historical Thought* (San Marino, California, 1967), p. 79.
6. Dale Van Kley, 'Pierre Nicole, Jansenism, and the Morality of Enlightened Self-Interest', Alan Charles Kors and Paul, J. Korshin, (eds), *Anticipations of the Enlightenment in England, France and Germany* (Philadelphia, 1987), p. 69.
7. Milton, *Catholic and Reformed*, pp. 173–4.
8. Patrick Collinson, *The Birthpangs of Protestant England* (London, 1988), p. 10; Milton, *Catholic and Reformed*, pp. 31–2.
9. Giuseppe Capecelatro, *Discorso istorico-politico dell'origine del progresso e della decadenza del potere de'chierici su le signorie temporali* (Naples, 1788).
10. Furio Diaz, *Per Una storia illuministica* (Garzanti, 1973), p. 9.
11. One of the few exceptions to the dismissal of seventeenth-century anti-curial polemic has been the work of Giorgio Spini, who draws parallels between the historiographical conceptions of Italian libertines and eighteenth-century writers. His comments, however, are very brief and his analysis consequently undeveloped; see for instance Spini's, 'Ritratto del Protestante come libertino', in T. Gregory, G. Spini, et al. (eds), *Ricerche su letteratura libertina e letteratura clandestina nel seicento* (Florence, 1981).
12. Carlo Gentile, in his *Pietro Giannone, E. Gibbon e il Triregno* (Bastogi, 1976) has at least attempted some comparative work, but its focus is restricted to Giannone and Gibbon.
13. Herbert Butterfield, *The Whig Interpretation of History* (Harmondsworth, 1973), pp. 14, 37.
14. Thomas Hankins, *Science and the Enlightenment* (Cambridge, 1995), p. 145. On the unprecedented fusion of science and religion in seventeenth-century England see Amos Funkenstein, *Theology and the*

161

Scientific Imagination from the Middle ages to the Seventeenth Century (Princetown, 1986).

15. On the lengthy delay in the proscription of Copernican ideas see the useful discussion in Domenico Sella's *Italy in the Seventeenth Century* (Longman, 1997).
16. James Byrne, *Glory, Jest and Riddle* (London, 1996), p. 110.
17. Collinson, *Birthpangs*, p. 83.
18. Roy Porter, *Gibbon Making History* (London, 1995), p. 17.
19. On the perception of the military and political threat posed by alliances of European Catholic powers in the seventeenth century see Milton, *Catholic and Reformed*; for a more vivid account see Jonathan Scott's 'England's troubles: exhuming the popish plot', in Tim Harris, Paul Seaward, Mark Goldie (eds), *Politics of Religion in Restoration England* (Oxford, 1990).
20. The politico-religious context in which Toland's views were formed are defined at some length in Rees Evans's *Pantheisticon. The Career of John Toland* (New York, 1991).
21. Okie, *Augustan Historical Writing*, p. 1.

CHAPTER 2   PRIESTCRAFT THEORY: TEXT AND CONTEXT

1. Trinitarianism is the doctrine that God is three 'persons' – Father, Son and Holy Spirit – and one substance; as opposed to the Unitarian (Socinian) view of the unipersonality of God.
2. Joseph Priestley, *A General History of the Christian Church from the Fall of the Western Empire to the Present Time* (4 vols, Northumberland, USA, 1802–3), vol. 1, preface, p. 12 (This is the continuation of Priestley's *A General History of the Christian Church to the Fall of the Western Empire*, 1790).
3. Elisabeth Labrousse, 'Reading Pierre Bayle in Paris', in Kors and Korshin, *Anticipations of the Enlightenment*, p. 11.
4. Peter Gay, *The Enlightenment: an Interpretation*, vol. 1 *The Rise of Modern Paganism* (London, 1973), p. 382.
5. Vincenzo Ferrone, *The Intellectual Roots of the Italian Enlightenment* (New Jersey, 1995), pp, 87–8, 147–50.
6. On the origin of some of the components of Luther's periodization of history, see John Headley's *Luther's View of Church History* (New Haven and London, 1963).
7. The *Magdeburg Centuries* is the title given to the *Ecclesiastica historia integram ecclesiae Christi* (1559–74) of Matthias Flacius Illyricus and others.
8. On the charge of miracles as fraudulent see for instance John Tyndale's *The Obedience of a Christian Man* (Marlborow, 1528); John Foxe's *Actes and Monuments of Matters happening in the Church* (London, 1563, 1st Latin edn 1554); Thomas Fuller's *Church-History of Britain, from the Birth of Jesus Christ untill the Year 1648* (1655).
9. John Wesley, *A Concise Ecclesiastical History from the Birth of Christ to the beginning of the Present Century* (4 vols, London, 1781), vol. 2, pp. 32, 56.

10. On the preservation of the legitimacy of apostolic miracles see also William Warburton's *A Critical and Philosophical Enquiry into the Causes of Prodigies and Miracles* (London, 1727).

11. The prevalence in English Protestant thought of the depiction of the medieval Church as ridden with priestcraft was only partly attenuated amongst pro-Laudian, High Church Anglicans in the 1630s; although before and after the 1630s some few High Churchmen continued to claim – with some considerable difficulty – that something could be rescued from the wreckage of the medieval Church.

12. *The Westminster Confession of Faith*, 1643 (London, 1962), p. 34. On the growing dominance of secondary causality within the Puritan community, see Barbara Donagan's, 'Understanding Providence: the Difficulties of Sir William and Lady Waller', in the *Journal of Ecclesiastical History*, 39, 3 (1988). It must not be assumed, however, that belief in the intervention of providence in the daily lives of Protestants declined at the same rate or to the same extent as it did in Protestant historical accounts. The depiction of historical events was of course usually relatively remote from contemporary daily concerns, with the consequence that providence in historical writing could be diminished or abandoned with little impact on personal piety. On the continued belief in some form of providential intervention in the lives of Protestants see for instance Alexander Walsham's '"the fatall vesper": Providentialism and anti-popery in late Jacobean London', in *Past and Present*, 144 (August 1994).

13. Roy Porter, *The Enlightenment* (London, 1990), p. 72; Peter Gay, *The Enlightenment: an Interpretation*, vol. 2, *The Science of Freedom* (London, 1973), p. 386.

14. H.A. Barnes, *A History of Historical Writing* (New York, 1963), p. 122.

15. Richard Field, *Of the Church* (London, 1606), pp. 82–5.

16. Peter Gay, *Modern Paganism*, p. 374.

17. Some High Churchmen, in their wish to salvage something from the history of the Church, did not want to condemn the papacy as the seat of the Antichrist. This was especially so in the decade of Laudian ascendency (1630s), and at times of diplomatic delicacy such as the negotiation of James I with Catholic Spain for a bride for his son Charles. The Westminster Confession of 1643 still proclaimed the pope to be the Antichrist and it remained so in the 1649 and 1690 parliamentary ratifications: its removal in 1690 would of course have been interpreted as a weakening of Anglican fundamentals, something Anglican prelates could ill afford in the bitter religious atmosphere of that decade.

18. Peter Harrison, in his *Religion and the Religions in the English Enlightenment* (CUP, 1990) notes the use of the comparative technique but dates its practice in England to late seventeenth-century Britain. Justin Champion claims the practice of comparative religion – the 'history of priestcraft ... the history and sociology of religion' – had its 'first moves' within deist thought in the 1690s ('Europe's Enlightenment and national historiographies: Rethinking Religion and Revolution', in *Europa. European Review of History* (1993), p. 84.

19. The Clarendon Code was composed of four acts designed to cripple the power of the Nonconformists: the Corporation Act 1661, the Act of Conformity 1662, the Conventicle Act 1664, the Five Mile Act 1665.
20. Scott, in his 'England's Troubles' (p. 110) argues that the seventeenth century should be treated as a continuity of crises (1637–42; 1678–83 and 1687–9) that were fundamentally about religion. While the Civil War and the other crises that he notes cannot be properly explained without reference to politics, economics and social class, Scott is certainly correct to point out the importance of religious division as a factor in seventeenth-century events. Champion (*The Pillars of Priestcraft Shaken* (Cambridge, 1992, pp. 16–17) notes the anti-popish critique of the Anglican Church was intermeshed with the danger of popish tyranny – as exemplified in the Spanish and French examples – and the continued growth of this critique means that the continuity of religious crises can be extended to 1720.
21. William Stephens, *An Account of the Growth of Deism in England* (London, 1696), pp. 3–6. For a similar analysis see also D.E. (anon.), *The Prodigious Appearance of Deism in this Age Modestly Accounted for in a Letter from a Deist to his Friend* (London, 1710).
22. Hugh Trevor-Roper, 'Religious Toleration in England after 1688', in *From Counter-Reformation to Glorious Revolution* (London, 1992), p. 276.
23. On the absolutism of French kings see Nicholas Henshall's *The Myth of Absolutism* (Harlow, 1992).
24. In the eighteenth century most of the Italian states were very weak in relation to the major European powers. Hence they continued to be prey to the vicissitudes of the political and military fortunes of the more dominant European powers. Thus the kingdom of Naples was a Habsburg possession from the Spanish War of Succession until 1734, when Spanish control was reasserted for another generation. The Duchy of Milan was in Austrian hands from early in the century until the French conquest in 1796–7. From 1737, with the extinction of the native Medici dynasty, the Grand Duchy of Tuscany was also a Habsburg possession, though never formally annexed to the main block of central European territories. Of the smaller states, Parma was assigned to a Spanish Bourbon prince in 1732, annexed by the Habsburgs in 1738 and granted independence once again under another Spanish Bourbon in 1748. The Este family survived as rulers in Modena mostly through Austrian support.
25. Sarpi used the pseudonyms of Pietro Soave and Lamindo Pritanio.
26. Allesandro Riccardi, *Ragioni del Regno di Napoli nella causa de'suoi beneficj ecclesiastici* (1708), p. 12.
27. The following three works constitute the history of the Church written by Orsi and continued by Becchetti: Giuseppe Agostino Orsi, *Della Istoria ecclesiastica* (21 vols, Rome, 1746–62); Filippo Angelico Becchetti, *Della Istoria ecclesiastica dell'eminentissimo Cardinale Giuseppe Orsi* (13 vols, Rome, 1770–81); Becchetti, *Istoria degli ultimi quattro secoli della Chiesa* (10 vols, Rome, 1788–96).
28. Fleury's most influential work was the *L'Histoire ecclésiastique* (1691–1720).

29. See Tommaso Vicenzo Pani's *Della Punizione degli eretici e del Tribunale della Santa Inquizione* (Rome, 1789).
30. It is difficult to define the precise nature of Italian Jansenism, which varied in its character depending on time and place. Rather than attempt any detailed theological analysis, it is more fruitful to understand Italian Jansenism as a hybrid of Jansenist, anti-curial and jurisdictionalist ideas, in which the following common elements can be identified: the desire for a return to Christian origins and an exaltation of the purity of the Church; moral rigour; an acquiescence to the will of sovereigns; and the independence of sovereign Churches from Rome. These elements, in one form or another, are present in the thought of most of the anti-curial writers surveyed in this book. Some of these elements, however, are also present in the thought of a number of anti-curialists who can hardly be considered Jansenist in theological outlook, as in that of Giannone for example.
31. On the early depiction of the reformers see Ottavia Niccoli, *Profetti e popoli nell'Italia del Rinascimento* (Rome and Bari, 1987).
32. To indicate but a few amongst many pro-curial propagandists who depicted the Reformation as priestcraft, see in the bibliography the works of Jacopo Moronessa, Lancelotto Politi (pseud. Ambrosius Catharinius), Thomas Bozio, Antonio Possevino, and Stanislaw Rezka.
33. Vincenzo Lodovico Gotti, *Veritas religionis christianae* (Rome, 1735–40).
34. D.M. Loades, *Politics and the Nation 1450–1660* (Fontana, 1979), p. 224.
35. Spini 'Ritratto del Protestante', pp. 177–8.
36. Gregorio Leti, *Il Nipotismo di Roma* (Amsterdam, 1667), pp. 36–8. Leti converted, nominally at least, to Protestantism but his conversion was more a sign of his anti-curial dissent than any evangelism, and he condemned the cruelty of the Protestants. For examples of Italian Protestant thought in the late seventeenth and early eighteenth century propounding very similar arraignments to those put both by English Protestants and Italian anti-curialists against the Curia see the Italian Savoyard Giovanni Legero's *Apologia delle Chiese Riformate delle Valli di Piemonte* (Haerlem, 1662); and Giacomo Picenino's *Apologia per i riformatori e per la religione riformata* (Coira, 1706).
37. Paolo Sarpi, *Trattato delle Materie Beneficiarie di Fra. Paolo Sarpi* (In Mirandola, 1676), pp. 1–2; this is a later edition of Sarpi's *Historia de Padre Paolo dell' ordine de'Servi sopra li Beneficii Ecclesiastici* (Colonia Alpina, 1675).
38. Pietro Giannone, *Istoria civile del Regno di Napoli* (4 vols, Naples, 1770; 1st edn 1723), vol, 1, p. 62.
39. 'Several Gentlemen', *The history of Popery* (2 vols, London, 1735), vol. 1, Introduction.
40. Lodovico Muratori, *Dissertazioni sopra le antichità italiane* (3 vols, Milan, 1751), vol. 3, *Dissertazione 58*, p. 255. The *Dissertazioni* are the posthumous translation of the *Antiquitates italicae medii* (6 vols, Milan, 1738–42), translated by the nephew of Muratori, Gian-Francesco Soli Muratori.

41.   Paolo Rivarola, *Storia del papato di Filippo de Mornay, cittadino Francese* (4 vols, Pavia, 1796–1802), vol. 2, pp. 186–7.

42.   On the early eighteenth-century movement for reform of the Church see Ferrone, *The Intellectual Roots*.

CHAPTER 3   FROM FREE CHRISTENDOM TO PAPAL DESPOTISM

1.   On Calvin's historical view, see his *Institutes of the Christian Religion* (1536), John Allen, ed. (2 vols, London, 1935), vol. 2, bk 4, ch. 5–7, 11.

2.   On Luther's scheme of Church history see Headley, *Luther's View*.

3.   One exception was, for example, the *Anglia sacra* (London, 1691) of Henry Wharton.

4.   The Anglican Nonjurors were staunch defenders of the divine right of kings. They were called Nonjurors on account of their refusal to take the oath of allegiance to William and Mary after 1688, because they had already taken oaths to James II.

5.   Laurence Howell, *A View of the Pontificate ... in which the Corruptions of the Scriptures and Sacred Antiquity, Forgeries in the Councils, and Encroachments of the Courts of Rome on the Church and State, to support their Infallibility, Supremacy, and other Modern Doctrines are set in a True Light* (London, 1712), p. 2.

6.   Howell, *View of the Pontificate,* preface pp. 6–7; main text pp. 139, 205, 317, 395, 406.

7.   Jeremy Collier, *An Ecclesiastical History of Great Britain, Chiefly of England* (2 vols, London, 1708), vol. 1, p. 80.

8.   George Gregory, *History of the Christian Church from the Earliest Period to the Present Time* (2 vols, London, 1790), vol. 1, p. 354.

9.   Thomas Gisborne, *A Familiar Survey of the Christian Religion* (London, 1799), pp. 437–8, 449–50.

10.   Bicheno's dating is vague on this point, but he seems to be referring to the fourth century.

11.   James Bicheno, *A Glance at the History of Christianity and of English Nonconformity* (Newbury, 1798, 2nd edn), pp. 7–8, 17–18 note A.

12.   *Latria* denotes worship reserved to God alone, and *dulia* that given to saints.

13.   'Several Gentlemen', *History of Popery*, vol. 1, pp. 10, 39, 355; vol. 2, p. 16.

14.   Joseph Priestley, *An History of the Corruptions of Christianity* (2 vols, Birmingham, 1782), vol. 2, p. 314.

15.   Priestley, *General History*, vol. 2, p. 292.

16.   John Angell (the Elder, d. *c.* 1764), *History of Religion* (4 vols, London, 1764), vol. 1, p. 38. Angell's *History of Religion* was formerly attributed to James Murray, under which name the work is still sometimes catalogued today. The biographical details of Angell in the *Dictionary of National Biography* (Leslie Stephen ed., vol. 1, London, 1885, p. 414) are confused and incorrect. See instead Alexander Wright, *The Two Angells of Stenography* (London, 1919).

17.   Wesley claimed he used Archibald Maclaine's translation of Mosheim

(*An Ecclesiastical History,* 2 vols, London, 1765) and Mosheim's original work; but in reality Wesley mostly relied on Maclaine.

18. Wesley, *Concise History,* vol. 1, pp. 262, 317–18, 320.
19. Joseph Milner, *The History of the Church of Christ* (5 vols, London, 1819, 1st edn 1794–1809; vol. 4 edited by Isaac Milner from the manuscript of J. Milner), vol. 3, pp. 116, 480, vol. 4, pp. 4–5.
20. Patrick Nisbet, *An Abridgement of Ecclesiastical History* (Edinburgh, 1776), pp. 96–7, 115–16.
21. John Brown, A *General History of the Christian Church,* 2 vols, Edinburgh, 1771), vol. 1, pp. 170, 184, 225, 279.
22. Cardinal Orsi's death prevented him progressing beyond AD 656 and Becchetti continued the work to the year 1587, the last volume of which was published in 1796. Orsi also wrote (against the Gallican Bossuet) the *De irreformabili romani pontificiis in definiendis fidei controversiis judicio adversus quartam cleri gallicani propositionem* (1739). There were other eighteenth-century pro-curial replies to its various Gallican or Febronian (Febronius was the pseudonym of J.N. von Hontheim, an anti-curial German cleric) critics; see the works (in the bibliography) of G. Marchetti, F.A. Zaccaria and G.A. Sangallo.
23. Giuseppe Piatti, *Storia critico-cronologica de' romani pontifici* (12 vols, Naples, 1765); Antonio Sandini, *Vitae pontificum romanorum* (Parma, 1739). See also the pro-curial and anonymous *Compendio della sacra storia … con le notizie storiche della Chiesa di Gesù Christo* (Rome, 1778).
24. The reappraisal of Lombard history is found in Bacchini's *L'istoria del Monastero di S. Benedetto* (Modena, 1696) – although Bacchini himself referred to the *Historia principum longobardum* (1643) of Camillo Pellegrino (1598–1663).
25. Muratori, *Dissertazioni sopra le antichità italiane,* vol. 3, *Dissertazione* 70, pp. 460, 468.
26. Arconati, *L'inquisizione processata, opera storica, e curiosa* (Colonia, i.e. Geneva), pp. 6–9.
27. Sarpi, *Trattato delle Materie Beneficiarie,* pp. 64–5.
28. Paolo Sarpi, *Storia particolare delle cose passate tra Sommo Pontefice Paolo V e la Serenissima Repubblica di Venezia negli anni 1605, 1606, 1607,* in *Opere varie del molto reverend Padre F. Paolo Sarpi* (2 vols, Helmstadt [i.e. Venice?], 1750), p. 1.
29. Giovanni Leone's pseudonym was Giovanni Simone Sardi. See also Tommaso Zefiriele Bovio's *Copia d'un lettera scritta a nostro signore Papa Paolo Quinto* (Pavia, 1606), which is more pious in tone but at the same time heavily pro-monarchical. He counterposes royal power to papal supreme jurisdiction, noting God did not send his son to judge the world but to serve it, and that Jesus died rather than disobey the king.
30. Giannone's *Istoria civile* was read with approval by Edward Gibbon and cited by Joseph Priestley. However, the English edition of the *Storia civile* (*The Civil History of the Kingdom of Naples,* London, 1729–1731) had only a very restricted diffusion and influence, partly because only a comparatively small section of it dealt with the history of the Church in

general. In any case, its analysis did not significantly differ from previous Protestant works.

31. For Giannone's conception of the importance of civil law and its imputed origin in Mosaic Law see his *Il Triregno*, Alfredo Parente, ed. (3 vols, Bari, 1940), vol. 1, 'Del Regno Terreno', p. 13. The *Triregno* was written in exile in 1731–3, but not published until 1867, although the text was known in manuscript form.

32. Giannone, *Istoria civile*, vol. 1, pp. 272–4, 293–5, 471; vol. 3, pp. 30–1.

33. There has been some debate on whether Capecelatro was a Jansenist, see for example Gennaro Auletta's *Un Giansenista napoletano del settecento: Mons. Giuseppe Capecelatro Arcivescovo di Taranto* (Naples, 1940). The much more recent summary by P. Stella does not even mention Jansenism in relation to Capecelatro, preferring the epithets reformist and jurisdictionalist (see Stella's summary in Vincenzo Cappelletti (ed.), *Dizionario biografico degli Italiani*, vol. 18, Rome 1975, pp. 445–52).

34. Eusebio Marcello Scotti's *Della Monarchia Universale de'papi* (Naples, 1789) was published anonymously. One possibility for authorship was an unknown individual, one Mineo, although he is sometimes only referred to as a collaborator. The other name advanced was that of Scotti, who is now considered the author. Scotti's work prompted a pro-curial reply from Francesco Antonio Zaccaria, *Il Discorso di un anonimo, della Monarchia universale de'papi, Napoli 1789* (Rome, 1791).

35. Scotti, *Monarchia universale*, p. 67.

36. Anonymous, *Istoria del pontificate romane e sue relazioni con le potenze della cristianità* (Geneva, 1785), pp. 73–5.

37. Little biographical detail is available on Rivarola, but for a reference to him see Renato Soriga's, *L'Idea nazionale italiana dal sec. XVIII alla unificazione* (Modena, 1941), pp. 116, 120–31; and Carmelo Caristia's, *Riflessi politici del giansenismo italiano* (Naples, 1965), p. 165. Rivarola translated Mornay's work possibly in collaboration with one Giuseppe Toietti, about whom biographical information is not available.

38. Rivarola, *Storia del papato*, vol. 2, pp. 285–6.

39. There are no biographical details available on Delle Piane; for passing references to him see Caristia (*Riflessi politici*, pp. 178–80, 321–2).

40. For a work combining a devastating critique of the papacy with elements of spiritual respect for the seat of St Peter see, for instance, *Il Papa; o siano ricerche sul primato dei questo sacerdote* (Eleutheropoli, 1783) of F. Catani. Catani concludes (pp. 165–7) with an open call to sovereigns to take the path of power over their Churches, and advocates a return to the times of Emperor Constantine. Similarly, see also the Jansenist Vincenzo Palmieri's *Istituzioni di storia ecclesiastica* (2 vols, Pistoia, 1789).

41. Pier Niccolò Delle Piane, *Storia cronologica de' papi* (Genoa, 1798), pp. 7, 129–30.

42. Carlo Denina, *Discorso istorico sopra l'origine della gerarchia* (Paris, 1808; composed c. 1779–80), p. 34.

43. Milton, *Catholic and Reformed*, pp. 49–50. On the offensive against Puritans see, for instance, Ormerod's *The Picture of a Puritane*.

44. Convocation of Canterbury, *A Representation of the present state of Religion, with regard to the ... growth of infidelity, Heresy, and Profaneness ... Drawn up by Upper House of Convocation* (London, 1711), p. 4.

45. Convocation of Canterbury, *A Representation of the present state of Religion ... rejected by the Upper House, but passed in the Lower House* (London, 1711), p. 7.

46. Ferrone, *The Intellectual Roots,* pp. 148–9.

47. Robert Howard, *The history of Religion. As it has been manag'd by priest-craft* (London, 1709), p. 278.

48. In exile, Radicati promulgated the clerical imposture theory in such works as *A Succint History of Priesthood, Ancient and Modern* (London, 1737; translated from his *Histoire abrégée de la profession sacerdotale ancienne et moderne,* 1736).

49. Spini, *Ritratto del Protestante,* pp. 177–8.

CHAPTER 4   CHURCH, STATE AND PRIEST-KINGS

1. Stuart Woolf, *A History of Italy 1700–1860* (London, 1991, 1st edn 1979), pp. 144–5.

2. Odorico Rinaldi, *Gli Annali Ecclesiastici tratti da quelli del Cardinal Baronio per Odorico Rinaldi* (5 vols, Rome, 1656–70), vol. 5, p. 589.

3. Don Antonio Rocco, *L'Alcibiade fanciullo a scuola* (Venice, *c.* 1650; written *c.* 1630).

4. On the concerns of Sicilian thinkers to preserve the balance of Church and state deemed essential to an acceptable political order see Woolf, *History of Italy,* p. 139.

5. Sarpi, *Storia particolare delle cose passate,* p. 1.

6. Sarpi, *Historia ... sopra li beneficii ecclesiastici,* pp. 17–21.

7. See for instance Guicciardini's *Storia d'Italia,* written in the 1530s.

8. For an anti-curial assessment of papal territorial claims see the anony-mous *Il Dominio spirituale e temporale del papa o siano ricerche sul vicario di Gesù Cristo e il principe di Roma* (London, i.e. Italy, 1783). This work stung the ever-energetic pro-curial propagandist Francesco Zaccaria into action; see his *Denunza solenne fatta alla Chiesa e ai Principi cattolici di un anticristiano: ... stampato in Italia colla falsa data di Londra, 'Il Dominio spirituale e temporale del papa o siano ricerche sul vicario di Gesù Cristo e il principe di Roma* (Assisi, 1783).

9. See Giovanni Battista Comazzi's *Politica e religione trovate insieme nella persona ed azioni di Gesù Cristo* (Cologne, 1709).

10. See for instance Muratori's *Ragioni della Serenissima Casa d'Este sopra Ferrara confermate e difese in risposta al dominio temporale della Sede Apostolica* (Modena, 1714).

11. See Lorenzo Valla's *De falsa credita et ementita Constantini Donatione declamatio* (1440).

12. Lodovico Muratori, *Annali d'Italia* (12 vols, Milan, 1744–9), vol. 4, p. 396.

13. Giannone, *Istoria civile,* vol. 1, pp. 382–6.

14. Giannone, *Il Triregno*, vol. 3, p. 219–20. The Carolingian dynasty endured from 730 to 887.
15. Scotti, *Della Monarchia*, pp. 33–4, 61–2, 127–9.
16. Capecelatro, *Discorso istorico*, preface pp. 5–6; main text, 17–22, 34–6, 38, 51–2, 57–8, 83–4.
17. Anonymous, *Istoria del pontificate*, pp. 9–10, 12–13, 15.
18. Rivarola, *Storia del papato*, vol. 2, 161–2; vol. 3, pp. 2, 75–6, 161–2.
19. Delle Piane, *Storia cronologica*, pp. 5, 202, 133.
20. Carlo Denina, *Discorso istorico*, pp. 34, 89; *Delle Rivoluzione d'Italia* (3 vols, Turin, 1769–70), vol. 1, pp. 397–8.
21. Headley, *Luther's View*, p. 199. On Calvin's view of papal tyranny see his *Institutes* vol. 2, bk 4, ch. 7 and 11.
22. Field, *Of the Church*, pp. 77–8; but see also Richard Crakanthorp's *Justinian the Emperor Defended against Cardinal Baronius* (London, 1616); Henry Foulis's *The History of Romish Treasons and Usurpations* (London, 1671, 2nd edn); Gilbert Burnet's *The History of the Rights of Princes in the Disposing of Ecclesiastical Benefices and Church Lands* (London, 1682).
23. G. Bennett, 'Conflict in the Church', in G. Holmes (ed.), *Britain after the Glorious Revolution 1689–1714* (London, 1982, 1st edn 1969), pp. 155–9.
24. Howell, *A View of the Pontificate*, pp. 8, 205–6, 232.
25. Gregory, *History of the Christian Church*, vol. 1, pp. 321, 350, 354, 361, 391; vol. 2, pp. 3, 12, 106.
26. See for instance John Toland's *Tetradymus. Containing ... Clidophorus; or, of the Exoteric and Esoteric Philosophy ... of the Antients* (London, 1720).
27. Arthur Young, *An Historical Dissertation on Idolatrous Corruptions in Religion* (2 vols, London, 1734), pp. 350–2.
28. Brown, *General History*, vol. 1, p. 187.
29. John Brown, *The Absurdity and Perfidy of all Authoritative Toleration of Gross Heresy, Blasphemy, Idolatry, Popery, in Britain* (Glasgow, 1780), p. 3.
30. Gisborne, *A Familiar Survey*, pp. 480–1.
31. Thomas Bray, *Papal Usurpation and Tyranny, concerning the Usurpations, Wars and Persecutions of the Popes, and Popish Clergy, with reference chiefly to Princes and States, to overturn their government* (London, 1712 – published as part one of Bray's collection of tracts entitled *Papal Usurpation and Persecution*), preface, pp. 1–2.
32. 'Several Gentlemen', *History of Popery*, vol. 1, pp. 376, 477; vol. 2, p. 113.
33. Angell, *History of Religion*, vol. 1, pp. 53, 82; vol. 2, p. 34. On anti-monasticism see M.S. Anderson, 'The Italian reformers', in H. Scott (ed.), *Enlightened Absolutism* (London, 1990), pp. 55–74.
34. Priestley, *An History of Corruptions*, vol. 2, pp. 305, 265; *General History*, vol. 1, pp. 388–9; vol. 2, pp. 331–2, vol. 3, p. 1.
35. Bicheno, *A Glance at the History*, pp. 7–8, 10.
36. Wesley, *Concise History*, vol. 1, p. 320; vol. 2, pp. 21, 117.
37. Milner, *History of the Church*, vol. 3, pp. 419, 494–5.

38. Nisbet, *An Abridgement*, pp. 95, 116, 122–3, 137, 146, 205.
39. Brown, *General History*, vol. 1, pp. 184, 187.
40. Headley, *Luther's View*, p. 198.
41. Anonymous (wrongly attributed to Isaac Casaubon), *The Original of Popish Idolatrie* (London, 1630, 2nd edn, translated from French; 1st edn 1624), p. 34.
42. Gay, *Modern Paganism*, p. 326.
43. Edward Gibbon, *The Decline and Fall of the Roman Empire, an Abridgement*, ed. D.M. Low (London, 1968), pp. 637–9.
44. Gibbon, *The Decline and Fall*, p. 740.
45. Anonymous, *The Thoughts of a Tory Author, concerning the Press* (London, 1712), pp. 1–2.
46. Milner, *History of the Church*, vol. 3. p. 97, vol. 4, p. 145.

CHAPTER 5   MARTYRS, FANATICISM AND EMPIRE DEFENDED

1. On Catholic martyrologies see also Bozio's *De signis ecclesiae* (2 vols, Rome, 1591), vol. 1, ch. 57.
2. Francesco Panigarola, *Lettioni sopra dogmi fatte da F. Francesco Panigarola minore osservante alla presenza, e per commandamento del Ser.^{mo} Carlo Emanuelle Duca di Savioa* (Venice, 1584).
3. Paolo Segneri, *L'Incredulo senza scusa ... Dove si dimostra che non può conoscere quale sia la vera religione, che vuol conoscerla* (Bologna, 1690), p. 195.
4. Gotti, *Veritas religionis christianae*, vol. 12, pp. 31–2, 125.
5. On the defence of the Inquisition see also Domenico Bernini*'s Historia di tutte l'heresie* (4 vols, Rome, 1705–9).
6. Anonymous, *Notizie storiche*, pp. 83–4.
7. Orsi-Becchetti, *Storia ecclesiastica* (52 vols, Rome, 1835–62 – a complete edition of Orsi-Becchetti), tome 118, pp. 40–2; this edition remains mostly as it was published, in *fascicoli* (pamphlets), which I have termed tomes.
8. Muratori, *Dissertazioni*, vol. 3, *Dissertazione* 60, p. 309. In some respects Tommaso Antonio Contin shared Muratori's views, At Venice in the 1760s and 1770s, Contin was the most authoritative representative of the Venetian reform movement, and was not alone in advocating a return to the jurisdictionalism of Paolo Sarpi. His *Dizionario dell'eresie, degli errori, e degli scismi* (5 vols, Venice, 1767–71), although containing a hard polemic against the Catholicism of the Counter-Reformation, also argued that heretical notions were justifications of error and venality. The *Dizionario* was Contin's expansion of Francois Pluquet's *Mémoires pour servir à l'histoire des égarements de l'esprit humain* (1762).
9. See for instance the preface to Pallavicino's *Il Divortio celeste* (Villafranca, 1643), and in the reprint and continuation of Pallavicino's work by Arconati, *Il Divorzio celeste* (In Regunea, i.e. Geneva, 1679).
10. Arconati, *Inquisizione*, pp. 9–11.
11. Giannone, *Istoria civile*, vol. 3, pp. 322, 333.
12. Capecelatro, *Discorso istorico*, pp. 42–3.

13. Delle Piane, *Storia cronologica de' papi*, pp. 260–4.
14. Woolf, *History of Italy*, p. 134.
15. Headley, *Luther's View*, p. 210.
16. William Turner, *The huntyng of the Romyshe foxe* (Basel, 1534), sig. F.vii.ʳ.
17. Job Throckmorton, *A Dialogue. Wherein is Plainly Laide open, the Tyrannicall Dealing of L. Bishopps Against God's Children* (1589), in Lawrence Sasek (ed.), *Images of English Puritanism* (Louisiana University Press, 1989), p. 50.
18. Henry Sacheverell, *The Perils of False Brethren, both in Church and State* (London, 1709), p. 12.
19. Collier, *Ecclesiastical History*, vol. 1, pp. 616–17; Milner, *History of the Church*, vol. 4, p. 201.
20. Howell, *View of the Pontificate*, pp. 218, 317.
21. Angell, *History of Religion*, vol. 2, p. 31.
22. Anonymous, *The History of the persecutions of the Reformed Churches in France, Orange and Piedmont from the year 1655* (London, 1699), pp. 8–9.
23. Gisborne, *A familiar survey*, p. 483.
24. Howell, *View of the Pontificate*, p. 395.
25. Brown, *A General History*, p. 335.
26. Gregory, *History of the Church*, vol. 2, pp. 126, 137; Wesley, *Concise History*, vol. 2, pp. 277–9; Priestley, *General History*, vol. 2, p. 488.
27. Calvin, *Institutes*, vol. 1, p. 91.
28. Collier, *Ecclesiastical History*, vol. 1, pp. 598–9.
29. Wesley, *Concise History*, vol. 1, pp. 5, 13; vol. 2, pp. 209–10.
30. Nisbet, *An Abridgement*, pp. 188, 223.
31. Giannone, *Il Triregno*, vol. 3, pp. 219–20.
32. Anonymous, *Istoria del pontificate*, pp. 32–40.
33. Delle Piane, *Storia cronologica*, pp. 251, 268.
34. Rivarola, *Storia del papato*, vol. 3, pp. 218–19; vol. 4, pp. 243–53, 407–8.
35. Wesley, *Concise History*, vol. 2, p. 93.
36. Bray, *Papal Usurpation and Tyranny*, preface, pp. 1–2.
37. Toland, *Christianity not Mysterious* (London, 1696), p. 173.
38. See for instance the anonymous *An account of the late persecution of the Protestants in the Valleys of Piemont ... in the year 1686* (Oxford, 1688); also *The History of the Persecutions of the Reformed Churches* (anonymous). On the reception of the Huguenot refugees in England see G.C. Gibbs, 'The Reception of the Huguenots in England', in Grell. Ole Peter, Israel, Jonathan I, and Nicholas Tyacke (eds), *From Persecution to Toleration, the Glorious Revolution and Religion in England* (Oxford, 1991).
39. Porter, *Gibbon*, p. 132.
40. Gregory, *History of the Church*, vol. 2, pp. 45, 47–52.
41. Gibbon, *The Decline and Fall*, pp. 778–9.
42. 'Several Gentlemen', *History of Popery*, vol. 1, pp. 342–3.
43. Brown, *General History*, p. 235.

CHAPTER 6   THE BOOK OF PRIESTCRAFT OPEN: FRAUD AND IDOLATRY

1. Henoch Clapham, *A Chronological Discourse touching, the Church; Christ; Anti-Christ; Gog and Magog* (London, 1609), sigs I, L. Gog and Magog were biblical characters under Satan's domination.
2. On Calvin and human nature see his *Institutes*, vol. 1, bk 1, ch. 4; bk 2, chs 1–3.
3. *Westminster Confession of Faith*, 1643 (Glasgow, 1985), pp. 39–40.
4. Robert Crowley, *A Briefe Discourse against the Outwarde Apparell and Ministring of the Popishe Church* (London, 1566), sig. A5r.
5. Henry More, *The Antidote Against Idolatry* in *A Brief Reply to a Late Answer to Dr. Henry More and his Antidote against Idolatry* (London, 1672, 1st edn 1669), p. 48.
6. As a comparison to English developments, see the work of Alan Kors on the French Enlightenment. Kors notes that within the deeply Christian and learned culture of the late seventeenth and early eighteenth centuries, 'there occurred inquiries and debates that generated the components of atheistic thought'. One must consider how 'a complex culture generated its own antithesis, the possibility of which it always had carried within' (Alan Charles Kors, *Atheism in France, 1650–1729*, vol. 1, *The Orthodox Sources of Disbelief* [Princeton, 1990], pp. 4, 379).
7. The five principles are: that there is one supreme God; that God ought to be worshipped; that Virtue and piety are the chief parts of the Divine worship; that we ought to be sorry for our sins and repent of them; that Divine Goodness dispenses rewards and punishments both in this life and after it. On earlier Reformation trends towards the use of reason in religion see Graf, H. Reventlow, *The Authority of the Bible and the Rise of the Modern World* (London, 1984).
8. On the perception of Islam and its use in religious polemic see Norman Daniel's *Islam and the West: The Making of an Image* (Edinburgh, 1960), and David Pailin's, *Attitudes to Other Religions* (Manchester, 1984).
9. See John Bale's *The Actes of Englysh Votaryes* (Wesel, 1546), p. 27; and Foxe's *Actes and Monuments* (1563), p. 1127b.
10. Matthew Sutcliffe, *De turcopapismo, hoc est, de turcarum & papistarum adversus Christi ecclesiam & fidem coniuratione, eorumq; in religione & moribus consensione & similitudine* (London, 1599), pp. 11, 109.
11. Perkins, *A Warning against the Idolatrie of the Last Times* (Cambridge, 1601), pp. 121–2.
12. The list of pagan elements taken up by the Church of Rome in Ormerod's *Pagano-Papismus* (London, 1606) provides an insight into the anti-Catholic comparative mentality; here I list just a few in paraphrase. Both papal and pagan Churches have in common a multitude of gods; gods for each country and city; household saints; gods for arts and sciences; for diseases; warriors commended to Mars, as Rome would have us commend ours to St George; gods for doors; for bees and apple trees; for learning; wealth; wine; gods for children; child

labour; and virgin gods (Mary). Rome also espouses idolatry; angel worship; and saint worship. Pagan kings sent altars ahead of them on travels, as the pope does his eucharist; heathens put golden crowns on the heads of their idols, as well as themselves. There are also images in temples; flagellation; shaved heads and beards; vestal virgins (nuns); witchcraft; sorcery and necromancy and jubilees. Papists believe in purgatory; sacrifices for the dead (purgatory sacrifice); special places in hell for each age and station of humanity. Catholics make holy water; candles for idols; and burn incense. They boast of miracles; give credit to vain and foolish apparitions, visions and phantasms.

13. Henry Ainsworth, *An Arrow against Idolatry. Taken out of the Quiver of the Lord of Hosts* (1640, 1st edn 1611), pp. 77, 80–3, 85–6, 93–5, 98–9. On the paganism charge see also Robert Jenison, *The Height of Israels Heathenish Idolatrie* (London, 1621); William Smith, *The Reign of the Whore Discovered and Ruine Seen* (London, 1659).

14. Herbert of Cherbury, *The Antient Religion of the Gentiles and Causes of their Errors considere'd* (London, 1705), pp. 271–2.

15. On the Anglican critique of Dissent see Humphrey Prideaux's *The True Nature of Imposture Fully Displayed in the Life of Mahomet* (London, 1697) which, along with Charles Leslie's *Socinian Dialogues* (1708–10) likened Unitarianism to Islam. Such critiques continued well into the eighteenth century; see William Russell's *Quakerism is Paganism* (London, 1674) and the anonymous *Fanatical Conversion; or, Methodism displayed* (London, 1779).

16. On anti-Anglican critiques see Smith's *The Reign of the Whore* (a Quaker anti-Anglican work); George Whitehead, *An Unjust Plea Confuted* (London, 1659); Delaune, *A Plea for the Non-conformists ... And how far the Conformists Separation from the Church of Rome ... justifies the non-Conformists Separation from them. ... To which is added, a Parallel Scheme of the Pagan, Papal and Christian Rites and Ceremonies* (London, 1684; edns in 1704, 1706, 1712, 1719, 1733, 1800, 1817, 1835, 1845 – a 'minor' work, but hardly without influence!). For an example of the general critique of Anglicanism by Puritans see Roger Crabb's *Dagons-Downfall, or the Great IDOL Digged up Root and Branch* (1657) – Dagon was a half man and half fish god worshipped by the Philistines. For a recent treatment of the Protestant idolatry charge, relating to the pre-Civil War seventeenth century see Milton, *Catholic and Reformed*, pp. 187–209.

17. For other late seventeenth- and eighteenth-century examples of the paganism comparative, see for instance the anonymous *The Anatomy of Popery: or, a Catalogue of Popish Errours in Doctrine, and Corruptions in Worship: together with the Agreement between Paganism, Pharisaism, and Popery* (London, 1673); Daniel Whitby, *A Discourse concerning the Idolatry of the Church of Rome* (London, 1674); Simon Patrick, *The Truth of the Christian Religion* (London, 1680); James Owen, *The History of Images and of Image Worship* (London, 1709); Arthur Young, *An Historical Dissertation on Idolatrous Corruptions;* and Conyers Middleton, *A Letter from Rome, shewing an Exact Conformity between Popery and Paganism* (London, 1729, in six edns to 1759).

18. Nisbet, *An Abridgement*, pp. 114–16, 139–40.
19. 'Several Gentlemen', *History of Popery*, vol. 1, pp. 72–3; vol. 2, pp. 15–16, 133, 136. On the more positive aspects of the Protestant view of Islam see N.I. Matar, 'Islam in Interregnum and Restoration England', in *The Seventeenth Century*, 6, 1 (1991); on the partial rehabilitation of Islam in the late seventeenth century see Champion, *Pillars* p. 104.
20. Brown, *General History*, vol. 1, p. 201; Wesley, *Concise History*, vol. 2, p. 140.
21. Martin Luther, *Letter to Pope Leo X* (1520), in Eric Cochrane and Julius Kirshner (eds), *Readings in Western Civilization*, vol. 5 (University of Chicago Press, 1986), p. 328.
22. Robert Howard, *The History of Religion. As it has been manag'd by Priestcraft* (London, 1694), pp. 305–7, 311. Treatises revealing the doctrinal frauds of popery were common and popular. Thomas James's *A Treatise of the Corruptions of Scripture ... by the Prelats, Pastors, and Pillars of the Church of Rome, for maintenance of Popery and Irreligion* (London, 1611), for instance, had editions in 1611, 1612, 1688 and 1843; Antonio Gavin's *The Frauds of Romish Monks and Priests* saw its fourth edition in 1704, and Crashaw's, *Falsificationum romanarum: et catholicarum restitutionum* (London, 1606) was still consulted well into the eighteenth century.
23. Gregory, *History of the Christian Church,* vol. 2, p. 80.
24. Wesley, *Concise History*, vol. 1, p. 268.
25. Howell, *View of the Pontificate*, pp. 108, 359, 392, 455.
26. Gregory, *History of the Church*, vol. 1, pp. 332, 407–8; vol. 2, p. 80.
27. Wesley, *Concise History*, vol. 1, p. 262; vol. 2, pp. 77–8.
28. 'Several Gentlemen', *History of Popery*, vol. 1, pp. 175, 240, 373, 477.
29. Brown, *General History*, vol. 1, pp. 145–6, 272.
30. Lancelotto Politi, *Compendio d'errori, et inganni luterani* (Rome, 1544), fols. 2v–3r.
31. For a discussion on the Tridentine revival and the decision of 1616 see Sella, *Italy in the Seventeenth Century*, pp. 206 ff.
32. Arconati, *L'Inquisizione processata*, p. 9.
33. Sarpi, *Trattato delle Materie Beneficiarie,* pp. 121–3.
34. Muratori, *Dissertazioni,* vol. 2, *Dissertazione* 43, pp. 601, 628; vol. 3, *Dissertazione* 59, pp. 285–6.
35. Giannone was not alone amongst Catholics to espouse Mosaic theology: French Jesuit priests who had returned from China having witnessed what they considered to be 'natural piety' also advocated it. In seventeenth-century England there was also a vibrant Protestant trend towards the ancient theology, as for example in the work of Robert Fludd: *Mosaicall Philosophy: Grounded upon the Essential Truth or Eternal Sapience* (1659). Such writers did not, however, use Mosaic law to reformulate Christian doctrine as did Giannone.
36. Giannone, *Il Triregno*, vol. 2, pp. 174–5.
37. On the corporeality of the soul see Giuseppe Ricuperati's, 'Il Problema della corporeità dell'anima dai libertini ai deisti', in Sergio Bertelli (ed.), *Il Libertinismo in Europa* (Milan and Naples, 1980). On John Toland's view of the soul see his *Letters to Serena* (London, 1704), letter

2, 'The History of the Souls Immortality among the Heathens'. Attacks on purgatory and the nature of the soul naturally produced defences of Catholic orthodoxy, see for instance Anton Filippo Adami, *L'Immortalità dell'anima provata* (Livorno, 1755).

38. Joseph Priestley, *An Inquiry into the Knowledge of the Antient Hebrews, concerning a Future State* (London, 1801), pp. 11, 31.

39. Giannone, *Istoria civile*, vol. 1, p. 461; vol. 2, pp. 315, 398, vol. 3, p. 339. The concept of purgatory is of course to be found earlier than the eleventh century, in the work of St Augustine. Gianonne used the term purgatory to refer to the specific conjunction of indulgences and purgatory.

40. Capecelatro, *Discorso istorico*, pp. 21–2, 69–70. It was just this type of analysis of clerical celibacy that stung the Curia, and prompted Antonio Zaccaria to polemicize against such 'detestible' ideas – see Zaccaria's *Storia polemica del celibato sacro da contrapporsi ad alcune detestibili opere uscite a questi tempi* (Rome, 1774). On the moral corruption of the clergy see also Capecelatro's *Delle Feste de' cristiani* (Naples, 1771).

41. Rivarola, *Storia del papato*, vol. 3, p. 19.

42. Scotti, *Monarchia universale*, pp. 21–2, 61–2, 65, 133.

43. On the use of *Pharisaism* as a comparative term of deprecation alongside the generic of paganism see, for instance, *The Anatomy of Popery* (anon.) and Henry Foulis's *The History of Romish Treasons and Usurpations*.

44. Rivarola, *Storia del papato*, vol. 2, pp. 104–5, 150–1; vol. 4, p. 17.

45. Blount, *The First Two Books of Philostratus* (London, 1680), pp. 19–21, 32–3, 112–13.

46. Besides the works of Thomas James and Antonio Gavin cited above, see for instance the *Popish Impostor: A Narrative. Setting forth the Frauds and Artifices of the Romish Clergy,* anonymous (London, c. 1735).

47. Radicati, *A Succint History of Priesthood,* pp. 19–20, 53–4.

48. Gibbon, *Decline and Fall*, pp. 181, 423, 638–9.

49. Toland, *Christianity not Mysterious*, p. 168.

CHAPTER 7   THE BIRTHPANGS OF 'DEIST' HISTORIOGRAPHY

1. On the difficulties associated with the term deist see D.A. Pailin, 'The confused and confusing story of natural religion', in *Religion* 24 (1994); Pailin, 'Herbert of Cherbury. A much-neglected and misunderstood thinker', in Creighton Peden and Larry E. Axel (eds), *God, Values and Empiricism* (Georgia, 1989).

2. David Pailin, 'British views on religion and religions in the age of William and Mary', in *Method and Theory in the Study of Religion,* 6–4 (1994), p. 354.

3. See, for example, Champion, *Pillars*, pp. 7–9, 11.

4. On this 'commonplace' see, for example, Harrison, *Religion,* p. 7.

5. The work of Popkin has been influential in this respect; see for example R.H. Popkin and A. Vanderjagt, *Scepticism and Irreligion in the*

Seventeenth and Eighteenth Centuries (Leiden, New York and Koln, 1993) and Popkin's *The History of Scepticism from Erasmus to Spinoza* (Berkeley, Los Angeles and London, 1979).

6. Pailin, 'Herbert of Cherbury', pp. 171–2, 177.
7. Kors, his Introduction to Kors and Korshin (eds), *Anticipations of the Enlightenment*, p. 2.
8. Convocation of Canterbury, *A Representation of the present state of Religion ... Drawn up by Upper House of Convocation,* p. 4. In their second report, Convocation also state that the Arian and Socinian heresies spread as a result of the attacks on the fundamental articles of the Catholic faith, see *A Representation ... rejected by the Upper House, but passed in the Lower House,* p. 4.
9. Labrousse, 'Reading Pierre Bayle', pp. 11, 15–16.
10. Howard, *History of Religion*, pp. 283, 288, 321–2.
11. Champion, *Pillars*, pp. 137–8.
12. Howard, *History of Religion*, pp. 278, 291, 302.
13. On Howard's Unitarianism see, for example, where he writes of the 'Being and Unity of God' (*History of Religion*, p. 315).
14. Dennis, *Priestcraft distinguished from Christianity* (London, 1715), Preface. p. 3; text pp. 1–2, 8–9, 31–2, 39. The analysis contained in this work is much the same as in his *The Danger of Priestcraft to Religion and Government, with some Politick Reasons for Toleration* (London, 1702).
15. John Trenchard, *The Natural History of Superstition* (London, 1709), pp. 6, 8–9.
16. Sydney Lee (ed.), *Dictionary of National Biography* (1899), vol. 57, pp. 198–9.
17. Champion, *Pillars*, pp. 99–100.
18. On Cherbury's Christianity and the lack of evidence for him as the founder of deism, see Pailin, 'Herbert of Cherbury'.
19. Field, *Of the Church,* p. 81.
20. Gay, *Modern Paganism*, p. 327.
21. Champion, *Pillars*, pp. 101, 106.
22. Evans, *Panthesiticon,* pp. 1, 20.
23. Isaac Newton, *Observations upon the Prophecies of Daniel and the Apocalypse of St. John* (London, 1733), pp. 13–14.
24. John Locke, *A Letter Concerning Toleration* (London, 1689), p. 26.
25. Bennett, 'Conflict in the Church', p. 155.
26. Stephens, *An Account of the Growth of Deism*, pp. 3–6. D.E., *The Prodigious Appearance of Deism,* pp. 4–7.
27. Arthur H. Powell, *The Sources of Eighteenth-Century Deism. An Inquiry into its Causes and Origin* (London, 1902), pp. 5–6, 13–14; John Coward, *Deism Traced to one of its Principal Sources, or the Corruption of Christianity the Great Cause of Infidelity* (London, 1796), pp. 25.
28. For an appreciation of Toland written within living memory of his life, see the biography of him prefaced to Toland's posthumous *A Critical History of the Celtic Religion and Learning* (London, 1740), esp. pp. 6–7.
29. John Toland, *An Apology for Mr. Toland* (1697), quoted in Evans, *Pantheisticon,* p. 24.
30. On the difficulties of defining republicanism, and locating archetypal

republican currents in the period 1680–1720 see David Wootton's 'The
Republican Tradition: From Commonwealth to Common Sense', in
Republicanism, Liberty, and Commercial Society, ed. D. Wootton
(California, 1994).

31.   Butterfield, *The Whig Interpretation,* pp. 32, 35.
32.   On Toland's concern for the Protestant succession see also the biog-
      raphy of Toland prefaced to his *Critical History of the Celtic Religion*
      and his *Anglia libera* (1701).
33.   John Toland, *Vindicius liberius: or M. Toland's Defence of Himself,*
      against the Lower House of Convocation (London, 1702), pp. 26–7, 162.
      On Toland's extemely wide definition of Christianity see Evans,
      Pantheisticon, pp. 146–7.
34.   Harrison (*Religion,* p. 87), and Evans (*Pantheisticon,* pp. 14–15) also
      describe *Christianity not Mysterious* as a work aimed at reform of the
      Protestant Church. Evans (p. 15) notes that Toland, on account of his
      religious concerns, cannot be written off as a 'sceptic or simple deist'.
35.   Toland, *Christianity not Mysterious,* pref. pp. 9, 21, text pp. 168–76. On
      Toland's belief that Christianity demonstrated the immortality of the
      soul and for more on the condemnation of superstition and idolatry see
      Toland's, *Letters to Serena* (pp. 19–20, 127–9).
36.   Angell, *History of Religion,* vol. 1, pp. 18–19.
37.   Convocation of Canterbury, *A Representation ... rejected by the Upper*
      House, but passed in the Lower House, p. 5.
38.   Toland, *Christianity not Mysterious,* pp. 159–63, 168–71.

CHAPTER 8   CONCLUSION: THE SPIRITUAL POLITICS OF
SOCIAL CLASS

1.   Christopher Hill has produced a range of studies, not least his
     Puritanism and Revolution (London, 1958), and *The world turned upside*
     down: Radical ideas during the English Revolution (London, 1972).
2.   On the 'third way' see for example Champion's 'Europe's
     Enlightenment and national historiographies'.
3.   See Weber's *Capitalism and the Protestant Ethic* (1904–5).
4.   On the Enlightenment and the French Revolution see, for example,
     William Church's (ed.) *The Influence of the Enlightenment on the French*
     Revolution (Lexington, 1974; 1st edn 1964).

Select Bibliography

Clandestinity

Where authors used pseudonyms, they are usually given in the main text of this work and can be located with the help of the Index – search under the real name of the author, which is always given in the text. Where it was not convenient to cite pseudonyms in the main text, they are provided below in parentheses after the author's name. Places of publication, as given in the texts themselves, will be given in the normal manner, even if they are false. Where the correct place of publication is known, this will be given after the false location. Where doubt still exists as to the correct location, there will be a question mark: (Helmstadt, i.e. Venice?, 1750).

Biographical Information

Little or no biographical detail is available on some writers; especially Italians, for the *Italian Dictionary of National Biography* is still making only very slow progress towards completion. In any case, the turbulent nature of Italian history has meant some writers have had little or nothing of their lives recorded. Where this is the case I have referenced whatever meagre information has been available to me; to find those references in the text search the Index under the author's name. Where there is abundant biographical material available on authors, I have only given references in order to warn of error, possible confusion or for other specific reasons.

PRIMARY TEXTS

Sixteenth Century

Anonymous, *The Fortresse of Fathers* (1566).
Bale, John, *The Actes of Englysh Votaryes* (Wesel, 1546).
Bale, John, *Acta romanorum pontificum* (Basle, 1558).
Bale, John, *The Pageant of the Popes* (London, 1574).
Barnes, Robert, *Vitae romanorum pontificum* (Basle, 1555, 1st edn 1536).
Bozio, Tommaso, *De signis ecclesiae* (2 vols, Rome, 1591).
Calvin, John, *Institutes of the Christian Religion*, ed. John Allen (2 vols, London, 1935).
Crowley, Robert, *A Briefe Discourse against the Outwarde Apparell and Ministring of the Popishe Church* (London, 1566).
Foxe, John, *Actes and Monuments of Matters happening in the Church* (London, 1563), ed. George Townsend (8 vols, New York, 1965).
Luther, Martin, *Letter to Pope Leo X* (1520), in Cochrane, Eric and Kirshner, Julius (eds), *Readings in Western Civilization*, vol. 5, (University of Chicago

Press, 1986).

Moronessa, Jacopo, *Il Modello di Martino Lutero* (Vinegia, 1556, i.e. 1555).

Panigarola, Francesco, *Lettioni sopra dogmi fatte da F. Francesco Panigarola* (Venice, 1584).

Politi, Lancelotto, *Compendio d'errori, et inganni luterani* (Rome, 1544).

Possevino, Antonio, *R.P. Antonii Possevini, Theologi Societatis Iesu, de sectariorum nostri temporis atheismus liber* (Cologne, 1586).

Rainolds, William, *Calvino-Turcismus. Id est calvinisticae perfidae, cum mahumetana collatio, et dilucida utriusque sectae confutatio* (Antwerp, 1597).

Rezka, Stanislaw, *De atheismus et phalarismus evangelicorum* (Naples, 1596).

Sutcliffe, Matthew, *De turcopapismo, hoc est, de turcarum & papistarum adversus Christi ecclesiam & fidem coniuratione, eorumq; in religione & moribus consensione & similitudine* (London, 1599).

Job Throckmorton, *A Dialogue. Wherein is Plainly Laide open, the Tyrannicall Dealing of L. Bishopps Against God's Children* (1589), in Lawrence Sasek (ed.), *Images of English Puritanism* (Louisiana University Press, 1989).

Turner, William, *The Huntyng and Fyndying of the Romish Foxe* (Basel, 1534).

Tyndale, John, *The Obedience of a Christian Man* (Marlborow, 1528).

Seventeenth Century

Ainsworth, Henry, *An Arrow against Idolatry. Taken out of the Quiver of the Lord of Hosts* (1640, 1st edn 1611).

Ainsworth, Henry, *Certayne Questions concerning (i) Silk or wool in the High Priest's Ephod; (ii) Idol Temples commonly called Churches* (London, 1605).

Anonymous, *The Original of Popish Idolatries* (London, 1630, 2nd edn, translated from French).

Anonymous, *An Account of the late Persecution of the Protestants in the Valleys of Piemont ... in the year 1686* (Oxford, 1688).

Anonymous, *The History of the Persecutions of the Reformed Churches in France, Orange and Piedmont from the year 1655* (London, 1699).

Anonymous, *The Anatomy of Popery: or, a Catalogue of Popish Errours in Doctrine, and Corruptions in Worship: together with the Agreement between Paganism, Pharisaism, and Popery* (London, 1673).

Arconati, Lamberti Giovanni Gerolamo, *Il Divorzio celeste* (In Regunea, i.e. Geneva, 1679); the first tome is by Ferrante Pallavicino, published in 1643.

Arconati, Lamberti Giovanni Gerolamo, *L'Inquisizione processata, opera storica, e curiosa* (Colonia, i.e. Geneva, 1681).

Blount, Charles, *The First Two Books of Philostratus, concerning the Life of Apollonius Tyaneus* (London, 1680).

Bovio, Tommaso Zefiriele, *Copia d'un lettera scritta a nostro signore Papa Paolo Quinto di Zefiriele Tomaso Bovio Veronese* (Padua, 1606).

Burnet, Gilbert, *The History of the Rights of Princes in the Disposing of Ecclesiastical Benefices and Church Lands* (London, 1682).

Campanella, Tommaso, *Atheismus triumphatus* (Rome, 1631).

Care, Henry (ed.), *A Pacquet of Advice from Rome* (5 vols, London, 1678–83; from 1679 entitled the *Weekly Pacquet of Advice from Rome*).

Burnet, Thomas, *De statu mortuorum et resurgentium liber* (London, 1720).

Cherbury, Herbert of, Lord Edward, *De religione gentilium, errorumque apud eos causis* (Amsterdam, 1663).

Herbert of Cherbury, Lord Edward, *The Antient Religion of the Gentiles and Causes of their Errors considered* (London, 1705).

Clapham, Henoch, *A Chronological Discourse touching the Church; Christ; Anti-Christ; Gog and Magog* (London, 1609).

Crabb, Roger, *Dagons-Downfall, or the Great Idol digged up Root and Branch* (1657).

Crakanthorp, Richard, *The Defence of Constantine: with a Treatise of the Popes Temporall Monarchie* (London, 1621).

Crashaw, William, *Falsificationum romanarum: et catholicarum restitutionum* (London, 1606).

Delaune, Thomas, *A plea for the Non-Conformists ... And how far the Conformists Separation from the Church of Rome ... justifies the non-Conformists Separation from them. ... To which is added, a Parallel Scheme of the Pagan, Papal and Christian Rites and Ceremonies* (London, 1684).

Field, Richard, *Of the Church, Five Bookes* (London, 1606).

Foulis, Henry, *The History of Romish Treasons and Usurpations: ... a Particular Account of many Gross Corruptions and Impostures* (London, 1671).

Fuller, Thomas, *Church-History of Britain, from the Birth of Jesus Christ, untill the Year 1648* (1655), ed. J.S. Brewer (6 vols, Oxford, 1845).

James, Thomas, *A Treatise of the Corruptions of Scripture, Councels, and Fathers, by the Prelats, Pastors, and Pillars of the Church of Rome, for maintenance of Popery and Irreligion* (London, 1611).

Jenison, Robert, *The Height of Israel's Heathenish Idolatrie* (London, 1621).

Leone, Giovanni Battista [pseud. Giovanni Simone Sardi], *Due Discorsi sopra la liberta ecclesiastica* (Venice? 1606).

Leti, Gregorio, *Il Nipotismo di Roma* (Amsterdam, 1667).

Locke, John, *A Letter Concerning Toleration* (London, 1689).

More, Henry, *The Antidote Against Idolatry*, in *A Brief Reply to a Late Answer to Dr. Henry More and his Antidote Against Idolatry* (London, 1672, 1st edn 1669).

Ormerod, Oliver, *The Picture of a Puritane ... Whereunto is annexed a Short Treatise, entituled, Puritano-papismus: or a Discoverie of Puritan-papisme* (London, 1605).

Ormerod, Oliver, *The Picture of a Papist ... Whereunto is annexed a Certain Treatise, intituled Pagano-Papismus: wherein is proved ... that Papisme is flat Paganisme* (London, 1606).

Pallavicino, Ferrante, *Il divortio celeste* (Villafranca, 1643).

Patrick, Simon, *The Truth of the Christian Religion* (London, 1680).

Perkins, William, *A Warning against the Idolatrie of the Last Times* (Cambridge, 1601).

Prideaux, Humphrey, *The True Nature of Imposture Fully Displayed in the Life of Mahomet* (London, 1697).

Rinaldi, Odorico, *Gli Annali ecclesiastici tratti da quelli del Cardinal Baronio per Odorico Rinaldi* (5 vols, Rome 1656–70).

Rocco, Don Antonio, *L'Alcibiade fanciullo a scuola* (Venice c. 1650, written c. 1630).

Russell, William, *Quakerism is Paganism* (London, 1674).

Sarpi, Paolo, *Historia della Sacra Inquisitione* (In Serravalle: Fabia Albicocco, 1638).

Sarpi, Paolo, *Storia particolare delle cose passate tra Sommo Pontefice Paolo V e ... Venezia negli anni 1605. 1606. 1607*, in *Opere Varie del molto reverend Padre F. Paolo Sarpi* (2 vols, Helmstadt, i.e. Venice? 1750).

Sarpi, Paolo, *Trattato delle materie beneficiarie di Fra. Paolo Sarpi* (Mirandola, 1676).

Segneri, Paolo, *L'Incredulo senza scusa ... Dove si dimostra che non può conoscere quale sia la vera religione, che vuol conoscerla* (Bologna, 1690).

Smith, William *The Reign of the Whore Discovered and Ruine Seen* (London, 1659).

Stephens, William, *An Account of the Growth of Deism in England* (London, 1696).

Stopford, Joshua, *Pagano-Papismus: Or, an Exact Parallel between Rome-Pagan and Rome-Christian, in the Doctrines and Ceremonies* (London, 1675).

Symson, Patrick, *The Historie of the Church* (London, 1624, 3rd edn 1634).

Toland, John, *Christianity not Mysterious* (London, 1696).

Toland, John, *Letters to Serena* (London, 1704).

Westminster Confession of Faith, 1643 (London, 1962).

Whitby, Daniel, *A Discourse concerning the Idolatry of the Church of Rome* (London, 1674).

Eighteenth Century

Adami, Anton Filippo, *L'Immortalità dell'anima provata* (Livorno, 1755).

Amidei, Cosimo, *La Chiesa e la repubblica dentro i loro limiti* (Florence, 1768), in A. Rotondò (ed.), *Opere di Cosimo Amidei* (Turin, 1980).

Angell, J. (the Elder), *The History of Religion* (4 vols, London, 1764; vol. 1 title page date of 1744 is a misprint).

Anonymous, *Notizie Storiche della Chiesa di Gesù Cristo,* (Rome, 1778). This work is the second part of the *Compendio della sacra storia del Vecchio, e Nuovo Testamento con le notizie storiche della Chiesa di Gesù Christo* (Rome, 1778).

Anonymous, *Il Dominio spirituale e temporale del papa,* (London, i.e. Italy, 1783).

Anonymous, *Istoria del pontificate romane e sue relazioni con le potenze della cristianità* (Geneva, 1785).

Anonymous, *Popish Impostor: a Narrative. Setting forth the Frauds and Artifices of the Romish Clergy* (London, c. 1735).

Anonymous, *Fanatical Conversion; or, Methodism displayed* (London, 1779).

Anonymous, *The Book of Martyrs, or The History of Paganism and Popery* (Coventry, 1764).

Anonymous, *The Thoughts of a Tory Author, concerning the Press* (London, 1712).

Becchetti, F., *Della Istoria ecclesiastica dell'eminentissimo Cardinale Giuseppe Orsi* (13 vols, Rome, 1770–81).

Becchetti, F., *Istoria degli ultimi quattro secoli della Chiesa* (10 vols, Rome, 1788–96).

Bicheno, James, *A Glance at the History of Christianity and of English Nonconformity* (Newbury, 1798, 2nd edn).

Bray, Thomas, *Papal Usurpation and Tyranny, concerning the Usurpations, Wars and Persecutions of the Popes, and Popish Clergy, with reference chiefly to Princes and States, to overturn their government* (London, 1712); published as part one of Bray's collection of tracts with the title of *Papal Usurpation and Persecution* (London, 1712).

Brown, John, A *General History of the Christian Church* (2 vols, Edinburgh, 1771).

Brown, John, *The Absurdity and Perfidy of all Authoritative Toleration of Gross Heresy, Blasphemy, Idolatry, Popery, in Britain* (Glasgow, 1780).

Brown, John, *A Compendious History of the Church of England and of the Protestant Churches in Ireland and America* (2 vols, Glasgow, 1784).

Brown, William, *Impiety, and Superstition expos'd: a Poetical essay* (Edinburgh, 1710).

Capecelatro, Giuseppe, *Discorso istorico-politico dell'origine del progresso e della decadenza del potere de'chierici su le signorie temporali* (Naples, 1788).

Capecelatro, Giuseppe, *Delle Feste de'cristiani* (Naples, 1771).

Catani, Francesco Maria, *Il Papa; o siano ricerche sul primato dei questo sacerdote* (Eleutheropoli, 1783).

Clarke, Samuel, *A Discourse concerning the Unchangeable Obligations of Natural Religion* (London, 1706).

Collier, Jeremy, *An Ecclesiastical History of Great Britain* (2 vols, London, 1708).

Comazzi, Count Giovanni Battista, *Politica e religione trovate insieme nella persona ed azioni di Gesù Cristo* (Cologne, 1709).

Convocation of Canterbury, *A Representation of the Present state of Religion, with regard to the ... growth of Infidelity, Heresy, and Profaneness ... Drawn up by Upper House of Convocation* (London, 1711).

Convocation of Canterbury, *A Representation of the Present State of Religion, with regard to the ... growth of Infidelity, Heresy, and Profaneness ... rejected by the Upper House, but passed in the Lower House* (London, 1711).

Coward, John, *Deism Traced to one of its Principal Sources, or the Corruption of Christianity the Great Cause of Infidelity* (London, 1796).

D.E. (anon.), *The Prodigious Appearance of Deism in this Age Modestly Accounted for in a Letter from a Deist to his Friend* (London, 1710).

Delle Piane, Pier Niccolò, *Storia cronologica de' papi* (Genoa, 1798).

Denina, Carlo, *Delle Rivoluzione d'Italia* (3 vols, Turin, 1769–70).

Denina, Carlo, *Discorso istorico sopra l'origine dell gerarchia e de'concordati fra la podestà ecclesiastica e la secolare* (Paris, 1808).

Dennis, John, *Priestcraft distinguished from Christianity* (London, 1715).

Dennis, John, *The Danger of Priestcraft to Religion and Government, with some Politick Reasons for Toleration* (London, 1702).

De'Ricci Scipione (ed.), *Raccolta di opuscoli interessanti la religione* (16 vols, Pistoia, 1783).

Douglas, John, *The Criterion: or, Miracles examined with a View to Expose the Pretensions of Pagans and Papists* (London, 1754).

Gavin, Antonio, *The Frauds of Romish Monks and Priests* (1704, 4th edn).

Giannone, Pietro, *Istoria civile del Regno di Napoli* (4 vols, Naples, 1770; 1st edn 1723).

Giannone, Pietro, *Opere postume di Pietro Giannone* (2 vols, Naples, 1770–2).
Giannone, Pietro, *Il Triregno*, ed. Alfredo Parente (3 vols, Bari, 1940).
Giannone, Pietro, *La Chiesa sotto il pontificato di Gregorio il Grande*, Mancini, P.S. (ed.), in *Opere inedite* (2 vols, Turin, 1859).
Giannone, Pietro, *Opere di Pietro Giannone*, Bertelli, Sergio and Ricuperati, G. (eds), in Ricciardi, R. (gen. ed.), *Illuministi italiani*, vol. 1 (Milan and Naples, 1971).
Gisborne, Thomas, *A Familiar Survey of the Christian Religion* (London, 1799).
Gotti, Vincenzo Lodovico, *Veritas religionis christianae* (12 vols, Rome, 1735–40).
Gregory, George, *History of the Christian Church* (2 vols, London, 1790).
Howard, Robert, *The history of Religion. As it has been manag'd by Priestcraft* (London, 1709).
Howell, Laurence, *A view of the Pontificate ... in which the Corruptions of the Scriptures and Sacred Antiquity, Forgeries in the Councils, and Encroachments of the Courts of Rome on the Church and State, to support their Infallibility, Supremacy, and other Modern Doctrines are set in a True Light* (London, 1712).
Marchetti, Giovanni, *L'Autorità suprema del romano pontefice* (Rome, 1789).
Marchetti, Giovanni *Critica della Storia Ecclesiastica e de'discorsi del ... Claudio Fleury* (2 vols, Bologna, 1782–3).
Middleton, Conyers, *A Letter from Rome, shewing an Exact Conformity between Popery and Paganism* (London, 1729).
Milner, Joseph, *The History of the Church of Christ* (5 vols, London, 1819, 1st edn 1794–1809); vol 4 edited by Isaac Milner from the manuscript of J. Milner).
Montegnacco, Antonio, *Ragionamento intorno a' beni temporali posseduti dalle chiese* (Venice, 1766).
Mosheim, Johann Lorenz von, *An Ecclesiastical History,* translated by Archibald Maclaine (2 vols, London, 1765).
Muratori, Lodovico Antonio, *Annali d'Italia* (12 vols, Milan, 1744–9).
Muratori, Lodovico Antonio, *Dissertazioni sopra le antichità italiane* (3 vols, Milan, 1751); the *Dissertazioni* are the posthumous translation of the *Antiquitates italicae medii* (6 vols, Milan, 1738–42) by the nephew of Muratori, Gian-Francesco Soli Muratori.
Muratori, Lodovico Antonio, *Ragioni della Serenissima Casa d'Este sopra Ferrara confermate e difese* (Modena, 1714).
Muratori, Lodovico Antonio, *Della Fallibilità dei pontefici nel dominio temporale,* posthumous, ed. C. Foucard (Modena, 1872)
Muzzarelli, Alfonso, *Dominio temporale del papa* (1789).
Newton, Sir Isaac, *Observations upon the Prophecies of Daniel and the Apocalypse of St John* (London, 1733).
Nisbet, Patrick, *An Abridgement of Ecclesiastical History* (Edinburgh, 1776).
Orsi, Giuseppe Agostino, *Della Istoria ecclesiastica* (21 vols, Rome, 1746–62).
Orsi, Giuseppe Agostino, and Becchetti, Filippo Angelico, *Storia ecclesiastica* (52 vols, Rome, 1835–62).
Orsi, Giuseppe Agostino, *Dell'Origine del dominio e della sovranità temporale de'romani pontifici* (Rome, 1742).

Orsi, Giuseppe Agostino, *Della infallibilità e dell'autorità del romano pontefice sopra i concilj ecumenici* (2 vols, Rome, 1741–2).

Owen, James, *The History of Images and of Image Worship* (London, 1709).

Palmieri, Vincenzo, *Istituzioni di storia ecclesiastica* (Pistoia, 1789).

Pani, Tommaso Vicenzo, *Della Punizione degli eretici e del Tribunale della Santa Inquizione* (2 vols, Rome, 1789).

Piatti, Giuseppe, *Storia critico-cronologica de' romani pontifici* (12 vols, Naples, 1765–8).

Picenino, Giacomo, *Apologia per I riformatori e per la religione riformata* (Coira, 1706).

Pluquet, François-André-Adrien, *Dizionario dell'eresie, degli errori, e degli scismi*, translated by Tommaso Antonio Contin (5 vols, Venice, 1767–71).

Priestley, Joseph, *A General History of the Christian Church from the Fall of the Western Empire to the Present Time* (4 vols, Northumberland, USA, 1802–3).

Priestley, Joseph, *An History of the Corruptions of Christianity* (2 vols, Birmingham, 1782).

Priestley, Joseph, *An Inquiry into the Knowledge of the Antient Hebrews, concerning a Future State* (London, 1801).

Radicati, Alberto, Count of Passerano, *A Succint History of Priesthood, Ancient and Modern* (London, 1737, translated from French).

Riccardi, Allesandro, *Ragioni del Regno di Napoli nella causa de'suoi beneficj ecclesiastici* (1708).

Rivarola, Paolo, *Storia del papato di Filippo de Mornay, cittadino Francese* (4 vols, Pavia 1796–1802).

Sacheverell, Henry, *The Perils of False Brethren, both in Church and State* (London, 1709).

Sangallo, G.A., *Dello Stato della Chiesa e legittima potestà del romano pontefice* (Venice, 1766).

Scotti, Marcello Eusebio, *Della Monarchia universale de'papi* (Naples, 1789).

Several Gentlemen, *The history of Popery, with such Alterations of Phrase, as may be more suitable to the taste of this age; and such additions, as may improve the history, strengthen the argument and better accommodate it to the present state of Popery in Great Britain* (2 vols, London, 1735).

Toland, John, *Vindicius liberius: or M. Toland's Defence of Himself, against the Lower House of Convocation* (London, 1702).

Toland, John, *Christianity not Mysterious* (London, 1696).

Toland, John, *A Critical History of the Celtic Religion and Learning* (London, 1740).

Toland, John, *Tetradymus* (London, 1720).

Toland, John, *Letters to Serena* (London, 1704).

Toland, John, *The Memorial of the State of England, in Vindication of the Queeen, the Church, and the Administration* (London, 1705).

Trenchard, John, *The Natural History of Superstition* (London, 1709).

Warburton, William, *A Critical and Philosophical Enquiry into the Causes of Prodigies and Miracles* (London, 1727).

Whitehead, George, *An Unjust Plea Confuted* (London, 1659).

Young, Arthur, *An Historical Dissertation on Idolatrous Corruptions in Religion* (2 vols, London, 1734).

Wesley, John, *A Concise Ecclesiastical History* (4 vols, London, 1781).
Zaccaria, Francesco Antonio, *Anti-Febbronio ... o sia apologia polemico-storico del primato del Papa* (Pesaro, 1767).
Zaccaria, Francesco Antonio, *Il Discorso di un anonimo, Della Monarchia universale de'papi, Napoli 1789* (Rome, 1791).
Zaccaria, Francesco Antonio, *Denunza solenne fatta alla chiesa e ai principi cattolici di un anticristiano: ... stampato in Italia colla falsa data di Londra, 'Il dominio spirituale e temporale del papa o siano ricerche sul vicario di Gesù Cristo e il principe di Roma* (Assisi, 1783).

SECONDARY TEXTS

Ambrasi, D., *Riformatori e ribelli a Napoli nella seconda metà del settecento* (Naples, 1979).
Anderson, M.S., 'The Italian reformers', in Scott, H.M. (ed.), *Enlightened Absolutism* (London, 1990).
Auletta, Gennaro, *Un Giansenista napoletano del settecento: Mons. Giuseppe Capecelatro Arcivescovo di Taranto* (Naples, 1940).
Baker, F., *John Wesley and the Church of England* (London, 1970).
Barnes, H.E., *A History of Historical Writing* (New York, 1963, 2nd edn).
Bennett, G.V., 'Conflict in the Church', in *Britain after the Glorious Revolution 1689–1714*, ed. G. Holmes (London, 1982, 1st edn 1969).
Bertelli, Sergio, *Ribelli, libertini, ortodossi nella storiografia barocca* (Florence, 1973).
Bertelli, Sergio (ed.), *Il Libertinismo in Europa* (Milano and Napoli, 1980).
Butterfield, Herbert, *The Whig Interpretation of History* (Harmondsworth, 1973).
Byrne, Peter, *Natural Religion and the Nature of Religion* (London and New York, 1989).
Byrne, James, *Glory, Jest and Riddle* (London, 1996).
Camic, C., *Experience and Enlightenment* (Edinburgh, 1983).
Caristia, Carmelo, *Riflessi politici del giansenismo italiano* (Naples, 1965).
Chadwick, Owen, 'The Italian Enlightenment', in Teich. M. and Porter, Roy (eds), *The Enlightenment in National Context* (Cambridge, 1981).
Champion, Justin, *The Pillars of Priestcraft shaken* (Cambridge, 1992).
Champion, Justin, 'Europe's Enlightenment and national historiographies: Rethinking Religion and Revolution', in *Europa. European Review of History* (1993).
Chiosi, Elvira, *Lo spirito del secolo. Politica e religione a Napoli nell'eta dell'illuminismo* (Naples, 1992).
Chitnis, Anand, *The Scottish Enlightenment* (London, 1976).
Clark, J.C.D., *English Society 1688–1832* (Cambridge, 1985).
Collinson, Patrick, *The Birthpangs of Protestant England* (London, 1988).
Croce, Benedetto, 'Studi sulla vita religiosa a Napoli nel settecento, L'arcivescovo di Taranto', in *La Critica. Rivista di letteratura, storia e filosofia*, 24, 2 (1926).
Daniel, Norman, *Islam and the West: The Making of an Image* (Edinburgh, 1960).

De Felice, Renzo, *Il Triennio giacobino in Italia 1796–1799* (Roma, 1990).
De Maio, R., *Società e vita religiosa a Napoli nell'età moderna 1656–1799* (Naples, 1971).
Diaz, Furio, and Saitta, A., *La questione del'giacobinismo italiano* (Roma, 1988).
Diaz, Furio, *Per una Storia illuministica* (Naples, 1973).
Diaz, Furio, 'Ludovico Antonio Muratori', in Cecchi E. and Sapegno N. (gen. eds), *Il Settecento*, vol. 6 of *Storia della Letteratura Italiana* (Garzanti, 1988).
Donagan, Barbara 'Understanding Providence: The Difficulties of Sir William and Lady Waller', *Journal of Ecclesiastical History*, 39, 3, (1988).
Drummond, A. and Bulloch, J., *The Scottish Church 1688–1843* (Edinburgh, 1973).
Evans, Robert Rees, *Pantheisticon. The Career of John Toland* (New York, 1991).
Ferrone, Vincenzo, *The Intellectual Roots of the Italian Enlightenment* (New Jersey, 1995; 1st edn *Scienza, natura, religione: Mondo newtoniana e cultura nel primo settecento* (Naples, 1982).
Funkenstein, Amos, *Theology and the Scientific Imagination from the Middle ages to the Seventeenth Century* (Princetown, USA, 1986).
Gay, Peter, *The Enlightenment: an Interpretation*, vol. 1 *The Rise of Modern Paganism*, vol. 2 *The Science of Freedom*, (London, 1973; 1st edn vol. 1, 1966, vol. 2, 1969).
Gentile, Carlo, *Pietro Giannone, E. Gibbon e il Triregno* (Bastogi, 1976).
Gibbon, Edward, *Decline and Fall of the Roman Empire* (6 vols, London, 1776–88).
Gibbon, Edward, *The Decline and Fall of the Roman Empire, an Abridgement*, by D.M. Low (London, 1968).
Gibbs, G.C., 'The Reception of the Huguenots in England', in Grell, Ole Peter, Israel, Jonathan I., and Nicholas Tyacke (eds), *From Persecution to Toleration, the Glorious Revolution and Religion in England* (Oxford, 1991).
Hankin, T., *Science and the Enlightenment* (Cambridge, 1995, 1st edn 1985).
Harrison, Peter, *'Religion' and the Religions in the English Enlightenment* (Avon, 1990).
Haydon, Colin, *Anti-Catholicism in Eighteenth-Century England, c. 1714–1780* (Manchester, 1993).
Haydon, C., Walsh, J., and Taylor, S. (eds), *The Church of England c. 1689–c. 1833* (Cambridge, 1993).
Headley, John M., *Luther's View of Church History* (New Haven and London, 1963).
Henshall, Nicholas, *The Myth of Absolutism* (Harlow, 1992).
Hill, J.E.C., *The World Turned Upside Down: Radical Ideas during the English Revolution* (London, 1987, 1st edn 1972).
Jacob, Margaret, *The Radical Enlightenment: Pantheists, Freemasons and Republicans* (London, 1981).
Kors, Alan Charles and Korshin, Paul, J. (eds), *Anticipations of the Enlightenment in England, France and Germany* (Philadelphia, 1987).
Kors, Alan Charles, *The Orthodox Sources of Disbelief*, vol. 1 of *Atheism in France, 1650–1729* (Princeton, 1990).
Labrousse, Elisabeth, 'Reading Pierre Bayle in Paris', in Kors, Alan Charles

and Korshin Paul, J. (eds), *Anticipations of the Enlightenment in England, France and Germany* (Philadelphia, 1987).

Levy, F.J., *Tudor Historical Thought* (San Marino, California, 1967).

MacNeill, John T., *The History and Character of Calvinism* (New York, 1967).

Marcialis, Maria Teresa, 'L'"Ame Matérielle' tra libertinismo e clandestinità', in Spini, G. and Gregory, T., et al. (eds), *Ricerche su letteratura libertina e letteratura clandestina nel seicento* (Florence, 1981).

Matar, N.I., 'Islam in Interregnum and Restoration England', in *The Seventeenth Century*, 6, 1 (1991).

Miller, S.J., 'The limits of political Jansenism in Tuscany: Scipione de'Ricci to Peter Leopold, 1780–1791', in the *Catholic Historical Review*, 80, 4 (1994).

Milton, Anthony, *Catholic and Reformed. The Roman and Protestant Churches in English Protestant Thought 1600–1640* (Cambridge, 1995).

Mullet, Michael, 'Radical sects and dissenting Churches, 1600–1750' in Gilley, Sheriden and Shiels W.J. (eds), *A History of Religion in Britain* (Oxford, 1994).

Niccoli, Ottavia, *Profetti e popoli nell'Italia del Rinascimento* (Rome and Bari, 1987).

Okie, Laird, *Augustan Historical Writing: Histories of England in the English Enlightenment* (London and New York, 1991).

Pailin, David A., *Attitudes to Other Religions: Comparative Religion in Seventeenth- and Eighteenth-Century Britain* (Manchester, 1984).

Pailin, David A., 'The confused and confusing story of natural religion', in *Religion* 24 (1994).

Pailin, David A, 'Herbert of Cherbury. A much-neglected and misunderstood thinker', in Peden, Creighton and Axel, Larry E. (eds), *God, Values and Empiricism* (Georgia, 1989).

Pailin, David A., 'British views on religion and religions in the age of William and Mary', in *Method and Theory in the Study of Religion*, 6–4 (1994).

Penco, Gregorio, *Storia della chiesa in italia* (2 vols, Milan, 1978).

Ramum, O. (ed.), *National Consciousness, History, and Political Culture in Early Modern Europe* (Baltimore, 1975).

Popkin, R.H. and Vanderjagt, A., *Scepticism and Irreligion in the Seventeenth and Eighteenth Centuries* (Leiden, New York and Koln, 1993).

Porter, Roy, 'The Enlightenment in England', in Teich, M. and Porter, Roy (eds), *The Enlightenment in National Context* (Cambridge, 1981).

Porter, Roy, *The Enlightenment* (London, 1990).

Porter, Roy (ed.), *The Enlightenment in National Context* (Cambridge, 1981).

Porter, Roy, *Gibbon Making History* (London, 1995).

Powell, Arthur H., *The Sources of Eighteenth-Century Deism. An Inquiry into its Causes and Origin* (London, 1902).

Pullapilly, Cyriac K., *Caesare Baronius Counter-Reformation Historian* (Notre Dame, Indiana, 1975).

Rendall, J., *The Origins of the Scottish Enlightenment, 1707–1776* (London, 1978).

Reventlow, Graf, H., *The Authority of the Bible and the Rise of the Modern World* (London, 1984).

Ricuperati, Giuseppe, 'Il Problema della corporeità dell'anima dai libertini ai deisti', in Sergio Bertelli (ed.), *Il Libertinismo in Europa* (Milan and Naples, 1980).

Ricuperati, Giuseppe, *L'Esperienze civile e religiosa di Pietro Giannone* (Naples, 1970).

Ricuperati, Giuseppe, 'Libertinismo e deismo a Vienna: Spinoza, Toland e il Triregno,' in *Rivista storica italiana*, 79, 3 (1967).

Rupp, G., *Religion in England, 1688–1791* (Oxford, 1986).

Scalfari, P., *Marcello Eusebio Scotti* (Rome, 1963).

Scott, Jonathan, 'England's troubles: exhuming the popish plot', in Tim Harris, Paul Seaward, Mark Goldie (eds), *Politics of Religion in Restoration England* (Oxford, 1990).

Domenico Sella, *Italy in the Seventeenth Century* (Harlow, 1997).

Sher, Richard, *Church and University in the Scottish Enlightenment* (Edinburgh, 1985).

Siebert, Frederick Seaton, *Freedom of the Press in England 1476–1776* (Urbana, 1952).

Soriga, R., *L'Idea nazionale italiana dal sec. XVIII alla unificazione* (Modena 1941).

Spini, Giorgio, *Ricerca dei libertini. La Teoria dell' impostura delle religioni nel seicento italiano* (Florence, 1983, 1st edn 1950).

Spini, Giorgio, 'Alcuni appunti sui libertini italiani', in Bertelli, Sergio (ed.), *Il Libertinismo in Europa* (Milan and Naples, 1980).

Spini, Giorgio , 'Ritratto del Protestante come libertino', in Gregory, T. and Spini, G., et al. (eds), *Ricerche su letteratura libertina e letteratura clandestina nel Seicento* (Florence, 1981).

Stella, Pietro, *Il Giansenismo in Italia/Piemonte* (3 vols, Zurich, 1966–74).

Thomas, Keith V., *Religion and the Decline of Magic. Studies in Popular Beliefs in Sixteenth and Seventeenth-Century England* (London, 1971).

Titone, Virgilio. *La storiografia del'Illuminismo in Italia* (Milan, 1975, 1st edn 1965).

Trevor-Roper, Hugh, 'Religious Toleration in England after 1688', in *From Counter-Reformation to Glorious Revolution* (London, 1992).

Tullio, Gregory, *Etica e religione nella critica libertina* (Naples, 1986).

Van Kley, Dale, 'Pierre Nicole, Jansenism, and the morality of enlightened self-interest', in Alan Charles Kors and Paul J. Korshin (eds), *Anticipations of the Enlightenment in England, France and Germany* (Philadelphia, 1987).

Venturi, Franco, *La Chiesa e la repubblica dento i loro limiti,* vol. 2 of *Settecento Riformatore* (Turin, 1976).

Venturi, F. (ed.), 'Riformatori lombardi, piemontesi e toscani', in Ricciardi, R. (gen. ed.), *Illuministi Italiani*, vol. 3 (Milan and Naples, 1958).

Walsham, Alexander, '"the fatall vesper": providentialism and anti-popery in late Jacobean London', in *Past and Present,* 144 (August 1994).

Woolf, Stuart, *A History of Italy 1700–1860* (London, 1991, 1st edn 1979).

Wootton, David, 'The republican tradition: from commonwealth to common sense', in Wootton, D. (ed.), *Republicanism, Liberty, and Commercial Society* (California, 1994).

Wright, Alexander T., *The Two Angells of Stenography* (London, 1919).

Index

For anonymous texts see under their titles.

Ainsworth, Henry, 60, 109–11, 137, 147
  estimation of reason in ancient religion, 109–10
Allen, William, 137–8
Amidei, Cosimo, 11, 43, 83, 150
Angell, John, 52, 79–80, 147
Anglican Church and Anglicanism, vii–viii, x, 9, 132
  anti-Anglican priestcraft charge implicit, 147, 156
  compared to papal priestcraft, 94, 128
  competition between it and Dissenters, 140–2
  critics of dismissed as antichristian, 134–5
  High Church and Churchmen, 9, 48, 75, 82, 85, 96, 136, 145; pressured to deepen critique of medieval Church, 82
  oppression of Dissenters, 76, 93, 140–1, 145, 157
  vicissitudes of royal leadership, 141
  viewed as popish and idolatrous, 32
  See also comparative polemic, Convocation of Canterbury
Anglomania, 6
anti-Catholicism, 9, 94–5
  anti-Catholic historiography, 13
  anti-Catholic writings read as anti-Christian, 24
  role of anti-Catholic polemic in rehabilitation of reason, 96, 99–100, 107
  Gordon Riots (1780), 94
  implicit in Dissenter priestcraft discourse, 146–7, 150
  informs polemico-historical views of Dissenters and deists, 75–6
  King James II, popish plots and fears of European Catholic powers, 30, 33–4, 62–3, 66
  as encompassing political, humanitarian and economic concerns, 34, 62–3, 75–6, 85, 143–5
  as a factor in Protestant unity, 9, 66, 129

See also Catholicism, Bayle, comparative polemic
antichrist, 6, 29, 51
anticlericalism,
  relative impact of pre- and post-Reformation ideas, 18–19, 27
  problems arising from imprecise usage of term, 15
  reason in relationship to Enlightenment anticlericalism, 104
anti-curialism/anti-curialists, 9–10
  limits of anti-curial Church reform programme, 41
  on critique of Church–state relationship, 66
  importance of medieval history to, 150
  view of papal temporal dominion and trespass of the Church on princely prerogatives, 42
  in a polycentric peninsula, 34
  alliance with princes, 44; limits of alliance, 69
  See also Church history
apostolic Church, x, 128, 135–6
  See also Presbyterianism
Arconati, Lamberti, 40–1, 55, 61, 90, 119
Aspinwall, Edward, 114
audience,
  for Christian and enlightened publications, 16–17
  the importance of, 18, 135
  see also anti-Catholicism, Anglicanism

Bale, John, 8, 106, 108
  adoption of Luther's historical scheme, 48
  on tyranny of Church over state, 74, 82
Baptists, 140
Barnes, Robert, 26
Baronius, Cesare,
  Annales ecclesiastici, 26, 54, 66–8
Bayle, Pierre, 158
  misinterpretation of his writings, 24, 132–3
Beccaria, Cesare, 37, 89
Becchetti, *see Orsi and Becchetti*
Bencini, Abbot, 25, 61–2, 135
Bennett, G., 141

intermeshing of temporal dominion
and Church supremacy, 37
poverty amidst splendour of Church,
66
see also papacy
Perkins, William, 108
Philosophes,
anticlericalism of similar to dissenting
Protestants, 16
attitude to ancient writers, 4
dismissive attitude to medieval period,
6
undue concentration on, 6, 21
their influence generally, also *vis-à-vis*
Protestant writings and audi-
ence, 5–6
importance attached to the desacralization of Church history, 8
importance attached to Protestant
analysis of medieval Church, 8
see also history
Piatti, Giuseppe, 54
Pistoia, Synod of, 39
Polignac, Cardinal, 38
Politi, Lancelotto, 116
Porter, Roy, 18, 27
Powell, Arthur, 143
priestcraft theory, viii, ix–x, 2, 6, 8–9
advantages of implicit accusation,
146–7
benign priestcraft of state and Church,
77–8, 159–60
Catholic view, 39
collusion of kings and emperors in
priestcraft, 50
crusades as evidence of medieval
priestcraft, 97–9
its deepening and chronological
stretching, 81–2
discrimination between Christian and
non-Christian views of, 24
libertine view, 61
Priest kings, 6
Protestant view, 26–7
spiritual intercession of Catholic
Church: seen as fraud by
Protestants, 113–14; by anti-
curialists, 117; corporeality of
soul as denial of intercession,
120–1
*See also Luther and Calvin, compara-
tive polemic, Church history,
anti-Catholicism, audience,
Anglicanism*

Presbyterianism, x, 9, 59–60, 65–6,
128–9, 139
as alternative to priestcraft, 12–13,
15–16, 126
anti-hierarchical element, 50–1, 126
persistence of its ideals, 129, 138
and social class, 9, 129
as vehicle for political expression, 129
*see also Dissenters, Puritanism, apos-
tolic Church*
Priestley, Joseph, 14, 23, 51–2, 85, 94, 96,
121, 126
Prophecy (biblical), *see Church history*
Protestant identity, 2
Puritanism, x, 136–7, 155
splintering of, 129
see also Presbyterianism, Dissenters

Quakers, 140-1

Radicati, Alberto (Count of Passerano),
63, 126–7, 149–50
his historiographical rationalism, 43
flight from Piedmont, 36

Rainolds, William, 39, 108, 124
reason,
practical polemical use versus explicit
theological defence, 96–7, 100,
103–4, 107
defence of reason did not preclude
belief in biblical prophecy, 30
Luther and reason as insufficient
guide in religion, 106
reasonable creed of Protestant versus
superstitious Catholicism, 42,
96–7
Muratori genuflects to reason, 42–3
formal Christian defence of reason did
not significantly transform their
historiography, 42–3
*see also anti-Catholicism, Luther,
Cambridge, Platonists, Herbert of
Cherbury, Ainsworth, Blount*
Reformation,
Catholic and Protestant polemic, x, 9
fulcrums of debate, 6
polemical aftermath, vii–viii, 6: class
factors in, x, 8–9, 23, 78, 85, 142,
see generally Chapter 8
economic, political, military consequences, 22–3
Reformation protagonists as frauds
and idolaters, 39